PROFESSIONAL PRACTICE IN HUMAN SERVICE ORGANISATIONS

PROFESSIONAL PRACTICE IN HUMAN SERVICE ORGANISATIONS

Catherine McDonald, Christine Craik,
Linette Hawkins, Judy Williams

Routledge
Taylor & Francis Group

LONDON AND NEW YORK

First published 2011 by Allen & Unwin

Published 2020 by Routledge
2 Park Square, Milton Park, Abingdon, Oxon OX14 4RN
605 Third Avenue, New York, NY 10017

Routledge is an imprint of the Taylor & Francis Group, an informa business

Cataloguing-in-Publication details are available
from the National Library of Australia
www.librariesaustralia.nla.gov.au

Internal design by Emily O'Neill
Index by Puddingburn Publishing Services
Set in 12/15 pt Adobe Garamond by Post Pre-press Group, Australia

ISBN-13: 9781742370392 (pbk)

We dedicate this book first, to all the past, present and future social work and human service students we have had the privilege to teach; and second, to all of the wonderful social workers who offer field-based educational experiences for our students.

CONTENTS

LIST OF TABLES

INTRODUCTION

The human services field constitutes a large and growing industry of increasing significance in the twenty-first century. Currently, it is the second fastest-growing industry in contemporary Australia (Healy and Lonne, 2009). It is also an industry with a range of vocational roles and widely varying levels of qualifications. In general, the pre-service education of people working in that part of the human services known as the 'community sector' is mixed. Often, people are working in the sector without post-school vocational education or university qualifications (Meagher and Healy, 2006; McDonald, 1999). As such, many people learn (or fail to learn) how to go about human service work 'on the job'.

In addition to making employees' early working careers in the field very hard, this situation creates considerable transaction costs for employers. Furthermore, learning 'on the job' inevitably creates workers attuned to the specific practices—either good or bad—prevailing in the organisation that employs them, irrespective of whether these are the most appropriate or effective forms or modes of practice for the presenting issues to which the organisation is attempting to respond. Some human service organisations have well-developed practices for managing the volume, scope, challenges and variety of work, while others do not. Often this is a function of size and age. Increasingly, it is also a function of the funding jurisdiction to which an organisation is oriented.

Organisations funded by governments are required to demonstrate conformity to high standards of operations in relation to administrative systems, information-management systems, organisational practices, and so forth. In some Australian states, funded organisations—either currently or in the near future—will be subject to formal audit of these by state governments. This book is designed to assist future workers in particular to both understand the importance of professionalism in organisational practices and to develop excellence in practice standards within human service organisations engaged in human services delivery.

Furthermore—partly as a consequence of the increased pressures on workers and organisations arising from the destabilisation of the welfare state and the increased pressures on human service organisations and their workforce to conform to funding bodies' contractual requirements—what workers do on a daily basis is increasingly prescribed by drives for efficiency and constrained notions of effectiveness. In these contexts, what might once have been considered core activities in the delivery of services have contracted to 'deliverables' couched in terms of key performance indicators (McDonald, 2006; Harris, 2003).

> *Transaction costs:* The expense to an organisation or individual that is incurred by undertaking an activity which is not recognised or compensated.
>
> *Audit:* A process wherein the activities of an organisation or an individual are closely scrutinised.
>
> *Deliverables or key performance indicators:* Nominated outcomes of the activities of an organisation or individual as agreed in a contract.
>
> *Intervention skills:* Skills used in human service work such as casework, counselling, case management, group work, community work and social planning.

Workers—both qualified and unqualified—will therefore be encouraged to apply core sets of practices centrally implicated in effective service delivery—practices that are both quite practical in nature and transferable across virtually all organisational contexts. Furthermore, many entrants to the human services have little experience of working in organisational contexts themselves. The first section of the book (Chapters 1 and 2) orients the reader to these contexts and explores the characteristics and peculiarities of working in human service organisations and in non-profit organisations. Chapters 3, 4 and 5 address core generic practices that all workers need to adopt, such as scoping the context, writing and recording, working with information and working across cultural and linguistic differences.

This book also acknowledges that human service work involves working with and through intra- and inter-organisational networks, within a context of complex service delivery systems. Effective work within these systems requires another set of attendant practices that are often not fully acknowledged or are often overshadowed in standard pre-service and in-service human service education and training devoted to developing intervention skills. These are discussed in Chapter 6. This book is designed to assist future workers to develop and maintain good practices in relation to their work over and above their intervention knowledge and skills—in relation to service users, their employing organisations and other workers and organisations in the industry.

The remainder of the book acknowledges and responds to the nature of work in all parts of the industry, which inevitably involves working with vulnerable people—for example, with children, the disabled, the elderly and the homeless. There is an imperative that people engaged in caring work carry out their duties in a manner which is constantly mindful of the range of inherent risks to these people, and are able to respond appropriately with sound practices within organisations. The work has inevitable ethical dimensions and implications at every point. Accordingly, skills in ethical reasoning and decision-making are essential. Further, the vulnerable nature of the people with whom the human service industry engages suggests that understanding the need for as well as having the capacity to respond positively to their issues and rights is particularly important.

The title employs the adjective 'professional' in relation to practice in the industry. We do not use this word to imply that the book contributes solely to professionalism as that term is understood in the sociology of professions. Generally, professionalism implies a particular type and level of knowledge, skills and commitments, differently articulated in and sometimes 'owned' by various fields such as social work and psychology. It is used here in a more colloquial sense to signify that there should be certain standards that both service users and employers can expect of all employees working in the industry, irrespective of educational background and/or qualifications. Accordingly, we focus on those generic skills that apply *across* the diversity of human service industry settings. This book is *not* designed to develop specific intervention skills such as counselling or group work. Rather, it is designed to develop accompanying sets of skills and practices that are also needed, but that are often addressed in quite limited ways in standard human service intervention texts. As we have done to a limited extent in these introductory comments, we will explain words and terms that readers may be unfamiliar with as the book progresses. Finally, we hope that, by reading this book and thinking about the issues and topics we discuss, readers' capacities to work in what is undoubtedly a fascinating yet at the same time very challenging field of the human services is enhanced.

CHAPTER ONE | Understanding organisations

SUMMARY

This chapter is designed to assist students and new workers to understand the nature, dynamics and functioning of human service organisations. After establishing why the context of organisations is important to the conduct of human service work, we explore key concepts related to organisations and key challenges of working in organisations, particularly but not wholly emerging from the contemporary context. Finally, the chapter discusses a number of important issues involved in being an employee, and hence being managed, before briefly discussing several issues related to managing ourselves.

THE IMPORTANCE OF CONTEXT

While everyone has some experience of organisations—for example, through attending school or university—most of us take them very much for granted. We rarely stop to consider the implications of an organisation for the range of people—for example, staff and service users—engaging with it. This is a very important issue for human service workers because the organisational context itself shapes how workers undertake their work, and ultimately the impact of their work on disadvantaged or troubled service users who are often heavily dependent on the organisation to which they have come for help. Think, for example, about the relationship that a person who has been homeless has with an emergency housing service, or that a person with a psychiatric disability has with a mental health service. It is also very important to remember that most people who become service users of human service organisations do so because they have little choice. As a consequence, how the organisation functions—especially at the front line—is important not only for ourselves as workers, but also for the people we want to assist.

Unlike many other forms of work, such as that done by builders, plumbers or electricians, human service work is nearly always undertaken in organisational contexts. These contexts are not uniform, however—they range from huge state-based bureaucracies to small non-profit or community-based organisations—each with its own unique sets of issues and experiences. While professions such as social work that operate within the human services field draw their legitimacy from their profession, they also draw it—perhaps even more so—from their employing organisation. Very often, those organisations (particularly if they are operated by a government) are established by statute and have an associated body of legislation that sets out their purpose and their powers. A human service worker working for a state government child protection service, for example, has quite significant powers in relation to children considered to be at risk, and a social worker working for Centrelink has substantial power in determining the eligibility of young people for income security.

Many newly graduated professionals have been taught the notion that they retain significant professional autonomy. This is not entirely true and, as we will discuss later, it is even less true in the contemporary context than it was 30 years ago. Organisations largely create the rules of the game—for example, the actual intervention practices a worker might undertake, as well as the specific duties and responsibilities of employees. Being employed in an organisation inevitably means being subordinate to someone, and for beginning workers it often means working in a position a long way down a daunting hierarchy. These positions imply that employees have to obey sets of rules established by the organisation. It is also important to reflect that employees draw the means of daily sustenance from their employers in the form of their salaries; furthermore, they spend a considerable part of their lives within the organisation.

Mostly, organisations operate in physical locations, demarcated from the surrounding community in which they are embedded by such devices as buildings, doors and counters. Some human service organisations deploy degrees of security rarely seen or experienced in other contexts, and in doing so they send clear messages to both their staff and their service users. Finally, organisations grant identities to their employees, often represented and projected via physical means such as ID cards, name badges or corporate clothing. In all, human service organisations are significant contexts for human services practice, and all human service workers need to develop the capacity to understand the contexts within which they ply their skills, and the implications for their practice.

> *Non-profit organisation:* An organisation that may not legally redistribute any surplus money it makes to individual shareholders. Any such surplus must be reinvested in the legally accepted goals and activities of the organisation.

> *Statute:* An act passed by a parliament or other legislature that is formally recorded.

> *Professional autonomy:* The rights of some professions, individually and collectively, to manage and govern their own work.

KEY CONCEPTS IN HUMAN SERVICE ORGANISATIONS

Distinguishing characteristics of human service organisations

It is generally accepted by key theorists that human service organisations are somewhat different from other organisations (see Hasenfeld, 1983 for a seminal account). Jones and May (1992) suggest that this group of organisations can (more or less) be distinguished by their purpose, their technology and their auspice. We begin with purpose. Usually, human service organisations are contrasted with for-profit organisations engaged in production or business. The primary purpose of that latter group, it is suggested, is to produce profit for owners and shareholders. For the most part (though there are exceptions, and these are growing in number), human service organisations nominate as their primary purpose the promotion of the care and wellbeing of people experiencing difficulties in their lives because of poverty, disability, illness or some other life hazard. While this might seem straightforward, distinguishing a human service organisation by purpose can have its difficulties, especially in what is known as a *mixed economy of welfare*. By this, we mean the entire range of organisations caught up in the over-arching business of the welfare state (a term characterising and describing the activities of those advanced industrialised countries that have actively promoted and provided many forms of welfare since the end of World War II). In Australia, for example, these can be public sector organisations, non-profit organisations or businesses. Consider the employment services sector, where a number of businesses such as Sarina Russo and Maximus are contracted by the Commonwealth government to provide services to the unemployed. Clearly, these organisations could claim that their purpose is to help the unemployed. However, their other very important purpose is to make a profit for their owners and shareholders. Other examples include businesses providing nursing home care and child care. Some of these are very controversial—such as boarding or rooming houses—because the poor conditions often found in them illustrate only too well that the main purpose is profit generation, often to the detriment of their hapless residents.

Another means of distinguishing human service organisations is through the 'technologies' they employ. 'Technology' here is really a metaphor for the types of activities and interventions deployed— for example, counselling or emergency relief. Hasenfeld (1983) is one of the main theorists suggesting this. He argues that we can distinguish between people-processing, people-sustaining and people-changing organisations. People-processing technologies are found in those organisations that assess people and provide a particular label, which then causes them to be treated in specific ways. In the Australian context, one of the main people-processing organisations is Centrelink. Clearly, when a person goes to a Centrelink customer-service office, his or her status is assessed and labelled as unemployed, sole parent, disabled or aged. Each of these categories attracts a particular payment with specific conditions attached to it. Hasenfeld originally thought that such organisations were not particularly interested in changing the attributes of their service users, a view he expressed in an era before 'welfare reform' (a development in policy by which income security payments became conditional on recipients behaving in required ways). Increasingly, and certainly in the case of Centrelink, the conditions attached to payments for unemployment require certain activities, which it is believed will change the dispositions of the unemployed from passive beneficiaries to active job-seekers.

People-sustaining organisations are those that provide some sort of service which allows people to live their lives, but which again is not interested in changing them. Some examples of these are aged care (for example, in-home care that is designed to allow people to 'age in place' or stay in their own homes), child care and many disability-support services.

In-home care: Domestic support or care services provided to the aged in their own homes.

Age in place: A principle of good practice in aged care that suggests people are happier in their own homes than in institutional settings.

Finally, people-changing organisations are those that are specifically set up to change the dispositions or personal attributes of the people who engage with them. There are many examples of these, including counselling services, educational services, family-support services and child-protection services. Jones and May (1992) argue that there is a fourth type of human service organisation: people-controlling organisations—the main purpose of which is control or restraint. Examples of these are corrective services and some mental health services (e.g. psychiatric hospitals).

The third feature said to characterise distinctiveness in human service organisations is auspice. By auspice, we mean the mandate or mechanism that authorises an organisation's existence. Usually, this is drawn from the legal form of the organisation. There are several of these in the human services: statutory organisations or Commonwealth and state government departments; for-profit business entities; and non-profit organisations. The last group is also split into four types: religious charities, secular charities, incorporated associations and companies limited by guarantee.

Religious charity: An organisation engaged in human services delivery sponsored by a legally recognised church, which is recognised as such by the Taxation Department.

Secular charity: An organisation engaged in human service delivery *not* sponsored by a legally recognised church, but accepted as a charity by the Taxation Department.

Incorporated association: A non-profit secular organisation given legal identity through state *Associations Incorporations Acts*.

Company limited by guarantee: A non-profit secular organisation given legal identity by the Australian Securities and Investment Commission (ASIC).

The common feature of the non-profit group is that they are all bound by what is known as the 'non-distribution constraint' (Hansman, 1980: 835), by which they are legally barred from distributing

any organisational surplus as profit and must reinvest any such surplus into the aims and objectives of the organisation.

Table 1.1: Characteristics of organisations

	Auspice	Technology	Purpose
Uniting Care nursing home			
State child protection service			
Neighbourhood centre			
For-profit employment service			
Welfare rights centre			
Private prison			
Smith Family charity			

EXERCISE

Identify the characteristics of the organisations in Table 1.1.

Organisational structure

Organisations are characterised by structure, by which we mean the
pattern of relationships—both horizontal and vertical—that exist
in any organisations. We all understand the vertical structure of an
organisation. At the top is the boss—the chief executive officer of a
private or non-profit organisation, the Director-General of a state or
Commonwealth department, the principal of a secondary school, or

the vice-chancellor of a university. Falling out in rows below the boss is a series of levels and roles, each charged with a part of implementing the objectives of the organisation, culminating in human service organisations—the people who deliver services—in the front line.

Buchanan and Hyczynski (2004: 5) state that organisational structure is a 'social arrangement for achieving controlled performance in pursuit of collective goals'. In the previous paragraph, we invoked one type of structure—the typical bureaucratic or hierarchical structure—but there are other models in which the degree of hierarchy is considerably reduced. Another famous theorist, Mintzberg (1989) suggested five dimensions that inform the type of structure in an organisation:

1. the degree of job specialisation including the vertical and horizontal division of responsibility and accountability
2. the criteria by which jobs are grouped together
3. the degree of formalisation of rules and regulations and the extent to which these are written down
4. types of integrative mechanisms
5. the centralisation of decision-making and the degree of delegation downwards.

EXERCISE

Discuss the organisational structures likely to be found in a neighbourhood centre, Anglicare and Centrelink.

Organisational culture

All organisations have cultures, and an organisation's culture plays an integral part in shaping how it functions, as well as how it is experienced by workers and service users. By culture, we mean the basic assumptions and beliefs—often hidden and unconscious—that represent the nature of the organisation and its relationship with the environment. Culture can be expressed in such practices as rituals, formal written statements, standards, rules and policies, artefacts, and formal and informal stories told about the organisation by its members. Employees rapidly learn an organisation's culture, as most organisations actively disseminate their formal culture at induction. The Red Cross, for example, has a video it shows staff and volunteers about its unique history. See, for example, that organisation's history drawn from its web page:

The Red Cross and Red Crescent Movement began almost 150 years ago when on a hot June day in 1859 Henry Dunant, a Swiss banker travelling on business in northern Italy, witnessed the aftermath of the Battle of Solferino a horrifying and bloody conflict between 300,000 soldiers from Imperial Austria and the Franco-Sardinian Alliance. In 1862 Dunant published his recollection of this experience as A Memory of Solferino and remained convinced that the power of humanity could be engaged to alleviate suffering on a global scale. Vulnerable people exist in all societies, he argued, and should be afforded the same care and consideration.

Some of the men wounded in battle lay where they fell for days bleeding and tormented by thirst, hunger, flies and burning heat. The dead were thrown into huge pits, along with others seriously injured but alive nonetheless. Amid the stench and sounds of pain and anguish, thieves moved from person to person, robbing both the wounded and the dead. Moved by the sight of the appalling injuries suffered by these young men, Dunant rallied villagers from the town of Castiglione della Pieve to assist and tend the wounded. These townsfolk were to become the first volunteers of the Red Cross.

Would there not be some means, during a period of peace and calm, of forming relief Societies whose object would be to have the wounded cared for in time of war by enthusiastic devoted volunteers fully qualified for the task? Such Societies could even render great service during epidemics or at times of disaster of flood and fire; the philanthropic motives underlying their vocation would bring them into action immediately wherever and whenever they could usefully intervene.

His matter-of-fact account, with its underlying message of hope and inspiration drew widespread support across Europe, bringing with it the salient reminder that suffering does not end once the battle has ceased. In

> *Geneva in October 1863 under the leadership of Henry Dunant, Gustave Moynier, General Guillaume-Henri Dufour, Dr Louis Appia and Dr Theodore Maunoir set up the International Committee for Relief to the Wounded. The Committee, later to become the International Committee of the Red Cross, chose as their emblem a perfectly formed red cross on a white background the simple inverse of the Swiss flag.* <www.redcross.org.au/aboutus_history_international_default.htm>

In some organisations—particularly religious charitable organisations—the culture is drawn directly from the spiritual orientation of the religious group or order auspicing the organisation.

EXERCISE

Discuss what you know about the culture of the Salvation Army.

As well as formal cultures, many organisations also have informal or covert cultures, which are more powerful because they are unspoken and unchallenged. In one large non-profit organisation studied by McDonald and Warburton (2004), there was a negative and unacknowledged cultural understanding of the relationship between the centre and the periphery, which led to considerable bitterness and conflict. Unfortunately, it is not uncommon for human service organisations to have cultures that are negative and dismissive about their service users. McDonald and Marston (2008b) found, for example, that many case managers at the front line of Australia's employment services have very negative attitudes towards the unemployed, especially the long-term unemployed. This orientation to service users more generally was also noted by Wearing (1998) in his study of the non-profit sector in New South Wales.

EXERCISE

From a service user's point of view, what is the dominant covert cultural orientation of Centrelink customer service officers?

Street-level or front-line workers

In 1980, Michael Lipsky wrote a very famous book called *Street-Level Bureaucracy*, in which he advanced the proposition that workers at the front line of human service organisations—particularly state-run organisations—were the ultimate shapers of social policy. How a service user actually experienced a particular policy orientation and associated program was mediated through a front-line worker's understanding of the policy and his or her personal orientation to the work and to the service users. This was the case, he suggested, because front-line workers in human service organisations had considerable autonomy in the way they went about their work. In 1993, Smith and Lipsky revisited the notion of street-level bureaucrats in the context of developments since the original book was published. In the later book, they noted that workers at the front line in the non-profit sector were the new street-level bureaucrats. To a certain extent this is true, in the sense that much service delivery that once was undertaken by the state is now undertaken by the non-profit or community sector. That said, and as we will discuss shortly, developments in government have changed the way bureaucrats monitor and oversee the work of contracted community organisations. Nevertheless, front-line workers still bear much of the responsibility for and risks inherent in human service delivery. In other words, front-line workers are vital.

KEY CHALLENGES IN HUMAN SERVICE ORGANISATIONS

Clearly there are many challenges facing people working in human service organisations, some of which we discuss here. The issues discussed largely arise from the contemporary environment in which human services operate.

New public management

In 1992 an extremely influential book, *Reinventing Government* by Osborne and Gaebler, was published, setting the tone for governments throughout the advanced industrialised world. Its central argument was that governments should run the public sector in much the same manner as private corporations. Subsequently, an entire movement in public sector administration—New Public Management (NPM)—grew up. This movement has reshaped the public sector, and in the process the relationships between the state and those non-state organisations contracted to fulfil state functions. With regard to the latter, the conditions of contracts now routinely specify what organisations will do, how they will do it and how they will organise themselves. Some of the major reforms include practices such as:

- increased use of purchase-of-service contracts (whereby the state hires non-state organisations to undertake their work), transferring significant swathes of service delivery out of the state's direct control
- introduction of performance targets (key performance indicators) for organisations and employees
- the prioritisation of efficiency as an operational principle
- the use of generic senior managers as opposed to people who are experts in the field.

Currently, all human service organisations—public sector and non-profit—are affected. One of the biggest implications for workers is the decreased trust of advocates of NPM in professionals, and the subsequent deterioration of their autonomy. Coupled with the increased use of information technology, the front line of welfare is now much more tightly controlled than it was in the past, and what autonomy and discretion workers once had is now increasingly designed out.

Quality assurance

Accompanying the rise of NPM and its associated distrust of professionals, a new method of managing the quality of service delivery has developed—quality assurance, a comprehensive and quite invasive method of assessing 'quality' in organisational functioning. Currently, all organisations—including human service organisations—are using formal quality assurance systems. Nationally, the

Quality Improvement Council (QIC) undertakes quality assessments of health and community service organisations around a whole range of matters. Increasingly, such accreditation is a requirement for funding. See Table 1.2 for the core standards used by QIC when accrediting organisations.

Table 1.2: Core standards summary

Section 1	Building quality organisations
Standard 1.1	Leadership and management
Standard 1.2	Human resources
Standard 1.3	Physical resources
Standard 1.4	Financial management
Standard 1.5	Knowledge management
Standard 1.6	Risk assessment and management
Standard 1.7	Legal and regulatory compliance
Section 2	Providing quality services and programs
Standard 2.1	Identifying and meeting community needs
Standard 2.2	Focusing on positive outcomes
Standard 2.3	Ensuring cultural safety and appropriateness
Standard 2.4	Confirming consumer rights
Standard 2.5	Empowering consumers
Standard 2.6	Coordinating services and programs
Section 3	Sustaining quality external relationships
Standard 3.1	Service agreements and partnerships
Standard 3.2	Collaboration and strategic positioning
Standard 3.3	Incorporation and contribution to good practice
Standard 3.4	Community and professional capacity building

Source: <www.qic.org.au>

Each organisation that applies for accreditation has to undertake a formal external review of its systems, and if they meet the standards the organisation is accredited for a number of years. In some states, quality accreditation is a condition of receiving government funds.

The rise of risk

As Power (1997) so eloquently suggests, risk has become a central concept employed in understanding the contemporary operating environments of organisations. Accompanying it is a management imperative to manage risk. This takes several forms. All organisations, including human service organisations, interrogate their organisational practices in terms of potential riskiness, and develop protocols and procedures to minimise it. These affect virtually all aspects of an organisation's functioning, and often involve deflecting considerable resources away from direct service delivery. There are several types of risk—financial risks (e.g. unanticipated expenditure), legal risks (where organisations are held liable for something), political risks (wherein governments or organisations are held responsible for failure or for poor outcomes) and reputational risk (where an organisation's reputation is put at jeopardy). Increasingly, governments manage risk associated with human service delivery by contracting it out. Look, for example, at the Victorian government's recently implemented Child First system of responding to and managing child protection (see case study).

Obviously, this has implications for the community-based family support agencies providing support to 'risky' families. As a consequence, those organisations are very concerned with making sure their front-line staff can manage the work.

Involving service users

Increasingly, it is accepted that good practice in human service organisations is practice that takes seriously the issue of listening to and involving service users. The degree of involvement can vary from organisation to organisation, depending on the values

Case study: Child First

Introduced in 2007, the Victorian government has legislated that the primary arena of intervention into families considered to be 'at risk' is non-profit family support services organised into regions. Characterised as secondary specialist services, and because of the Child First model, government-funded non-profit family services agencies have increasingly targeted the most vulnerable families with the most complex problems. The *Children, Youth and Families Act* 2006 authorises these organisations to accept referrals from the Department of Human Services' Child Protection Service as well as from other sources. Child Protection itself assesses cases, makes formal notifications and undertakes any court proceedings deemed necessary. After investigation, and when no application to the Children's Court for a protection order is made, the case is transferred to a non-profit family services organisation. In Victoria, 6 per cent of notifications result in a protection order, so intervention by Child Protection in the bulk of cases is time-limited and episodic. For most families at risk of harming their children (that is, experiencing significant difficulties), therapeutic intervention and family support are undertaken by the non-profit sector. Furthermore, the department has, through the provisions of funding contracts, enjoined agencies to connect with each other in localised service delivery systems. One agency is nominated as lead agency, which takes referrals from Child Protection, assesses their needs and manages further referral for intervention to one of the other partner agencies. If there is no 'space' in the system, the lead agency (or another contracted for the task) has the role of 'managing' the case until intervention is able to commence. From a risk perspective, the agency charged with that management has a very tricky job to do. By definition, these are high-risk cases, yet as they wait for assistance to lower that risk, the non-profit organisation 'managing' these families inevitably faces what may well be an escalating risk of harm occurring to the notified children *because* there is no intervention.

orientation of the management. In some organisations, involvement of service users is largely confined to providing information—either routinely handing out information in written form or responding to specific requests for information. A more in-depth approach would be forms of consultation with service users—surveys, focus groups or consultation meetings. In some organisations, the relationship between the organisation and the service users is more like a partnership, whereby users are formally involved on advisory or planning committees. Finally—and as is becoming more common in disability services—some organisations delegate control to service users, who may be involved in selecting staff.

Hardina (2005) outlines ten characteristics of what she calls an 'empowerment oriented organisation', a number of which relate to the involvement of service users. These are that an organisation:

1. includes service users/consumers in organisation decision-making
2. creates partnerships to design and evaluate programs
3. delivers culturally appropriate services
4. minimises power differentials between service users and staff
5. promotes team-building and collaboration
6. promotes psychological empowerment of workers by giving them more autonomy to make decisions that affect their work
7. creates an administrative leadership structure that is ideologically committed to empowering service users and staff members
8. increases employee job satisfaction through the provision of fringe benefits and other incentives
9. encourages staff to advocate for improvements in service delivery and service user resources
10. increases the political power of organisation constituents.

Even though there may be formal systems in place to maximise service users' involvement, it may still be difficult to put into practice. This can be the case if an organisation does not deliberately try to accomplish the fourth point on the list above. We address this issue in considerable depth in Chapter 9.

BEING MANAGED AND MANAGING OURSELVES

Supervision and accountability

There are at least two types of supervision operating in human service work. One is professional supervision, where a professional supervisor works with a person to discuss their approach to cases and to develop their professional capacities. We discuss this type of supervision in more depth in Chapter 7. Of more interest in this chapter is the formal supervision a line manager undertakes in relation to his or her staff. This supervision is concerned primarily with accountability. Even though administrative supervision is essentially about working with employees to meet the organisation's goals and targets, it nevertheless should still be centrally concerned with helping people achieve their potential.

Coulshed and Mullender (2001: 165) list what an employee should expect from administrative supervision. According to them, a supervisor will:

- help them with their workload and caseload management, balancing the overall workload fairly among employees in the unit
- monitor all the work undertaken in the unit to ensure it complies with the organisation's policies and procedures
- provide a sounding board for a worker to think through issues or worries
- keep employees in touch with developments in the organisation
- give feedback about an employee's performance
- ensure that employees keep up to date with the management of information.

It is well known that poor supervision and poor leadership at the front line lead to poor performance, low job satisfaction, low levels of organisational commitment and high degrees of turnover (Elpers and Westhuis, 2008; Mary, 2005). Finally, an employee can expect that their experience of supervision is positive and if (for whatever reason) it is not, then an employee and his or her colleagues have every right to make that known to the organisation.

Case study: Supervision

Mario is a new recruit to the state Child Welfare Department. He has undertaken a six-week induction and training course and is now on the job in an inner-city local office. Over the course of the first eight weeks, several issues arise, largely to do with him being given a number of very complex and serious cases to manage. On five occasions he has gone to his supervisor for advice and has been brushed off. He feels increasingly frightened and demoralised. He asks his colleagues whether this is normal and they say it is. One day, he goes out for lunch and comes back to find his supervisor at his desk. She dresses him down for not filling out the records properly and for not contacting a school about one child. He explains that he (a) didn't know he had to, (b) that the file did not indicate he should be doing these things, and (c) he's unsure of the protocols of contacting a school. She tells him that he will do poorly at his first performance appraisal with her and she will be recommending that he be put on performance management for three months before review. Mario feels desperate, and after talking it over with his partner he formally resigns. Unfortunately, the whole episode has upset him so much that he thinks he will never be a good worker.

Discussion questions
- What is the problem here?
- What approach should Mario's supervisor have taken?
- Was resigning the best option?
- What other option should Mario have pursued?

Performance appraisal

All employees in all organisations are accountable to their employers. Overall, this is a good thing because it is one of the means by which human service organisations maintain quality in service delivery. Increasingly, formal performance appraisal is the mechanism used to assess a worker's performance. If it is done well, performance appraisal is a useful tool for helping a worker to think about his or her goals, and to think through ways of achieving these through, for example, targeted staff development. In many human service settings—for example, those where observable change in the service user group is slow—performance appraisal can be used as a professional tool to reflect on what is going well, what is not, and how progress is defined and evaluated. Usually, performance appraisal takes place on an annual basis, involves an intensive session with a supervisor and results in a written record of decisions made, goals identified and supports nominated.

Coulshed and Mullender (2001: 175) suggest that performance appraisal in human service organisations should:

- reflect a partnership approach
- be systematic
- be task-focused
- solve problems
- be respectful, valuing the employees' strengths
- be empowering through giving the employee a voice
- be based on a written agreement.

Staff development

Staff development is an important part of any human service worker's development plan. Most workers, when graduating, are not yet fully formed as professionals and will need additional learning to reach their full potential. Furthermore, in the fast-changing contemporary environment, the notion of lifelong learning has become increasingly important. Lifelong learning is a concept that has become very popular over the past two decades, especially with governments. It recognises that the contemporary contexts in which people work are becoming more complex, and that contemporary workers increasingly are knowledge workers. Employees working as professionals in human service organisations are examples of knowledge workers. Engaging in professional practice involves significant analytical skills, as well as the ability to draw on different bodies of knowledge, interpret these in context and develop a plan of action. Engaging in staff-development activities as an active learner helps employees to become lifelong learners.

Clearly, supervisors play an important part in developing, promoting and matching people to staff development opportunities and processes. Supervisors should not only help people to identify and engage in learning activities; they should provide people with the means of demonstrating the application of their learning in the workplace.

It is also important to understand that most human service professional groups are required to undertake continued professional education to remain accredited by the professional body. The Australian Association of Social Workers, for example, says that:

> *Continuing professional education is a commitment each member makes to professional development as an accountable social worker. The purpose of the AASW CPE policy is to promote continued learning by social work practitioners that may be integrated into professional practice. The goal is to ensure that social workers maintain up to date knowledge and skills as the foundation for professional endeavour in all fields of practice.* (AASW, 2006)

Staff care and self-help

Again, we address this issue in considerably more detail in Chapter 7. Nevertheless, it is important to acknowledge in this introductory chapter on understanding organisations that working in a human service organisation can be both demanding and stressful. Read, for example, the following excerpt:

> *inadequate compensation, large caseloads, long hours and on-call responsibilities, voluminous paperwork, frequent policy change coupled with stringent state and federal policy requirements, issues of personal safety, inadequate training and supervision, involuntary service users facing complex problems, lack of adequate resources to serve service users . . .* (Westbrook et al., 2006: 38)

While this quotation is referring to working in child protection, many of the same issues are experienced in other types of human service organisations. Prior to addressing the issues of managing your own health and stress, it would be helpful to identify what factors you think would be important to self-care in the human services.

EXERCISE
Identify at least four factors that you think will be central to your self-care when working in a human service organisation.

The importance of critical reflection

When working in the human service field, it has been clearly demonstrated over and over again that it is the relationship you develop with the service user that matters above almost everything else. Workers in this field need to understand that, underneath it all, it is how they relate to and treat the human being in front of them that counts. If, as a worker, you cannot recognise and understand the impact of your own experiences on the ways in which you interpret issues (and the ways in which these experiences have impacted on your life opportunities and life choices), then you have little hope of being able to cut through the dominant discourses of our society. Similarly, you will have little capacity to recognise and understand what shapes the life opportunities and life choices of your service users.

This is why we value and use critical reflection in our day-to-day practice. Critical reflection is an effective way to learn to understand how and why you react the way you do to certain issues. It will assist you as a worker to develop a deeper understanding of what is going on with your service users—which basically means assisting you in developing understanding and empathy. Critical reflection contributes to an atmosphere of inquiry, the realisation of the importance of lifelong learning and the 'wanting to know' among human service workers and their organisations. You need to be able to develop critical reflection as a habit that is part of everyday practice.

What do we mean by critical reflection?

At different times throughout this book, we will talk about *critical reflection* and *critically reflective practice*. When we do so, we are talking about a lens through which good workers evaluate their reactions, understandings and the work they do. Understanding what *you* have done, and why, and developing insight into where your thoughts and actions come from and how effective your processes are is essential when working in the human services area. Your evaluation of the 'where' and 'why' will also guide your ideas about how you might use this experience for future work. As a worker in the human service field, you need to be able to evaluate your thought processes and follow your 'journey of learning' around these thought processes. To do this, you need to be able to reflect on your own experiences in life, as well as your feelings and values, and identify aspects of your social location that have contributed to the position you hold on any issue or situation. After all, we ask our service users to reflect in such a way on the how and why of where they are, and we know critical reflection works for them. So why shouldn't we be following the same processes as workers?

With regard to critical reflection, human service workers need to:

- be able to demonstrate their beginning understandings of a situation or issue and to begin to tease out the meaning of the issue or incident for them
- deconstruct their first interpretations of a situation—what it is that led to your initial understanding and to your way of thinking, your values, assumptions, behaviours (what role does the impact of your social location—for example your age, gender, class, race, culture, religion, ability, sexuality—have on the ways in which you think, behave and understand)
- understand the contribution of the new experience (whether that be a reading, a workshop, discussion, work with a service user, a team meeting, supervision or an organisational issue)

- after reflecting, challenging and evaluating (through discussion, often in supervision), to demonstrate where they sit now with a particular issue or situation.

In short, a worker needs to be able to 'reconstruct' the meaning for him or her that has come out of this issue or experience.

We often tell our students that understanding critical reflection is a bit like looking at a maths equation. We don't want to give you the equation (or the issue, problem, situation) and just hear the answer; we want you to be able to demonstrate and understand the process of working it out. We like to see the 'journey' of learning, and want you to be able to articulate your understanding of this journey.

CONCLUSION

As we indicated in the Introduction, human service organisations form the context of professionals' experience and that of the people they serve. In many ways, this chapter serves as the foundation for other themes that will emerge in subsequent chapters. And as will become clear, many of the issues we touched on here will be taken up in more depth in subsequent chapters.

Chapter review questions

1.1 Identify three reasons why the organisational context is important.

1.2 What are people-processing, people-sustaining, people-changing and people-controlling organisations?

1.3 What is an organisation's auspice?

1.4 What do we mean by organisational culture?

1.5 What is New Public Management?

1.6 Why do organisations undergo quality assurance?

1.7 What characteristics should an employee expect of a good performance appraisal?

1.8 Why is critical reflection important?

OTHER RESOURCES

'Our Community', development material for Community Organisations, <www.ourcommunity.com.au/index.jsp>.

Quality Improvement and Community Services Accreditation, <www.latrobe.edu.au/aipc/qicsa>.

AASW, 2006, Continuing Professional Development, <www.aasw.asn.au/document/item/89>.

KEY READINGS

Jackson, A.C. and Donovan, F.D. 1999, 'Maximising People's Contribution', in *Managing to Survive: Managerial Practice in Not-for-profit Organisations*, Allen & Unwin, Sydney.

Gardner, F. 2006, in *Working with Human Service Organisations*, Oxford University Press, Melbourne.

Hughes, M. and Wearing, M. 2007, *Organisations and Management in Social Work*, Sage, London.

CHAPTER TWO | Leadership in human service organisations

SUMMARY

This chapter explores leadership in human service organisations. We start with a discussion of why leadership is important to new human service workers. We then provide an overview of broader issues of management in the human services. This includes an overview of the concept of leadership and some theories and models that have been used to understand it. We then look at different ways of understanding the role human service workers can play in managing human services and in exercising leadership. Examples of how workers can exercise leadership and influence the development and delivery of services in their organisation are discussed. Finally and importantly, the chapter looks at how recent ideas of good leadership have a lot in common with core professional values. Throughout the chapter, workers are encouraged to think about how they can learn from the leadership of colleagues as well as ultimately exercise leadership themselves— even if they do not hold management positions.

WHY IS LEADERSHIP IMPORTANT?

As a new worker starting out in the human services field, you may wonder 'Why is leadership important to me?' Many new graduates enter practice with a strong commitment to work with individuals or families and no real interest in dealing with bureaucracy or aligning themselves with 'management'. Others may feel that, as a new, inexperienced worker in the organisation, they will just have to fit in, follow the procedures set and certainly have no role in leadership—even if they want to.

This can lead to a feeling of helplessness or a belief that they have no power or influence on their role and the duties they perform. It can also lead to workers being in a position where they feel they have no rights and are potentially open to bullying or exploitation by managers. We discuss the importance of power and how you can conceptualise and exercise power as a worker in more detail in Chapter 9; for now, though, it is important to note that an understanding of the manager's role and of how leadership can be exercised is central to being able to deal with the inevitable tensions that can arise in human service work.

Leadership is important to all human service workers in several ways. First, as outlined in Chapter 1, if you are to work in an organisation, the way it is managed and how others exercise leadership will have a direct impact on the quality of your work and your job satisfaction. If you understand more about management and leadership, it may help you to work constructively; it may also help you to identify when things are not going well and work out strategies you can use to raise concerns. A second and very important aspect is that you can play a leadership role in many ways within your work setting, and through this you may be able to influence the quality of service offered to the users of the organisation. Examples of this will be provided throughout the chapter. A third reason is that you are likely, at some point, to be asked to comment on your employing organisation's leadership. Finally, though it may not seem likely now, you will almost certainly move into team leadership positions, perhaps even more senior positions.

In the early years of human service activity, professionals tended to be left largely alone to undertake their service user-based work. From the 1980s onwards, there was a shift towards a stronger role for managers within human services and public service organisations (Lawler 2007). While this managerialism may have brought increased efficiency and accountability, it also came at a cost to professional staff in terms of more control and structure for human service workers. This resulted in a reduction in their job satisfaction and ultimately a reduction in the quality of their work, as staff became disengaged and constrained due to limited opportunities to exercise professional judgement. In this context, leadership (as opposed to management) can be seen as a way to increase effectiveness and improve services while allowing for more creativity, job satisfaction and individual responsiveness in a way that recognises professional training and the complex situations in which human service workers operate.

Managerialism: A uniquely Australian term used to signify that New Public Management-inspired reforms are operative.

It has been argued that as human service organisations become more complex with changes in funding for and fragmentation of services, it has become more important for staff members to be able to understand how the organisation works (Coulshed and Mullender, 2001). In their book *Management in Social Work*, these authors provide an overview of organisational theory and frameworks for undertaking management functions within human service agencies, and the points they raise are valuable for new human service workers. They are also simple to understand. Coulshed and Mullender (2001: 11) argue that workers need to 'think like a manager' and be able to look critically at their organisation, the work they undertake and the standards to which they themselves work. This 'critical eye' provides the opportunity to see the service that they and their agency provide from the perspective of service users. It also promotes analysis of the quality of service and issues that may not otherwise be considered due to a preoccupation with one's own role.

It is also important to note that, through understanding management principles and processes, human service workers can better understand how they fit within the system and when changes are needed to ensure quality service. The following quote summarises this point well: 'The relevance of management studies to social work might lie in helping us to see when it is the system, not ourselves, which is at fault and when standards are not good enough and need changing.' (Coulshed and Mullender, 2001: 12) Examples of how workers can influence the quality of their service will be considered later in the chapter.

While human service workers may not immediately see that management or leadership are core parts of their role, a closer examination will show that in fact they are central. Chenoweth and McAuliffe (2008: 15), in their introductory text for social work and human service practice, identify eight domains of practice in which they believe social workers and human service practitioners have a legitimate place. Organisational practice, management and leadership is one of these domains. The others are: work with individuals; work with families and partnerships; group work; community work; social policy; research and evaluation; and education and training. Chenoweth and McAuliffe make the important point that social workers and human service practitioners are not the only workers/ professionals who have legitimacy in these domains; they do, however, have a key role to play and a unique opportunity for influence, given the breadth of their training.

While human service workers often move into positions of leadership after they have worked in the field for a number of years, there are also examples of human service workers taking up this role early in their working careers. The first position one of the authors undertook in the human services field was coordinator for a small, newly funded community organisation. While she had a community-based management committee to provide overall direction and to help identify community issues and concerns, and a co-worker with excellent knowledge of the community (but no training in human service work), most of the day-to-day planning and management functions fell to her. The broad training provided by her social work education—particularly in areas such as policy, community work, group work and management issues—provided an excellent foundation to help her understand how to establish new services and to work with a wide range of funding bodies, community groups, human service organisations and government departments.

MANAGEMENT IN HUMAN SERVICE ORGANISATIONS

A lot has been written about management in organisations. As suggested in Chapter 1, a key difference when considering management of human services is that most do not have profit as their primary motive—unlike business, where management theory first was developed. Much of the research on leadership has also been in for-profit organisations (Packard, 2009). That said, as also outlined in Chapter 1, an increasing number of for-profit organisations are now operating in the human service area. For the purpose of this chapter, we will focus on understanding theories of leadership and management as they are applied to human service organisations. This will assist you to develop an understanding of your employing organisation and the challenges it faces in providing social and community services.

In *The Handbook of Human Services Management*, Patti (2009) provides a comprehensive overview of management and organisational theory and practice as they are applied to human services. The book is a key resource for human service management and has contributions from a wide range of practitioners and academics. The central theme of the book, in Patti's words, is 'how to manage human service organisations in ways that lead to the provision of high quality, effective services to consumers' (2009: ix). The book has a strong focus on issues and approaches important for managers. However, the way the organisation is run will affect not only the quality of service to consumers but also the satisfaction of workers within it and their capacity to achieve their goals. Patti (2009: 3) defines management—also referred to as *administration*—as 'one of the methods of practice employed by human service workers to achieve their professional and organisational objectives'. He sees management and leadership as core to human service work. This view may not be shared by workers new to the field, but a lot can be gained by thinking about opportunities for leadership and this is what we hope to give you a feeling for in this chapter. It is also important to understand how management requirements may impact on your capacity to work in the organisation.

Patti sees management as essential to the optimum functioning of human service organisations. He discusses the range of managerial roles in human services and outlines key roles. For the purpose of this chapter, we will not discuss these roles; however, by listing them we can get an idea of the huge range of roles a manager can undertake. These are: communicator, boundary spanner, futurist-innovator, organiser, resource evaluator, policy practitioner, advocate, supervisor, facilitator and team-builder/leader (Patti, 2009: 10–11).

Patti (2009: 13) identifies three levels of management authority: the executive level (e.g. CEO); the middle level (program directors); and the supervisory or technical level (e.g. team leaders). He notes that workers who do not have a specific management function can also contribute to the 'managerial processes', particularly as facilitators and team-builders. Activities such as membership on agency or inter-agency committees and providing feedback on the impact of policies and procedures at the grass-roots level are examples of this.

The role of your managers will be set out within the organisational structure. The degree of autonomy and support you have in your position will be apparent from your job description or duty statement. It is important for you to have a clear understanding of what is expected of your manager and how much autonomy you will have. Do take the time to familiarise yourself with what is expected. This should be done through reading the agency formal documentation and by speaking with your manager and with colleagues. If there is something you do not understand—ask. Do not leave it until an issue arises to find out that certain things are expected of you, or conversely, should have been provided by your manager.

If you do not feel that your needs or rights are being properly considered, do not ignore this and potentially end up feeling stressed or trapped; rather, spend some time reflecting on the situation, explore possible action you can take and seek advice from other workers or managers. If this does not help, consider seeking input from professional bodies or your union. The importance of maintaining professional relationships and strategies for dealing with conflict is addressed later in this book (Chapters 6 and 8) and will help you in understanding constructive ways of dealing with poor management. The role of their manager is a very significant one for any human service worker, but particularly so for someone new to the field. It is worth spending a short while considering what you do or can expect from your manager.

EXERCISE

Take a few minutes to think about managers with whom you have worked, perhaps at a placement agency or in a human service setting.

- Write down the three keys things you see as being integral to the manager's role.
- Think of an example of where a manager performed his or her management role well.
- Think of another example where you feel a manager did not perform well. What made the difference? Was it personal qualities? The structure of the setting? Something else? Discuss your examples in pairs/groups and see whether there is shared understanding about what was/wasn't done well and why. Also see whether you can reach agreement about what the role of the manager should be in the situations you discussed and what is needed for it to work well.

What will you expect from managers? Factors that may influence this will be:

- your previous experiences, both good and bad
- your colleagues' perceptions
- your personality
- your understanding of the organisation and its focus and aims.

LEADERSHIP IN HUMAN SERVICE ORGANISATIONS

While most human service workers are able to understand the role of managers, leadership is more difficult to define, and there are wide-ranging views about how it does and does not differ from management (Lawler, 2007; Gardner, 2006; Patti, 2009; Jackson and Donovan, 1999). Many writers consider—as do we—that management involves a line responsibility for the day-to-day work of a group of staff, whereas leadership can both be a component of management and also be exercised by others within the organisation. In his article on leadership in social work, Lawler (2007: 126) clearly states that the literature on leadership is now of the view that 'they do constitute different phenomena, with management focusing more on efficiency and regulation, as leadership focuses more on change and motivation'.

Packard (2009) provides a comprehensive overview of historical and current views of leadership, and notes that a wide range and mix of approaches have been and continue to be used in organisations. This is quite a complex area, and it is useful to quote Packard for an overview of these approaches:

> The earliest research on leadership focused on traits, which were originally seen as innate characteristics of leaders. This area of study has broadened to include skills and competencies as well as more innate traits. Next, research in to group dynamics examined interpersonal and task behaviours as they impacted group effectiveness. The notion of leadership style evolved from this work, often used in a continuum from autocratic or directive styles to participatory approaches. Eventually, researchers explored the notion that there is no one 'best way' of leading and identified contingencies that would suggest the best approach. Current theories commonly include elements of several of these earlier models. (2009: 146)

Human service workers keen to understand more about theories of leadership (and management) could read Packard's chapter in full and read the *Handbook of Human Services Management* more widely (Patti, 2009). Those with a particular interest in the management of smaller non-profit organisations will find a lot of practical and local information in Jackson and Donovan's book *Managing to Survive* (1999), which is written primarily for managers and board members of smaller organisations within the human service sector. Their earlier book, *Managing Human Service Organisations* (Donovan and Jackson, 1991) is a more detailed account that provides some valuable information to help readers understand and support management of human services from an Australian perspective. Coulshed and Mullender (2001) also provide some practical and very accessible guidance on management within social work; while written from a British perspective, this book is still very relevant to human service practice and management in Australia.

Within the human services, there are many definitions of leadership. Packard uses Northouse's definition of leadership as 'a process by which an individual influences a group of individuals to achieve common goals' (2009: 144). This fairly straightforward definition makes sense to us. Packard focuses on program and agency leadership; however, he also notes that leadership can take place at other levels, including groups, teams and more broadly communities and countries. For the new worker, it is at the group or team level that they have the potential to exercise leadership.

More recent writings on leadership have shifted away from a concern with the personal qualities of a leader to an understanding of dimensions of leadership and how important characteristics can be developed (Lawler, 2007; Jackson and Donovan, 1999). Another important way of understanding management and leadership is provided by considering the concepts of transactional and transformational leadership. Lawler (2007: 126) describes these as follows: 'Transactional leadership (or "management") has a focus on stability, efficiency, formal authority, coordination, results and control. Transformational leadership has a focus on effectiveness, change and the development of co-operation, motivation and values.'

The introduction of values is where leadership starts to show a clear connection with human service workers, and social work in particular. Values are central to professional practice—as articulated, for example, through a Code of Ethics (AASW). Hughes and Wearing (2007: 79) refer to more recent theories of leadership as 'new leadership', where the leader is seen as influencing organisational culture and articulating shared values and purpose. Throughout their chapter on leadership, Hughes and Wearing (2007) identify a strong potential role for social work in particular in leadership within human service organisations. We will revisit the question of leadership and human services values and practice standards at the end of this chapter.

Opinions about how a manager should exercise leadership and about what makes a good manager or leader vary greatly. It is interesting to note that research has shown when workers are asked about leadership they often see leadership as what managers do or should do (Gardner, 2006). Donovan and Jackson (1991) also state that in human service organisations there is a tendency to focus on what should be done without considering factors that may impact on decision-making. Hughes and Wearing (2007: 78) state that while the common image of a leader in an organisation is a 'purposeful, active change agent', they see this as a construction that does not match people's lived experience in organisations. They make the following observation about how decisions can be made in organisations: not all decisions are handed down to social workers from 'on high' and as a *fait accompli*. Many are experienced by front-line workers as being negotiated in process, with real and sometimes unintended consequences.

This supports our view that human service workers do have more opportunities to influence decisions than they realise. It is a matter of looking for these opportunities and building your own confidence and capacity to make a contribution. It is also useful to understand that not all actions and decisions of managers are made in perfect, planned circumstances. Consider the following case study, which illustrates both the capacity for workers to influence service delivery and the difficulties managers can have when seeking to implement change.

Case study: Gathering statistics

Lisa is a new worker in a family support agency. When she joins she is told by her manager, Maria, that her employment is part of an expansion of services for the agency, brought about by new funding from the state government. She is told that it will be important for continued funding of her position that statistics are accurately kept. Lisa is happy with this as she is keen to keep working in the program and is interested in seeing details on the types of service users/situations the program encounters and the range and number of outcomes.

When Lisa meets her co-workers, she starts to hear many complaints about the manager. Workers are unhappy with the changes she has introduced and particularly unhappy about the need to keep lots of detailed statistics, which they see as irrelevant. Several of her co-workers tell her that Maria has changed since she took on the management role, and that the statistics she has told them to keep do not make sense for the new program, in which Maria has never worked. They tell her that they aren't really bothering to keep the statistics and will make up entries when they are forced to put in their monthly reports.

Lisa becomes more and more worried, as she knows that her continuing employment depends on the extra funding and that the statistics are needed to prove the amount and type of work they are doing. She is also concerned because she agrees with the other workers that the statistics kept do not make sense and do not reflect all of the work done. She starts to worry that she will not have a job for long, so although she is really enjoying the work and it is in her area of interest, she decides to look for a new position in another agency.

Discussion questions

- What do you think has happened here?
- Is there something Lisa could have done to try to improve her situation?
- What do you think may be happening between Maria and the other staff?
- If you were asked by Maria to help in this situation, what would you suggest?
- What could the other workers do if they were unhappy with the changes?

EXERCISING LEADERSHIP AT THE FRONT LINE

Now that we have given an overview of management and leadership in the human services and spent some time thinking about what a manager 'should do', or what may impact on their ability to manage, it is time to think about what role you might play as a worker in a human service agency. We start by considering some of the roles workers can undertake in the management of their organisations and then move on to discuss examples of how human service workers can contribute to management and leadership in their organisation. We want you to think about how you can exercise leadership; what you can do to improve the quality of service to your consumers and what you can do to improve your own and others' job satisfaction.

As outlined at the start of the chapter, we believe that it is possible for front-line workers to exercise leadership and that this is a core part of their role/domain of practice within the human services field. Jackson and Donovan (1999: 9) discuss the relationship between management and leadership; their view is that very few activities are purely leadership or purely management, but most activities are both. For new human service workers, a useful distinction may be made between roles where workers have a formal responsibility for other staff or activities, and broader leadership functions that can be exercised apart from these formal roles.

The role of front-line workers in management

Chenoweth and McAuliffe (2008: 19) provide a clear overview of management responsibilities. They state:

> *Management responsibilities, which are often administrative in nature, include recruiting and employing staff, training volunteers, negotiating funding arrangements and budgets, evaluating services, developing policy, public speaking and coordinating services.*

They provide the following examples of management responsibilities:

- being responsible, as a senior social worker, for a staff team in a major hospital and coordinating organisational responses to staffing issues
- managing a community agency responsible for coordinating women's health services across a region
- managing a government funding program for community agencies that provides gambling support services in rural areas
- managing a multicultural community agency responsible for providing language programs to linguistically diverse communities
- providing clinical supervision within a child protection agency (Chenoweth and McAuliffe, 2008: 19).

While many positions requiring management and leadership skills are often administrative, leadership skills are also important in non-administrative positions. Human service workers can move to management positions—most typically as senior workers/practitioners—and they can also be administratively accountable to or for workers from different disciplines other than their own. Organisational skills and the ability to work constructively with other disciplines are identified as some of the key factors important to human service management.

It is important to understand that while leadership opportunities may come with line management or administrative accountability, they do not always have to go together and in some cases administrative responsibly can in fact detract from the capacity to exercise good leadership. It is important to strike a balance between administrative responsibility and the opportunity to exercise leadership. Sometimes the administrative responsibility can give legitimacy to your role in areas you can influence, but in other situations it can take the focus away from areas in which human service workers can make a real contribution, and tie up their time and resources with bureaucratic procedures and processes.

Case study: Centrelink

A good example of this is the history of social workers working with administrative staff in settings such as Centrelink. As a new and the sole social worker in a new Centrelink office, Sue was keen to find better ways to support the staff who worked at the front counter, dealing with myriad inquiries and concerns from the public, sometimes having to deal with people who were either very distressed or at times very angry. The opportunity to take on the team leadership of this group of staff presented and she gladly accepted, seeing this as a way of both supporting the staff and of influencing the quality of service offered to people attending the office. The problem was that the team leader role carried a range of other responsibilities with it, including monitoring attendance, drawing up rosters and ensuring that staff were up to date with policy and procedural changes. All this detracted from Sue's capacity to provide a social work service to people attending the office. As there were no social workers amongst the other staff, this meant that there was less time to see service users or to undertake other social work activities such as service development, monitoring of policy or liaising with other service providers in the community. Eventually Sue decided that there were other ways to provide support to the front-line staff and to influence the quality of service provided for service users. An experienced administrative staff member was appointed as team leader and Sue acted as mentor for new front-line staff and attended team meetings. She also provided input on service user needs, inter-personal skills training and community needs awareness. Acceptance of Sue in this consultative role was certainly assisted by her time as team leader, where she established her legitimacy and developed a strong appreciation of the issues facing front-line staff and the competing demands placed on them.

The role of front-line workers in leadership

Leadership in social work in particular can often be exercised laterally, not only from above, as illustrated by the Centrelink case study. A common situation where line management or team leadership is not an issue is when a human service worker influences his or her fellow workers to engage in appropriate practice through example, or by discussing how they would work in a particular situation. (See the Migrant Resource Centre case study later in this section for an example of this).

Coulshed and Mullender (2001) argue that all workers are managers; they also explore similarities between the skills involved in direct practice and in management. Central to this are interpersonal skills, working towards change and an understanding of group work theory and practice. The role of case manager is used to illustrate core aspects of human service work practice that provide good preparation for management because they require workers to utilise skills in areas such as negotiating, liaison and advocacy, as well as working within a budget. From this it should follow that workers in the human service field already possess the skills to exercise good leadership.

Examples of human service workers exercising leadership include:

- monitoring the quality of the service offered by the agency, either through a formal role in evaluation or by informal observation and feedback
- maximising service user orientation/focus through raising issues, staff training or commenting on proposed changes
- human service workers participating in management team of organisations (e.g. the senior social work role in Centrelink at the local level and in area management forums)
- participating in professional organisations such as the AASW
- participating in organisational working parties
- participating in unions (e.g. the Australian Services Union)
- serving on boards of other organisations (e.g. on the management committee of the local community centre or youth housing service).

The ability to appreciate the skills and knowledge of others as well as exercise leadership in a multidisciplinary setting is critical to successful work in human services. Lawler sees the concept of 'interprofessional leadership' as a key way that human service workers can exercise leadership in the human services (2007: 131).

A number of authors have discussed the importance of working towards change in an organisation (e.g. Gardner 2006; Coulshed and Mullender, 2001). We believe that this focus on organisational change and on improvement in the quality of service provision can be accomplished by human service workers exercising leadership. Coulshed and Mullender (2001: 16) state that workers within an organisation can contribute to change or innovation. They note: 'These do not always have to come from the outside; changing the agency from within occurs quite frequently and one need not be in a position of power to influence agency practice.'

Gardner (2006) discusses the concept of 'working actively' in the organisation. She looks at ways to work within the organisation for change and at times to resist change. The view she presents sits well with the definition of leadership we have promoted throughout this chapter.

Gardner also argues that while many workers at the lower end of an organisation often feel powerless and unable to voice their concerns, they in fact can initiate/resist change more than they realise. She makes the important point that:

> *workers are so focused on working with service users that they have no energy left to change or challenge the organisation. Often too, workers somehow loose the capacity to stand back from their organisation to see it more clearly, to be able to identify—as they would with an individual or community service user—how it works and how change may be possible, and then to take active steps to achieve this.* (Gardner, 2006: 128–9)

While workers will at times undertake a clear leadership or management role for a set period of time or purpose, it is also important for workers to be alert to opportunities for 'situational leadership'. By this we mean that there will be times when it is important to initiate action or show leadership in addressing an immediate issue or concern. What we hope to do by giving a brief overview of management and introducing the concept of leadership at human service worker level is to encourage you to always be open to the possibility of change and to have the confidence to make an effort.

Some strategies can that be used to work towards change include raising the issue, gathering information, promoting the case for change more formally, building support and actively advocating for change. These strategies can be used whether you seek small or larger scale change, and whether or not the change is wanted within or outside the agency (Gardner, 2006: 135). We believe that these strategies are concrete examples of exercising leadership.

Case study: Migrant Resource Centre

Jack is a worker in a Migrant Resource Centre. He has been there for about a year and is responsible to the team leader of the settlement program. A new worker, Ahmed, is employed to work as part of the settlement team with one of the emerging communities; he has limited experience in human service work and has been employed because of his cultural understanding and language skills. Jack notices that Ahmed is working very long hours and overhears him arranging for service users to contact him at home on weekends and evenings. He is also suspects that Ahmed is not keeping case notes for many of his contacts due to lack of time and the belief that he will be the only person working with the service users. Jack knows that Ahmed is meant to be receiving supervision and support from the team leader; however, this team leader is very busy due to another worker leaving. Jack also is aware that Ahmed is anxious to do a good job and is reluctant to approach his supervisor with any concerns in case this is seen as him not coping. Given these factors, Jack is also reluctant to speak to the team leader about his concerns, but he is beginning to feel that service users who see Ahmed are not getting an appropriate service. He can remember feeling like this when he started at the service a year earlier.

Discussion questions
- List some specific actions Jack could take.
- Should he advise the team leader?
- What are the longer term or broader issues Jack should be considering?
- What other factors may be relevant to the team leader not supporting Ahmed?

While a manager has the authority of his or her position to give weight to the wish for change, this does not mean that the change will be accepted without proper planning and support, as illustrated in the earlier Gathering statistics case study where Maria had difficulties exercising her management role. Conversely, as a worker you may not have a clear organisational mandate to identify issues/ areas of concern, but you still have the potential and the professional or ethical imperative to do so. This is illustrated by the Migrant Resource Centre case study above and will be considered further in the next section on leadership and professional values.

Another example of leadership that human service workers can exercise is to work with others to maximise services. Munn and Munn (2003) describe this role as that of 'social innovator', and describe the important function that social workers can play in their local community by working with both formal and informal networks to respond to change and develop services. This is an example of the importance of understanding the broad human services field and as well as having the capacity to understand and value the work of other disciplines. A human service worker in a rural area may be the only funded and qualified worker in the town—certainly a government employee may have the job security and continuity that other project funded positions will not. In this role, the human service worker can assist the community by resourcing and supporting local networks. This could be by acting as a convenor of a local welfare network, assisting with funding applications for much-needed local services or helping to coordinate local action/lobby groups. This is a role that can be played in other communities; however, there is likely to be a wider range of workers who can participate in this way in metropolitan settings. Other examples of leadership in this cross-agency discipline include the role of human service workers in disaster-recovery action.

Now that we have explored the importance of human service workers influencing the quality of service through exercising leadership, and have considered skills workers have in their practitioner role that can equip them to do this, let's consider another case study where leadership can be exercised. This case study involves both internal organisational change and work with a range of services.

Case study: Emergency funding for youth

Sonia is an outreach worker for a local government youth services program. One of the major issues faced by young people in her area is insufficient money for food and school costs for young people who either live away from home or come from families on very low incomes. There is a small amount of funding available from council for the youth counsellor to help out his service users; however, this is rarely enough and can only be provided to ongoing service users of the youth counselling program. As the youth counsellor only works one day per week, young people cannot access any of the funds on other days. Sonia is aware of many young people who cannot access any funds. The local community advice bureau receives some government funding to provide emergency relief; however, young people do not attend this service as they feel unwelcome there and the workers have said they do not want young people attending the service as they are concerned that their older service users will feel threatened by them. A number of church-based services also provide emergency relief when funds are available but they do not open during any regular hours. Sonia would like to improve young people's access to emergency relief funding and also improve the capacity of local services to work with young people more generally. She has raised this as a concern with the Social and Community Services manager, who says that emergency relief is not the council's role and the extra funding was made available to cater for young people who couldn't access the community information and support centres.

Discussion questions
- What options are open to Sonia?
- What can she can do to improve access within council?
- What action could she take to improve capacity of local agencies to work with young people?
- Is this part of her job? Why?

LEADERSHIP AND PROFESSIONAL VALUES

From our discussion of aspects of leadership in human services, it is clear that leadership is far more than line management and is not only the responsibility of those in designated leadership positions.

As a human service worker, you will have an ethical duty to look more broadly than your own day-to-day practice, and to do all you can to improve services provided by yourself and the organisation for which you work.

An example of this broader focus is provided by the Australian Association of Social Workers' (AASW) Code of Ethics, which clearly shows the importance of working at a broader level. Within this code, the purpose of social work is stated as follows:

> *The social work profession is committed to the pursuit and maintenance of human wellbeing. Social work aims to maximise the development of human potential and the fulfilment of human needs, through an equal commitment to:*
> * *working with and enabling people to achieve the best possible levels of personal and social well-being*
> * *working to achieve social justice through social development and social change (AASW Code of Ethics, 1999).*

Examples of how this can be done are provided through the AASW Practice Standards (2003), which were developed to guide practice and to provide a means of accountability. Practice Standard 2—Service Management states that:

> *All social workers, regardless of their organisational position or the context of their practice, have the responsibility to manage their own service provision and practice in a way which is consistent with these standards. This may involve management of staff and other Agency resources. The term 'social work manager' therefore applies to all social workers.* (AASW, 2003: 13)

This reinforces the points we have stressed throughout this chapter: that leadership is not just the role of the manager and that ethical work in the human service field involves taking a broader view, raising issues or taking action rather than just believing it is someone else's responsibility. Leadership is one way in which you are able to influence the quality of work undertaken and a practical demonstration of your willingness to work with others to improve services and address important issues of social justice and equity.

CONCLUSION

Through this chapter, you will have begun to understand the meaning of leadership in the human services and explored how you can exercise leadership as a new human service worker. We hope that you will also have begun to think about the role of managers in human services and to consider how you may use this, either as a worker or in a management position, to improve the quality of service more broadly.

Chapter review questions

2.1   Why is leadership important to human service workers?

2.2   What impact has managerialism had on human service workers?

2.3   How are management and leadership similar and different?

2.4   As a new worker in a human services organisation, what do you need to know about the organisation's management?

2.5   In what ways can a front-line worker exercise leadership? Give three examples, either from your experience or that you can see yourself undertaking.

OTHER RESOURCES

Centre for Social Leadership, < www.socialleaders.org>.
Community Leadership Centre, <www.ourcommunity.com.au/leadership/leadership_main.jsp>.

KEY READINGS

Coulshed, V. and Mullender, A. 2001, 'Management as Vision, Strategy and Leadership', in *Management in Social Work* (2nd ed.), Palgrave, Houndsmills.
Gardner, F. 2006, 'Working Actively within the Organisation', in *Working with Human Service Organisations*, Oxford University Press, Melbourne.
Hughes, M. and Wearing, M. 2007, 'Leadership, Decision Making and Risk', in *Organisations and Management in Social Work*, Sage, London.

CHAPTER THREE | Scoping the context

SUMMARY

This chapter is designed to illustrate how, when beginning work in a new organisation, workers can systematically approach developing an understanding of the context in which they are engaging. It involves scoping the ideological, political and legal context in which service delivery is undertaken, both within and between organisations, and in terms of the broader social context of a transforming welfare state.

WHY IS CONTEXT IMPORTANT?

As a human service worker, you often need to achieve a balance between your duty of care to your service users, your co-workers and your organisation. In order to achieve this, you have to be aware not only of the ideological, political and legal context of your organisation and how it fits into the bigger and ever-changing welfare landscape, but also of the tensions between your political and ideological beliefs and the needs of your service users. We have spoken to human service workers on many occasions who tell us that they leave their political and ideological beliefs out of their work with service users and organisations. Protestations notwithstanding, our position is that this cannot be done.

> *Ideology and ideological belief:* A doctrine or set of beliefs, usually informed by a set of political ideas.

Working in the human services field is inevitably political work, shaped and defined by legislation and the dominant ideological beliefs current at any particular time. What the workers to whom we referred above are really saying is that they do not properly understand the context of their work—certainly not enough to reflect on its impact on their implicit beliefs about service users, about the problems they confront and about their organisations. In effect, not being able to engage in critical reflection on all aspects of the context means such workers are in danger of neglecting their duty of care to their service users and to their agencies. Further, as a human service worker, you cannot advocate effectively if you are unaware of the political, legal and ideological position of yourself, your service users, your organisation and the industry as a whole.

> *Critical reflection:* A process by which workers research, evaluate and improve their own practice. It is intended to enhance a worker's ability to move beyond ideology and to scrutinise his or her own practice in relation to personal and professional values and commitments.

Duty of care: An imperative that applies to a range of situations; an obligation that a sensible person would have in the circumstances when acting towards others and the public. If the actions of a person are not made with care, attention, caution and prudence, their actions are considered negligent.

THE BIG PICTURE

Before we delve into the ways in which workers can interpret and understand the political, ideological and philosophical pressures and demands of working in the human services, we need to look at the bigger picture. It is necessary that we develop an awareness of the human service landscape: who works where, the relationships between the government and non-profit sectors, and some of the major bodies of law that shape the overall context of practice.

Developing an awareness of the industry and its labour force

Meagher and Healy (2006) state that the caring professions—those professions that focus on looking after people's physical, developmental, emotional and basic practical needs such as housing and income support—constitute a growing and expanding industry in the current climate. Certainly, the Commonwealth government agrees. The health and social care industry (in which human service organisations are located) is large. The industry is the fastest growing industry in Australia, set to expand to 24 per cent of all employment over the next five years. The industry is set to continue to grow by nearly 4 per cent until 2013 and 2014 (Department of Education, Employment and Workplace Relations, 2009) and produce an extra 170 000 jobs. Social workers, youth workers, criminal justice workers, welfare workers, community development workers, mental health workers, disability support workers, residential care workers, housing workers and employment placement workers, to name just a few, make up the many different backgrounds of workers in the growing human and community services field.

In terms of where the work is located in the current human service labour market, community services, welfare, education and health are the leading areas of employment for workers:

> *The bulk of employment in some caring occupations, such as counsellors and psychologists, was spread across the three main human service industries in 2001. Of all those reporting working as a counsellor in their main job, 39% were employed in community services, 26% in education, and 21% in health.* (Meagher and Healy, 2006: 29)

Human service workers are employed by an enormous range of agencies and organisations—of all sizes and with different auspices—all of which impact on how an organisation functions and how it is experienced by service users. In Australia, these range from many religious-based and secular charitable organisations to government bodies that deal with health, child protection, aged care and almost anything else one can think of. Employment in the human services industry is vast and varied, and as a result many fields of practice that could benefit from close and open dialogue with each other (for example, family violence and child protection) are often distanced in terms of funding, understanding, philosophy, evaluation practices and outcomes for service users.

An interesting trend that can be extrapolated from the Meagher and Healy (2006) study is that between 1996 and 2001, there was a definite change in the structure of employment in community services industries. Data from this time period show that there is a trend towards deinstitutionalisation of certain service user groups (such as people with a disability) accompanied by a corresponding trend in the deprofessionalisation of those working with this group of service users. What this means is that while service users are less likely to be living in an institutional setting (and much more likely to be living in home-based and community-based care and treatment options), correspondingly the workers who work with them are likely not to hold a professional qualification. As a professional worker in the human services field, this will have an impact on you in terms of how you work with this group of lesser qualified colleagues as well as service users. It has implications for the resources available to carry out your work and also for the ways in which you are able to work with other workers who may have a different understanding and interpretation of the many factors that contribute to service users' situations.

Understanding the role of the state and the non-state sectors in service delivery and the relationships between them

It is important to take a moment to understand how we came to be in the position in which we find ourselves in Australia in terms of organisations and agencies providing welfare services within the contemporary human services landscape. When Australia was settled as a colony of Great Britain, the colonial government policies of the day rejected the British approach to social support, and avoided any collective approaches to welfare activity. It has been well documented that settler societies in Australia and New Zealand were adamant that there would be no 'poor laws' and the associated workhouses in the new colonies (Thomson, 1998; Dickey, 1987; Mendelsohn, 1979). That approach was understood to promote unwanted dependency by the poor on institutional charity. The settling of the new world was seen as an opportunity to do things differently, and the understanding was that there would be plenty of work so people wouldn't need welfare. Poverty would only belong to those who brought it upon themselves. (The 'gendered bias' of this philosophy and what would happen to the many young women left 'holding the baby', so to speak, needs to be remembered, but that is a subject for another discussion.)

> *Poor Laws:* A system of poverty relief established in Elizabethan England, wherein landholders residing in parishes paid a 'tax' for the relief of the poor in that parish.

> *Workhouses:* Also known as 'indoor relief'. Part of the poor law system of relief, they were harsh institutions in which the destitute were forced to live and work.

As a result of this, government intervention to promote the welfare of the destitute was kept at a minimum. Support for those who couldn't support themselves was expected to come from families, neighbours or the Christian charities that were establishing themselves in the new colonies. The authorities at this time made a firm decision not just to stay out of the business of assisting the poor, but also to promote the idea that to be poor or to need help meant that a person was somehow morally deficient (Thomson, 1998). The reliance on religious charities and the accompanying lack of any legislation by governments to regulate these charities resulted in a system where judgement, discrimination and substandard service delivery towards those deemed the 'undeserving poor' was rife.

> ***Deserving and undeserving poor:*** The deserving poor were those considered to be destitute through no fault of their own (e.g. orphans); the undeserving poor were those able-bodied people who had the capacity to work but who (apparently) chose not to.

This legacy of the beginnings of welfare in this country has meant that a philosophy which distinguishes between the so-called deserving and undeserving poor still filters through in various forms of government legislation, charitable activity and income support today. (Think, for example, of the single mothers mentioned previously, and the ways in which they are still judged in government departments such as Centrelink.) Our welfare history has also left us with a welfare system that resembles a patchwork quilt—and it is a quilt that, in the traditions of all good families, has been handed down through the generations to the present day. Unlike the United Kingdom, where local government plays a major role in the provision of welfare and child protection, Australia has a welfare system that involves all three tiers of government (local, state and federal). It also involves other agencies and organisations deriving from those earlier charities (for example Anglicare, Kildonan, the Benevolent Society, St Vincent de Paul, the Brotherhood of St Laurence, the Salvation Army, the Smith Family), plus a whole raft of smaller community agencies largely set up because of developments in social policy from the 1970s onwards.

The welfare service delivery system varies from state to state within Australia—for example, the involvement of local government varies dramatically—and these days most organisations compete fiercely against one another for government funding. As a worker in the human services area, your work will be influenced by this history as well as by the present purchase of service contracting arrangements (discussed later). You will have to be aware of this in order to negotiate the 'system'.

> *Purchase-of-service contracting:* A system whereby a government buys the services of a non-state organisation to deliver human services it deems appropriate. The relationship between the purchaser (the state) and the provider (the non-state organisation) is managed via a legally binding contract.

The implications of these complexities mean that the major funding bodies for employment in the human services industry include federal, state and local governments, alongside various charitable and religious-based organisations and many smaller non-government agencies. The chances are that, as a worker in the human services industry, you will be employed by or your position will be either directly or partially funded by one of the three tiers of government. This can have major implications for the kinds of work you can do and the kinds of support you have for your work, as well as for the work you cannot do. Further, it may well place service users in different boxes or categories that will not be a good fit for them or address their needs adequately. You only need to look at the restrictions on Centrelink workers, child protection workers and immigration workers to gain an understanding of the importance of legislation and governance on your role in the human services industry. Legislation often defines who deserves what and who doesn't in terms of income support, legal protection and residency. Such categorisation of needy people constrains the work of a human service worker. So how do you negotiate your way around this minefield?

Big-picture influences on the organisational context

As a worker in the human services field, you need to have a good understanding of the dominant frameworks for conceptualising and responding to 'social problems'. The ways in which social issues and social problems are interpreted and understood in our society are constantly changing and adjusting, depending on the trends and philosophies of those in power. As these changes filter down to practice contexts, so do the dominant frameworks we use to understand and respond to these social problems.

Working in this line of work, it is our responsibility to be vigilant and consistent in interpreting, evaluating and critically analysing not only the motives behind the ways in which many social problems are conceptualised and interpreted by society, but also the ways in which the dominant frameworks for practice prescribe how we respond to these. Dominant prescriptions for how human service workers should respond to service users in certain categories may be based on flawed agendas of those in power. These agendas may serve the interests of a very few, often at the expense of your service users.

> *Critical analysis:* Similar to critical reflection; a process by which a worker thinks rationally and systematically about a situation or context using knowledge about injustice, discrimination and structural inequality.

A recent example of a 'dominant prescription' in Australia would be the way in which the behaviour of asylum seekers was portrayed to the public by the Howard Coalition government, and to a certain extent by the Labor government under Julia Gillard. Asylum seekers have been represented as 'queue jumpers', as 'un-Australian' and as a group not to be trusted. Federal government funding requirements and the practice procedures that flowed from this agenda meant that many human service workers had their frameworks for practice dictated in no uncertain terms. Workers had to be aware of the ways in which this group of service users was conceptualised and the corresponding ways in which this impacted on the work they were able to do. This often meant working in different ways—for example, gaining a firm understanding of the new legislation, the new categories of visas and the loopholes, and developing a working knowledge of which organisations were still able to offer services to this group of people. It meant that it was harder to work in an empowering way with people who were judged and ostracised by the wider community, as well as harder to educate those in that wider community about the reality of their lives.

Working through this period of time demonstrated the very real need for human service workers to think critically and to strive for an intelligent and humane understanding of the bigger picture in which our work is situated and the impact this can have on our service users. You need to scrutinise the bigger picture by asking questions about how service user issues are defined by those who hold the power to define them. What structures at the local, state, federal or global levels (whether they be legal, political, religious or social) are working to oppress, discriminate or contribute to your service users' issues? Why is this the case? Read the following case study and answer the questions posed.

The first step in gaining an awareness of the bigger picture is to have a clear understanding of structural discrimination and to use this as a lens through which to adapt any framework for practice to ensure that you are working for the best outcome for your service users. The next step in understanding the bigger picture is for you as a worker to gain some insight into the not so obvious ways in which this structural discrimination can be built into prescriptions for practice. Human service workers are often 'encouraged' to respond to these 'social problems' in specific ways.

> *Structural discrimination:* Discrimination against a person or group on the basis of race, cultural background, gender, race, age and/or disability.

This does not mean that you need to become critical for the sake of it when new frameworks and ways of working are introduced by

Case study: Access to community health services
You are a social worker, working in a community health centre. Part of your job is to facilitate access to the services of the community health centre for various groups in the local community, including newly arrived asylum seekers who are waiting for their immigration status to be finalised. You know that this is a very stressful time for this group of people. They have spoken to you often about the reasons why they were forced to flee their country, and the grief of having to leave family members behind. Many of the families with which you work have not been able to contact those they left behind, and are not even sure whether they survived. They have also talked about their journey to Australia, a journey that often took years, during which time they were attacked and assaulted and had few if any medical or dental services. Recently, the elderly citizens' exercise group has approached you. They are complaining about having to share the resources of the centre (e.g. the bus, the meeting rooms, etc.), with these new groups. They feel that, as they have always been here volunteering and working in the centre, they have more of a claim to these resources than the people who only just got here. They are angry and racist in their comments to you about the asylum seekers, and are demanding that you give them priority access to the centre's resources for the coming term.

Discussion questions
- What steps can you take to diffuse this situation?
- What do you think may be contributing to the exercise group's racist attitude?
- How may this impact on your already traumatised group of asylum seekers?
- In what ways could you increase each group's understanding of each other and their needs?
- Who would you feed this situation 'up' to and what would you be asking for?

governments and peak bodies. It does mean, however, that you need to ask yourself some questions about who is doing the defining, the prescribing and why. There are numerous examples of this in the human services field at the present time, with the dominance of frameworks and practices—based, for example, on medical models of interpreting presenting issues. These often serve to pathologise and blame individuals rather than situate their issues within broader social structures. An example of this would be the way the current system of employment services pathologises and blames the unemployed for their predicament, thereby authorising punitive and intrusive responses (see McDonald and Marston, 2008b). It can also be found in some of the ways in which the evidence-based practice approach is used.

'Evidence-based' approaches to the human services

As a human service worker, you will need to develop an informed position regarding the rise and adoption of evidence-based practice and research-informed practice in the human services industry. These approaches to practice are more than informed suggestions about ways forward. Indeed, as with everything in the social world, they contain and propel a moral agenda. Evidence-based practice in particular has been marketed to human service workers in many fields of practice as the most suitable model for workers to implement. One only needs to examine the terms and conditions of funding submissions and the tenders from any government department to gain an understanding of the ways in which this approach has saturated the human services. Your ongoing funding may well depend on the reporting and evaluation of practice through an evidence-based framework. So what is it and what are the implications of this saturation?

Evidence-based practice is derived from medical discourses, from a profession where scientific debates prevail. Evidence-based practice in the human services field draws on the tradition of evidence-based medicine in which decisions made about the care of patients (in our case, service users) will come from knowledge gained from rigorous scientific studies and a rational approach to decision-making. O'Connor and colleagues (2008) argue that this implies human service workers have an ethical responsibility to develop their knowledge base and ensure best outcomes for service users through consistently drawing from the most up-to-date research-based knowledge available. No one would deny that this is the kind of practice we want to achieve; however, evidence-based practice frequently draws only on the most up-to-date knowledge in certain areas. As a result, it can assume a one-size-fits-all approach and often fails to take into account the complexities of the human condition.

> *Discourse:* A particular system of beliefs held in common by a group or field of activity that shapes understanding, communications and practices in that field.

Evidence-based practice is built on the medical and scientific premise that your service user has a specific problem or problems that can be isolated and treated. It is geared towards precise measurement, monitoring and evaluation, and promotes an over-simplified view of practice that can measure the treatment of the specific symptoms. It often cannot address the complex multiple layers of the life experience of your service user, or an understanding of the inequalities or oppressive practices that have also contributed to your service user's issues. Beddoe and Maidment (2009: 67) argue that the primary difficulty with evidence-based practice is that the human condition is very complex and that: 'service users frequently have multiple layers of issues to address, including practical and psychological concerns relating to structural inequality'.

Evidence-based practice claims to be scientific and objective, and as a worker you obviously want 'best practice' for your service users. However, you also need to be mindful that evidence-based practice *is* derived from the medical profession—or, more specifically, from a white, male, Westernised medical discourse that often does not understand or honour vast amounts of knowledge located outside its own domain. As a human service worker, you need to be respectful of other bodies of knowledge that can contribute to the work you are doing with your service users, such as feminist or Indigenous ways of understanding the issues your service users experience. You need to bring in ways of understanding diversity arising from gender, culture, race, class and age, as well as the oppression inherent in these categories at multiple levels.

We are not suggesting that you dismiss the entire genre of evidence-based practice. This would certainly be detrimental in today's climate. We are asking that you look sceptically at the dominant forces in the industry and be equally sceptical about calls for overly simplistic ways of measuring the human condition. At the same time, we suggest that you work with your service users to address their disadvantage and lessen the impact of pathologising practice and other prescriptions that 'blame the victim'. Reflect on the case study below and the questions we pose.

Case study: Inter-generational issues

Kara is a support worker in a family support agency. She works mainly with families referred to her from Child Protection. She receives a referral to work with a 28-year-old woman, Natalie, a mother of two children aged 13 and 14. According to the referral, Natalie has been sending her children to school hungry and they are often not turning up to school at all. The secondary college they attend made a notification on the grounds of neglect. The referral from child protection suggests that Natalie needs assistance with parenting and budgeting, and there is some suggestion that the children may be witnessing violence. Once Kara begins to work with Natalie, a history emerges of inter-generational poverty and abuse. Kara learns that Natalie ran away at the age of 12 due to sexual abuse, and lived with various relatives, one of whom also abused her. By the time she was 14, she was no longer attending school and would not leave her house. At 16 she had her first child to her 27-year-old cousin, who is currently in jail for assault. Natalie is now alone with her children, unable to work due to acute anxiety, and as she is not fulfilling her 'looking for work' criteria, she has had her income docked by Centrelink.

Discussion questions
- What are some of the bigger-picture structural issues that are contributing to Natalie's situation?
- Evidence-based practice would suggest that, as her worker, you need to be assisting Natalie to comply with Centrelink protocol by getting her to look for work, learn to budget and become a more assertive parent. What complexities does this miss in Natalie's situation?

Every agency and organisation within which you work in the human services field will have these 'bigger picture' issues and pressures to contend with. The trick is to be able to see these tensions, to be able to analyse and understand what is going on and to work within the parameters of this understanding for the best outcome for your service users. Some of the most positive ways forward in being able to work within these boundaries involve having a firm understanding of the major bodies of law that shape practice and govern organisations, and a comprehensive knowledge of the context of your specific organisation.

UNDERSTANDING THE MAJOR BODIES OF LAW

The work of human service organisations is governed by various laws or Acts of parliament, whether it is federal legislation, state legislation or local council regulations. Knowledge is power, and having a good grasp of the 'rules' that regulate your work, and an understanding of the ways in which these rules are interpreted by various government bodies and legal institutions, is extremely important. Furthermore, service users are often not given the information they require, or told the direction they need to take, because their worker is not familiar with the legislation within which the issue sits.

We are not advocating that you have your head around all the legislation in all areas of the work you do; however, you need to know many of the basic legal tenets of the work that is the main business of your organisation, and where to look for further information when you need it. Legislation governing the work we do in the human services field reflects the chaotic mixed economy of welfare in which health, welfare and community services are delivered in Australia. Some legislation that directs your work is federal, and is therefore national in its coverage of that specific issue—for example, the *Social Security Act* 1991, which sets out the parameters for income security and the *Family Law Act* 2008, which sets out residency, contact rules and procedures for separating parents. These acts, along with the *Aged Care Act* 1997, the *Migration Act* 1958 and the *Disability Act* 2006 are consistent no matter in what state or territory you find yourself working.

Much of the legislation that will govern your work on a day-to-day basis is state legislation. Legislation governing housing (*Residential Tenancy Acts*), family violence, sexual assault, mental health and child protection is all in the form of state Acts, and as such is different in every state and territory of Australia. You will find that some of these are similar in various states and some are very different. In a recent national comparison of child protection systems, for example, it was found that, despite some differences in legislative structures and some differences in the ways in which this legislation is interpreted and enacted, Australian states and territories are providing very comparable models of child protection intervention (Bromfield and Higgins, 2005). Australia has eight different child protection systems because each state and territory has responsibility for its own health and welfare issues. This means that there is no single definition of child abuse consistent throughout Australia. Problems can emerge when service users who are under investigation in one state for child protection issues move interstate.

This volume of state-specific legislation can lead to other issues. In the crimes (sexual offences) and family violence area, for example, there are no consistent national definitions covering child sexual abuse or domestic violence. This means that what you may be able to address in a court of law in one state may not necessarily even be in the legislation of another. This has implications with service users who often need the protection of the law as they move around the country (whether they be children or adults), and often works to the advantage of perpetrators.

The Attorney-General's Departments, either nationally or at a state level, are responsible for regularly reviewing Acts to keep them up to date with changing times and changing community attitudes. It is your responsibility as a worker in this field to keep abreast of the changes and to familiarise yourself with new provisions to Acts of parliament. Often the best way to do this is to ensure that you find out who is offering training and workshops on revised or new legislation, and book yourself into this training.

Your agency or organisation should have copies of the legislation and legal frameworks that guide or control the everyday business of your agency. Take time to familiarise yourself with these documents. If they are not available, look them up. Legislation is available on the Attorney-General's website for every state in Australia. Alternatively, go to the website of the Australian Legal Information Institute at <www.austlii.edu.au>. Also ensure that you (or your agency) are a member of professional and industry peak bodies, as their communications are a good way to stay informed about any changes.

> *Professional body:* A professional body is an organisation giving recognition and providing membership to many of the professions. Examples include the Australian Association of Social Workers, the Australian Psychological Association and the Australian Medical Association.

> *Peak body:* A peak body is an industry-based organisation that is formed to represent the issues of providers in that industry. Examples include the Australian Council of Social Service, Jobs Australia and the Chamber of Commerce.

Some of the implications for day-to-day practice may not be quite so straightforward. The legislation and its guiding principles may set you at odds with other human service workers in your area, who may be working with the same service users as yourself. For example, interpretations around 'best interests of the child' have different weightings and meanings depending on whether you work from state-based child protection legislation or state-based family violence protection legislation, or the current *Family Law Act* 2006.

THE ORGANISATIONAL CONTEXT

As we have seen in the previous discussion of the industry as a whole, there are many factors that need to be taken into consideration when assessing the context of practice. In an organisation where the main goal is the delivery of human services, there can be multiple masters, and the worker may be accountable to many organisational and community stakeholders. As you begin to understand the legal, political and ideological context within which your organisation functions, you will also begin to understand the many inconsistencies and conflicting priorities that the workers within the organisation must confront and work through on a daily basis. It is no easy task to weigh up and balance the needs, wants and rights of the service users, the community, the government and other professional workers while keeping within your finite allocation of resources.

As discussed in Chapter 1 and according to Berg-Weger and Birkenmaier (2000: 90), many issues contribute to the contemporary environment of organisations. These include the instability and constant volatility of funding sources, social policy and pressures of accreditation and political affiliations, along with balancing the needs of your service users with the survival of the organisation. Organisations may also be conflict ridden and seem to have no shared value system. Cleak and Wilson (2007: 30) argue that many human service organisations have vague goals that are contested by workers as well as by external stakeholders. As a human service worker, you need to be aware of these different demands and develop skills that will enable you to manoeuvre and work effectively. Here are some additional insights that complement those offered in Chapter 1.

Understanding the ideological orientation of the organisation and the normative imperatives that arise from this

In order to be as effective as possible in your work with and on behalf of your service users, it is important to understand the ideological orientation of the organisations for which you work and those with which you network, together with the implications of this for the work you will be able to do. When you take into consideration the fact that you can find yourself working for a large government bureaucracy, a small community agency, a religious-based organisation, a collective or perhaps a 'profit-based' organisation, it is no wonder that there are many different ideological perspectives in the human services.

While it is very important to have a firm understanding of the policies, procedures and legislation that govern the day-to-day work within an organisation and the expectations upon the workers that arise from this, it is equally important to have a good appreciation of the informal rules, the language and the rituals through which an organisation defines itself. In Chapter 1, we introduced the notion of organisational culture. An organisation's culture provides an indication of how a worker will be treated by that organisation: whether a worker can be original and imaginative in the ways in which they work, or whether the organisation only has room for one dominant mode of working. If you do not have a good understanding of the culture of your organisation and how this reflects its values and ideology, you will have trouble working out what the implications are for the ways in which you work, and the ways in which you will be able to advocate for your service users. How can you go about working out the culture, and ideology of your agency?

> *Organisational culture:* The attitudes, beliefs, personal and cultural values shared by people and groups in an organisation that significantly impact on the way people interact with each other and with others outside of the organisation.

Every organisation or agency has annual reports, written values, mission statements and goals. Is the work you are doing with service users and other professionals reflective of these goals and values, or is there a mismatch? What do the service users think of the way they are treated by the organisation? Are they valued, empowered, listened to and respected? Are the workers within the organisation valued, empowered, listened to and respected? Often the ways in which the workers are treated are indicative of the ways in which service users are viewed. Worker evaluations, service user evaluations and outside audits are all good methods of collecting and reviewing information that will enable you and your agency to reflect on the reality of the work that is being done as well as on the culture of the organisation. They are also good methods of developing recommendations and ways of moving towards what you really want to be doing. A worker or an organisation that is resistant to this kind of scrutiny will often already know that they are not practising as they should. Again, read the following case study and think about the questions posed.

Case study: Organisational culture

You are a new graduate worker in a community agency. During your orientation, you read much about the mission and value statements of your new agency, which claim that the organisation reflects the local community in that it has a multicultural focus and is sensitive to the needs of the local Indigenous community. As you progress through your first few months in this agency, you begin to get an uneasy feeling that all is not as it seems. You realise that there are very few service users and no workers at all from any culturally and linguistically diverse backgrounds. Members of the local Indigenous community do not use your services and prefer to travel an extra 30 minutes to another agency, and there is no system in place for interpreting services or translation of any of the agency's written material.

Discussion questions
- As a new worker, what can you do about this?
- What can you do to ensure that these observations are validated and become more than anecdotal observations?
- To whom can your observations be given?
- Where to from here?

Understanding and dealing with the tensions between you as a human service worker and the organisations in which you work

Working in the human services field is never going to be all smooth sailing. What we expect and want from our organisations and the people with whom we work very rarely meets our expectations. Whether you are employed by a government or non-profit organisation, there can be many reasons why you may find yourself frustrated, and you need to find ways to identify, work through and deal with these tensions.

O'Connor and colleagues (2008: 185) outline four key reasons for these tensions:

1. Organisations control access to social resources. Workers often compete within their organisations for the distribution of these resources.

2. The knowledge and practice context of the work carried out by human service workers is often contested by service users, community attitudes, government policy and other workers.

3. Organisations are often a target for social change by their own workers or workers in other agencies.

4. Human service workers often have to confront issues of autonomy and control over their work.

These points demonstrate that workers can be under pressure from within their own organisation to work in certain ways and follow certain protocols, as well as coming under pressure from outside their organisations, from other professionals, service users and community attitudes to work in certain ways. We cannot stress enough that communication is often the key to negotiating your way through these tensions. Being able to state your case clearly and listen to that of others within your organisation can often lead to workable compromises in terms of the struggle for resources within organisations.

Understanding the bigger picture, as we have discussed previously—particularly in terms of having a good grasp of who is defining social problems, how they are doing it and why—is often the key to navigating pressures and tensions from outside your organisation. Being able to communicate this understanding, feeding this information up to those in government departments and remaining informed are all ways in which you can find a way through many of the frustrations and tensions you will experience.

As we will discuss in more detail in Chapter 6, a human service worker will have to work with workers from other disciplines and workers with other agendas. It is very important to be able to negotiate these relationships as respectfully as you can, in order to provide the best possible outcome for your vulnerable service user group and to deal with some of those tensions. There has been much research of late that clearly demonstrates the fact that service users lose when there is poor networking and poor communication, and this can often arise as a result of professional or agency rivalry.

The reality is that, as a worker, you will work with professionals, non-professionals and agencies, who may well be working from a different philosophical position than yourself. You will also be working with workers from other professions who have different ideological positions and who are focused on different outcomes—for example, nurses, doctors, lawyers, mental health workers, the police and the courts. The trick is to look for the positives and strengths in this diversity, to seek the ways in which this can assist your service user and work towards their goals. If you appreciate each profession, and strive for some understanding of where each worker and agency is coming from, you can be working towards solutions.

This does not mean that you remain silent about victim blaming and discriminatory practices, but it does mean that you work together, keeping this and your agenda for your service user in mind. Part of your work for particular service users may include the need for you to educate your co-workers about your position. This can be informal, or you may choose to make it formal. You could, for example, facilitate an education session with local general practitioners around domestic violence, or an education session with child protection workers around child sexual abuse and the importance of the relationship the child has with the non-offending parent.

CONCLUSION

This chapter has focused on how you can begin to scope the context of your work in any organisation. We have looked at why it is essential to gain an understanding of the bigger picture, and the structural dimensions which impact on your service users and the work that you do. Once you are able to use this critical analysis as a lens through which to see how your work is situated, you will have a better understanding of the issues contributing to the lives of your service users and the ways in which you and your organisation are situated to respond to these.

Chapter review questions

3.1   Why is it important to be able to understand the context of the organisation and the ways in which this impacts on your service users?

3.2   Who are the workers with whom you will be working and what might be their backgrounds?

3.3   What bearing could this have on the work that you do?

3.4   How can you become aware of who is defining social issues, why they are doing this and the potential impact on some of your clients?

3.5   Why is it important to have a basic understanding of the legal frameworks in which your work is situated?

3.6   How can you ensure that the work you are doing is consistent with the stated values and missions of your organisation?

OTHER RESOURCES

All Federal Acts of Parliament, <www.austlii.edu.au/au/legis/cth/consol_act>.

All state-based legislation is available at state government websites. For example, find Victorian legislation at: <www.legislation.vic.gov.au>.

Centre for Culture, Ethnicity and Health, <www.ceh.org.au/resources/publications/aspx>.

KEY READINGS

Beddoe, L. and Maidment J. 2009, *Mapping Knowledge for Social Work Practice, Critical Intersections*, Cengage, Melbourne.

CHAPTER FOUR | Recording and report-writing

SUMMARY

Note-taking, recording, report-writing and associated documentation are the major means of communication in the human services sector—both formally and informally. This chapter looks at factors common to all professional writing in this field. We then consider various forms and methods of writing for effective communication within and across different levels of practice. Some of these are specific to particular areas of work, within the context of legislation and principles that are common to all human service practitioners.

INTRODUCTION

As indicated in Chapter 1, what we write is dependent on the context. This means workers need to appreciate how specific contexts may influence the actions and interpretations of all involved. Further, the language we use creates the ways in which we both see and understand context (Hartman, 1991). 'Language is used to accomplish particular practical purposes and to construct and maintain social realities.' (Schneider, 2001: 231) Language is also determined by our capacity to engage in critical reflection, acknowledged by many recent writers as the most significant component of professional practice (e.g. Fook, 1996; Allan, 2009; Halfpenny, 2009). Critical reflection by a practitioner focuses on his or her practice in relation to how knowledge is generated about those with whom the practitioner is working, and the place of power in this process, together with reflection upon the influence of the practitioner's values, feelings and emotions. (D'Cruz et al, 2007).

The nature and significance of recording and report-writing have extended beyond them being seen as 'a mechanism to facilitate theory building, research, and teaching' (Cumming et al., 2007: 239) to being viewed as an essential component of all our practice. While many human service workers view recording and report-writing as a necessary burden, some see it as an integral part of their professional responsibility. Cleak (2009: 1) refers to research undertaken by O'Connor et al. (2008) that suggests workers in clinical settings spend one-fifth of their time recording. A senior social worker in a hospital recently estimated that approximately half of her time was spent writing reports or providing verbal reports. In contrast, the estimated time spent on this activity by a support worker in a small non-profit organisation was around 30 per cent and for the deputy CEO it was 90 per cent.

Our focus on recording and report-writing relates to its significant place in service delivery. Reference is also made to associated writing skills required for organisational responsibilities and community engagement (e.g. emails, minute-taking and press releases). The human service worker is part of an organisation that is there to address the service user's needs. These days, service users may be assisted by a team of professionals. This means that workers need to share information within and between teams belonging to a more or less dispersed network, communicating often by information technology. In this context, the term 'professional relationship' takes on a different meaning.

Research into the impact of data protection legislation in the United Kingdom found that human service practitioners experience ongoing tension between two different discourses, the legal-administrative discourse and the therapeutic discourse (Jenkins and Potter, 2007: 133). In a culture where fear and risk are constantly present, quality and timely recording is a critical component of human service work. In the first part of this chapter, we provide examples of the purpose and nature of recording and report-writing.

WHAT IS RECORDING?

> *A well-constructed record provides concrete evidence of change, information for analysis, and indications for future action . . . [serving] as the basis for individual reflection, supervisory discussion, and peer consultation. For program evaluation, future planning, justifying and obtaining funds, measures of quality assurance and research.* (Miley et al., 1998: 260)

Recording draws on information and knowledge from a wide range of sources, and includes description, analysis and professional judgement. Clear distinctions need to be made between fact and opinion where input is obtained from a third party.

As we discuss in more depth in Chapter 10, Australian citizens have the right to access information—personal and public—held by federal and state governments and government-funded agencies. In Victoria, for example, the Department of Human Services' policy is that, where appropriate, services users should be able to access their personal information directly, without the need to make a formal application under the Victorian *Freedom of Information Act*. For these reasons, it is vital that workers take great care when recording.

Records and reports in any human service work require a variety of writing skills. Work in a specialist area such as child protection will be focused on the individual, but much writing a worker does will be broader or for different purposes.

The different types of recording and reports within a specialist role such as child protection include: case notes; initial report or notification; minutes of case-planning meetings; case plans recording the child's goals and strategies; assessment reports; affidavits for care and protection court proceedings; court reports; letters to stakeholders affected by a decision; and reports for external (e.g. ombudsman) and internal audiences (e.g. memo to manager).

WHY RECORD?

When things go wrong there is a tendency to judge practice on the basis of the written record. (Taylor, 2008: 29)

Shaefor and colleagues usefully remind us that 'if it is not documented in the record, it was not done' (Shaefor et al., 2003: 181). They propose that the purposes of recording concern accountability in relation to four major parties: the service user, the worker, the organisation and the state. For example, it is used:

- to provide an accurate account of services provided (worker/ organisation)
- to identify changes in policy, service delivery and staff deployment (worker/organisation)
- for evaluation and future research (worker/organisation)
- for overall legal and policy requirements (organisation/state).

Recording plays a critical role in decision-making in contexts such as child protection, the Family Court and the Guardianship and Administrative Tribunals.

Besides documenting every contact with or in relation to the service user, the risk (minimal though it is in Australia) of charges being brought against a worker necessitate that even cancellations

Case study: Recording 1

Angela places a high priority on recording because: 'I need to record what is said and happens at the time. I can't rely on memory. For legal and professional reasons I retain a record of every service user contact on the database system, whether it be by phone, fax, letter or email. This is especially relevant to cases, which may end up in court, or those that the media may pick up, for which a speedy report to the minister or parliament may be required. We can't foresee the longer-term implications. We're accountable to the service user, their advocates, as well as to the government and our profession.'

of appointments should be noted. As Boyle et al. (2006) point out, careful documentation helps reduce a worker's liability if a service user sues them, or when an official investigation is carried out. Further, Cumming et al. (2007: 241) recommend familiarity with professional associations' codes of ethics and practice standards documents regarding the significant role of recording in relation to 'ethical risks' and professional accountability.

Recording for assessment, planning and reporting were integral factors developed in 2008 by the AASW Mental Health Practice Standards. They stipulate the necessity to:

- maintain records of activity as required by accountability standards within the agency
- develop a service plan with the service user that takes account of short- and long-term goals, and identifies how the case manager will support these goals
- review, revise and monitor the plan regularly with the service user
- integrate data-gathering to form a tentative assessment of community needs and resources
- regularly monitor the assessment formed.

Apart from the above formal necessity to maintain a reliable record of services rendered, there are several other advantages associated with a systematic recording plan. These include the visibility of specific goals and outcomes, a record of progress or otherwise, and data development enabling evaluation of effectiveness of practice, both individually and organisationally (Bloom and Fischer, 1983).

Case study: Recording 2

Angela's experience of a particularly critical incident related to the rejection of an application for refugee status for a woman with mental health issues. The woman's lawyer asked for extra time because the woman was pregnant and suffering pre-natal depression, so she was not well enough for an interview. This went on for several months. After childbirth, the woman was still unwell, experiencing psychotic episodes and unable to be interviewed. Consequently, she sought a decision from the departmental worker without an interview. Angela said that the interview was essential. The woman recovered so the interview proceeded. The woman claimed that she was a victim of domestic violence. Angela's assessment was that the situation was more related to family problems. Her status could not be defined as 'refugee', so her application was refused and a notification letter was sent to the service user and her representative. Approximately two weeks after the letter of rejection was sent, the woman's lawyer phoned and said that there was an error in notification and that the service user had received an additional letter that referred to the grant of a resident visa (i.e. permanent status). This was the result of an administrative error of which Angela was unaware. After checking the files she found that she had sent the correct notification letter to the service user, but that administration had sent an incorrect letter. The lawyer accused Angela of precipitating a suicide attempt by the woman because her case had been refused. Angela was concerned because over a six-month period she had responded to all of the woman's requests for additional time and extensions of the processing period. This was documented in her file and on the departmental database. Angela again advised the lawyer that application could be made to the Refugee Review Tribunal, drawing attention to what had been advised in the previous correspondence. Later the lawyer advised Angela that her service user's case had been approved by the Refugee Review Council.

Discussion question
- What more could Angela have done to remedy the situation?

HOW TO RECORD

Key questions that apply to everything we write are:

- Who is the audience?
- What is the purpose?
- What do I want to communicate?
- When should I record this?
- Which form of writing should I use?

Case study: Recording 3

Angela makes detailed handwritten notes, similar to a process record. She then writes an analysis of the case upon which a decision is made, drawing upon all information from the service user and other research documented, taking account on occasions of certain professional codes of ethics (e.g. where information on which the decision is based has been obtained primarily through an interpreter).

An important skill that is often overlooked is the development of our own version of 'shorthand'. While laptops have become the norm for note-taking at meetings, and computers are integral to interviewing in offices such as Centrelink, in many face-to-face encounters with service users, whether in the worker's office or in the service user's home, workers are still reliant on manual note-taking. In relation to case recording, Shaefor et al. (2008: 191) suggest a system of note-taking whereby case notes keep a chronological record of activities providing basic data that may be drawn upon at any time. In transferring the original notes into formal records, O'Hara and Weber (2006: 112) recommend that the report be simple and short, with sentences in the active voice, paragraphs confined to one point, avoidance of abstract words and jargon, a factual and objective style, and avoidance of judgement and subjectivity.

Workers need to develop writing skills in a range of writing styles to effectively document all aspects of their work and to convey the correct message to different audiences. Most organisations have specific computer- or paper-based systems with guidelines for documenting the how, when, why and what of practice. Reamer (2005) has developed a framework for conceptualising functions of documentation more broadly. He notes that for practice related to clinical, supervisory, management or administrative duties, our recording serves six main functions:

1. assessment and planning
2. service delivery
3. continuity and coordination of services
4. supervision
5. service evaluation
6. accountability to service users, insurers, agencies, other providers, courts and review bodies.

TYPES OF PROFESSIONAL RECORDING AND REPORTING

Cleak (2009: 15) identifies four main types of professional report-writing required of human service practitioners in their contact with service users. These are:

1. file notes, progress notes or client records
2. referrals to other professionals and agencies
3. reports on progress or outcome of interventions
4. assessments.

Some specific methods are listed below.

The diary or log book

Activity logs that document chronologically the contacts between worker and service user, as well as relevant tasks, goals, activities, future plans, other parties involved and time spent, are retrospectively valuable for reliability and accountability (Shaefor et al., 2003: 262).

In terms of time management and planning, a diary indicating daily events, appointments and calendar deadlines for certain tasks is invaluable. Cleak and Wilson (2007: 77) provide a useful tool.

Journal

A journal records material usually drawn upon to substantiate personal/professional reflection upon progress and outcomes. It is more commonly used by students to complement their learning plans. Cleak and Wilson (2007: Ch. 8) provide detailed guidelines for journal writing as a reflective learning tool.

Note-taking

Note-taking provides the basis for most records. Unlike lecture notes and log books, notes kept about service users may be subpoenaed, so at first contact it is appropriate to let the service user know why notes are being taken and to obtain permission to take notes during the interview.

Process recording

Process recording is 'a narrative account of an interaction with another individual' (Woodside and McClam, 2006: 319), a detailed account of communication that takes place between the interviewer and the interviewee. It is primarily used as a student learning tool with particular attention to critical reflection upon the record of the student's subjective reactions to the service user and situation. Contents should include a description of interaction with the service user, reflection upon how and what the service user communicated (including non-verbal behaviour) and the theory, skills and values drawn upon during the interaction.

A useful format for recording and reflecting upon process notes is reproduced in Table 4.1.

Table 4.1: Process recording sheet

Dialogue	Skills used	Feelings and responses	Reflective analysis	Supervisor comments

EXERCISE

Role-play an assessment interview between a worker and a hostile young father who has been referred by Child Protection to a parenting program run by a non-profit organisation. Fill out the process record in relation to that interview (see Table 4.1).

The following questions are useful to ask when reflecting upon the interview:

- Which aspects of the interview did I find most challenging and why?
- What might I have done differently?
- What specific micro-skills did I use in this interview?
- In what ways did the personal issues discussed during the interview reflect macro societal concerns?
- What needs to happen now with this 'case'?

Source: Beddoe and Maidment (2009: 30)

Narrative recording

In the human services, narrative recording is used predominantly as another learning tool for students engaged with individual service users. It is a detailed record of everything that is expressed in an interview, using the 'I said, she/he said' style of writing (Wint and Healy 1998: 97). Reissman and Quinney (2005) have used narrative frameworks elsewhere, such as for research interviews and professional storytelling at team meetings. Variations of narrative recording are critical incident and critical issue recording.

Critical incident recording

The ability to think critically is a key factor in responding effectively to the complexity and uncertainty of the human service environment. The critical incident concept has been applied in numerous ways. Davis and Reid (1983) refer to critical incident analysis as a useful method for detailed study of a person's specific experience grounded in a particular situation, and for capturing what is unique or common about an event. Hettlage and Steinlin (2006) regard the Critical Incident Technique as a useful tool for exploration in planning, project evaluation and empowerment activities.

The Critical Incident Technique was developed by Flanagan (1954) for the Aviation Psychology Program of the US Army Air Forces during World War II. Benner (1984) applied the technique to nursing, opening the way for its use in the qualitative study of professional practice, examples of which may be found in research regarding professional competencies (Gonzi et al., 1993) and professional expertise (Fook et al., 2000). Hettlage and Steinlin (2006) refer to the mutual benefit for both researcher and the researched of using the Critical Incident Technique as a research tool, with interviewees gaining a better understanding of their own behaviours in the process of structured reflection upon their experience while providing the information sought by the interviewer.

In health care, the Critical Incident Technique is used as a tool to help clinical staff better understand their practice from the viewpoint of a variety of roles (e.g. physician, nurse, clinical educator), as well as through reflection on the handling of a medical emergency or a common problem with a patient or a colleague. As an adult education learning tool, the critical incident exercise plays a dual role, which has been built into the curriculum of many human service programs. An individual's learning is enhanced by reflecting upon their own experience while exposing peers to a diversity of contexts and situations, learning through narrative and dialogue with each other: 'The simple act of asking a person to describe an incident that was critical to them elicits valuable concrete information about how that person experiences their world.' (Fook, 1996: 194)

The process of reflecting on the incident itself is a learning experience for that worker/person. As well, it potentially unearths all sorts of theoretical assumptions of which the worker is not always aware, which makes it a particularly valuable tool for teaching the integration of theory and practice. The ability to think critically is a key factor in responding effectively to the complexity and uncertainty of the human services environment. A critical incident may be:

- an incident that went unusually well
- an incident in which things did not go as planned
- an incident that is very ordinary and typical
- an incident that we think captures the essential nature of what our work is about
- an incident that was particularly demanding.

Increasing attention, both locally and internationally, is now being given to situation and response strategies when a particular type of critical incident (such as natural disaster or unforeseen acts of violence) impacts upon a group, a community or a nation.

Critical issue recording

A critical issue usually comprises factors spanning a period of time, relating to a group of people, an organisation or a community that is having a significant impact on others. A critical issue generally arises from involvement in areas such as program planning, staff training, research, policy evaluation or community development. It may be an issue that was particularly complex, one that raised conflicts or doubts, or one that caused us to reflect upon ourselves or the nature of the work in which we are engaged, the concepts upon which we draw, our values or our role in that context, raising questions about our obligation to take action and, if so, under which auspices.

The major factors involved in reflecting upon the experience are:

- why the incident or issue was critical to us at the time
- what were our concerns, thoughts, feelings and demands.

Intake summary

Most agencies have a standard pro-forma document for efficiency and consistency in information obtained at first point of contact with service users. However, the extent and depth of material recorded varies between organisations, and is dependent on the agency's auspice, statutory role and service provision. Legally, agency records are the property of the employer (Cleak and Wilson, 2007: 81).

Data generally required includes: agency and worker identifying data; date; identification (name, address, family status); referral source; reason for referral; background summary and social history; previous contact with agency; summary statement of presenting situation; and recommendations. Summary recording also refers to progress notes, intake summaries and referral reports.

Case notes

Case notes are the written account of each contact with or in relation to a service user. These provide a chronological record of communication, actions and events that may not be covered in other documentation. Case notes should be brief, factual and pertinent to the current situation of the service user (Cleak, 2009: 15).

Case records

A case record contains the information gained, plans agreed upon, decisions made and actions taken. Taylor (2008: 28) highlights the essential role of case-recording skills in records that increasingly are documented via IT. This standardised IT-based system of recording often facilitates inter-professional shared access and enables more systemic case administration, including availability of material for longer term quantitative and qualitative analysis.

Table 4.2: Case records

Identifying data: name, phone, address, family members—genogram	• Initial assessment of issue and situation • Issues person/s present with each person's strengths and needs
Initial and subsequent goals and objectives and review schedule	• Plans of how goals will be achieved • Tasks assigned to worker, family, other
Referral materials	
Service agreement/ plan	• Ideally developed in collaboration with and signed by service user
Case activity log	• Date, activity, comment • Related to plan and goals • Only records what is relevant to the issue • Records facts based on evidence and observations, e.g. verbal and non-verbal language, what was said, what happened, what you saw
Correspondence Reports	

Source: Costello, 2007

With increasing legislation being passed regarding rights and professional responsibilities, Jenkins and Potter (2007: 134) highlight the need for professionals to obtain their consent for the recording and to inform them of provisions and procedures regarding access to records. A critical factor determining accuracy of case notes is the period between communication with the other parties and documentation. Content of dialogue should be documented almost immediately for greater accuracy.

Action sheets/activity logs

Action sheets or activity logs are useful tools that complement case notes by documenting all the worker and the service user focused upon, relevant tasks such as the goals sought, activities, other parties involved, future plans and resources sought/required to achieve these.

REPORT-WRITING

Hamilton (in Cleak 2009: 51) describes a report regarding service users as a record of the professional accumulation of information, reflections and knowledge about a person and their situation, together with an analysis and application of this knowledge in the context of the person's needs and the service system available to respond. The report format will vary according to its purpose and organisational context. Shaefor et al. (2003) identify thirteen points that contribute towards a quality report. These apply to reports regarding individual service users as well as systems.

1. Specify the purpose of the report.
2. Decide upon the format and writing style appropriate for the report.
3. Organise the information in a logical structure with headings and sub-headings.
4. Use the minimum number of words to address purpose of report.

5. Use clear, simple and direct language/terminology.

6. Sentences should be succinct—fifteen to twenty words is the recommended length.

7. Where possible, use the active voice.

8. Construct paragraphs around a single idea, stating the central point in the first sentence, then finishing with a summary of the key point in the final sentence.

9. Avoid language that is vague, hazy or unclear in meaning.

10. Avoid clichés.

11. Ensure time for at least one draft and, where possible, obtain feedback from peers or another staff member before submitting to the supervisor.

12. When uncertain of the meaning of words, use a dictionary.

13. Maximise the use of tools on the computer to edit, and to check spelling and grammar.

Court reports

In general, a report for the Children's Court should include:

- an account of your involvement with the child or young person and the family (including your own direct involvement or the involvement of the agency or service)
- a description of the abuse or neglect of the child, if appropriate within your expertise
- a professional assessment of the family's situation, their strengths and weaknesses
- your major concerns about the child's wellbeing (including past, present and future concerns)
- the capacity and willingness of the child's parents or caregivers to care for and protect the child in the future.

Professionals must inform families that a report is being written for the Children's Court hearing, keeping them informed of the actions and reasons for writing the report.

The report will be a document of the Children's Court and is read by the magistrate and the legal representatives for the department, the child and family. The child and family will also usually read the report or have the contents explained to them. Below are factors specific to court reports from National Centre Against Sexual Assault's guidelines, in addition to the points identified by Shaefor et al. (2003).

- Present the information as a chronological account of your involvement with the child or young person, using precise dates.
- Distinguish between fact and professional assessment.
- Draw on facts and link these to your professional knowledge, training and theory.
- Provide examples to support your assessments and conclusions. For example, if you say 'Mary was withdrawn', then you need to say how and why.
- Distinguish between your own observations (first hand) and information from other sources (hearsay).
- State your sources of information.
- Keep within your own area of expertise and knowledge.
- State your conclusions and recommendations about the future care of the child or young person (avoid introducing new material at this point).
- Title the report 'Report to the Children's Court in Relation to (name of child)'.
- Include names of all relevant family members on the title page.
- State your role, the role of your agency and the services it provides.
- State when the child and family became involved with you and your agency, and why.
- Describe the nature of your involvement with the child and family.
- Describe the number and type of contacts you have had with the child or family in the body of the report, or attach it as an appendix.

- State your concerns for the child's welfare and the basis for these.
- Describe the strengths and weaknesses of the family.
- State your conclusions and, if appropriate, your recommendations.

Some agencies require that the report be signed by the individual worker (author) and counter-signed by the worker's supervisor or agency director. The envelope should be marked 'confidential'.

Professional letter-writing

Hogan's (2001) proposal for letter-writing as part of the counselling process is that it is an ethically valuable means of shared record-keeping, taking into account more open access to data under freedom of information (2001: 15). The contents of this kind of letter include identifying data (e.g. name, date and place), review of previous contact, points raised, future goals, plans, commitment and agreements. More formal letters require careful planning, succinct writing and a clear statement of the subject-matter, purpose and a contact person (if not the writer). A simple but sometimes omitted factor in letters sent by 'snail mail' these days is the date!

Recording internet communication

Communication by email has become an instant, speedy means of communication, blurring the boundaries between informal (personal) and professional messages. Johnson (2009) identifies three types of email: email providing information; email requesting information; and email requesting action. Sending single-topic emails obtains a speedier response, avoids confusion when sorting into themed mailboxes or when searching by subject at a later date. The importance of keeping personal and professional emails separate is obvious—but how often have we failed to adhere to this? How often have we forwarded emails on to others without thinking? We have little control over what happens to our message after it has been sent. The best safeguard is to avoid using email to communicate information that should not be made public (2009: 22). When attaching a file, always refer to it in the email message, stating the reason for sending the attachment.

Effective professional email communication is dependent upon:

- the policies and procedures of your organisation
- the inter-agency system in operation
- the personal organisation and 'use' of emails received and sent.

As practitioners, we are responsible for implementing the first two factors. Organisational email policies and procedures developed by the IT section of our organisation and authorised by management are those to which we sign agreement on commencing employment.

Johnson's (2009) guideline about avoiding sending information via email that should not be made public is helpful. However, the increasing dependency of our health and welfare systems upon speedy communication via email in lieu of telephone contact has necessitated the development of inter-agency systems for transferring confidential information about service users across agencies. An example of this is the Service Coordination of Tools Template (SCoTT) System, used by health services in Victoria. This is a database-driven e-referral system aimed at streamlining and coordinating referral processes, using standard documentation. The documentation includes agreed-upon standard referral processes, which require acknowledgement that the referral has been received and feedback about the outcome. Security integral to the system ensures limited access to material transmitted, guaranteeing confidentiality. A critical component of the system is client consent.

Use of the SCoTT system among organisations comprising the South West Primary Care Partnership (Victoria) has resulted in improvements in the content of referrals, confidentiality, more efficient data-collection and increased sharing of relevant knowledge about referral and outcome; it has also strengthened inter-agency relations (Sinnott, 2007). Alongside this, however, is the frustration experienced by workers due to the initial additional time consuming task.

The third factor in regard to our organisation and 'use' of emails received and sent is our personal/professional responsibility. Research in the business sector (Benjamin, 2008) found that 55 per cent of employers retain and read their employees' emails. McGhee (2009) recommends four ways to take control of your email in box:

1. Set up a simple and effective email reference system.
2. Schedule uninterrupted time to process and organise email.
3. Process one item at a time, starting at the top.
4. Use the '4 Ds for Decision Making' model.

The '4 Ds for Decision Making' refers to the choices available when opening each message—that is, deciding whether to:

- **Delete** it
- **Do** it
- **Delegate** it, or
- **Defer** it.

McGhee finds that this approach enables us to handle our daily emails more speedily, thereby enhancing our mindset.

Snopes.com provides advice that is particularly relevant to human service practitioners regarding messages about 'worthy causes' or 'matters of concern' that seek your support and ask you to forward them on to others. Through this process, the host sender acquires lists of 'active' email addresses, which may then be used for other purposes. Moreover, email petitions are not acceptable to government. The simple message is: do not sign, respond or forward emails of this kind. If you are concerned about the nature or source of an email, <www.snopes.com> may shed light upon whether the message is spam.

The increasing use of texting between workers and service users raises questions about our recording responsibility for information communicated in this manner. What are the methods for recording

SMS service user communication on our agency databases? Do we need different policies to record services provided by a medium other than our conventional face-to-face and telephone counselling (for example, online counselling) techniques?

Minutes of meetings

The minutes of a meeting are an official record of what takes place. This includes:

- a summary of the date, times that the meeting begins and ends and meeting venue
- the names of all people present and apologies received
- key points regarding all items discussed (whether on the agenda or not)
- motions and who made them, highlighting actions agreed upon, with the names of those responsible for implementation
- items deferred and motions for further discussion—these should be noted to agenda at the next meeting
- the date for next meeting.

It is wise to prepare a draft as soon as possible after the meeting. When reporting on lengthy or complex discussions, it is a good idea for the supervisor or a colleague present at the meeting to read the minutes before distribution.

Submission-writing

The guidelines and application forms of the potential funding organisation are the starting point for any submission-writing. An essential component in the application, or attached, is an organisational statement (no more than one page). This should include:

- organisation mission and purpose
- origins of organisation
- current operations

- future vision
- structure of organisation
- administrative procedures
- financial processes.

Material to support the need for funding could include reports (e.g. annual report), AGM minutes, survey results or a program flyer. Guidelines for report-writing are generally applicable to submission-writing, the major difference being that in a submission one is seeking funds for a program or research that is still an idea, for evaluating a new service or developing alternative ways of addressing local needs. The following submission-writing guidelines are from the Commonwealth Department of Health and Ageing (2006):

- Start with a description of the impetus of the submission. Where did it come from—a public meeting, the outcomes of a research project, an advertisement in the paper?
- State the nature and dimensions of the problem that a successful submission will address—provide clear and concrete information. Describe your understanding of the cause of the 'problem' and what the 'problem' is—explain how you identify this cause–effect relationship.
- Indicate supporting evidence, including research reports, current best practice, policy guidelines.
- Describe how the 'problem' is currently dealt with, how adequate these approaches are and their deficiencies.
- Explain the possible alternative courses of action, their benefits and deficits.
- State clearly what your proposal is and how it will address the problem—describe the proposed methods and what will be achieved.
- Indicate clearly how the service/project will be monitored and evaluated.
- Describe the organisational and accountability structures.
- Indicate who will be responsible for what.

- Describe how and when reports—say, to a funding body—will be delivered.

- Describe the required budget.

- Create a schedule of tasks and completion dates.

- State the contact details of your referees.

- Give the details for the contact person for the submission.

Media releases

Ross (2004) provides the following comprehensive guide to writing a media release, examples of which have been adapted to the human services field. The purpose of a media release is to provide newsworthy information to the media about recent or coming events—for example, the opening of the local youth-managed community café—in the hope that they will run the story. This information should be provided in writing rather than verbally, to minimise the chance of mistakes.

The media release should be brief and to the point. One page is recommended (background information, photos, etc. can be attached separately), starting with the main points, using bold text to make it easy for the journalist to extract the most important points. It must be consistent and accurate, with dates, times and numbers. A media release should answer the following questions: Who? What? When? Where? Why? How? How much? How many? And how do people access it? To make the story 'newsworthy', it needs to be topical/timely, politically/economically significant, atypical, of human interest and heart-warming. Use quotes to liven up the story, taking into account the tone/style of the publication to which you are sending the media release and who will be the readers.

Read the targeted publications to identify the relevant editors and journalists, developing a media list that is appropriate to our organisation. The media release should be sent to 'The Editor' (preferably by name). Media releases may be sent by fax or email, but a hard copy with any photographs or other enclosures should follow. It is important to check deadlines, especially for monthly or weekly publications, but to avoid sending it too far in advance of the event. A follow-up call a few days after sending the media release is a good idea, to double check that it has been received by the right person, and whether any further information is required; this also acts as a reminder.

CONCLUSION

Human service workers require a diversity of writing skills in providing service to individuals and raising community awareness about shared issues. Recording and report-writing are critical components of this work.

Chapter review questions

4.1   Why are recording and report-writing critical components of our work in human services?

4.2   What major legislation impacts upon our recording and report-writing?

4.3   What types of records are essential when communicating with service users?

4.4   How might recent developments in information technology and related legislation affect our recording?

4.5   What other types of writing are useful for our organisational and community roles?

OTHER RESOURCES

The Owl at Purdue (Purdue Online Writing Lab), <http://owl.english.purdue.edu/sitemap>.

Report Writing (Central Queensland University) <www.dtls.cqu.edu.au/clc/2_1_3.html>.

How to write reports in plain English, <www.plainenglish.co.uk/reportsguide.pdf>.

AASW Code of Ethics 1999, <www.aasw.asn.au/document/item/92>.

The Practice Standards for Social Workers: Achieving Outcomes, AASW, 2003, 1.6 and 1.7, <www.aasw.asn.au/document/item/16>.

Snopes, <www.snopes.com> and/or <www.truthorfiction.com>; <www.snopes.com/inboxer/petition/Internet.asp>.

CHAPTER FIVE

Information development and management in human service organisations

---

SUMMARY

This chapter is designed to assist students and new workers appreciate why information development and management—especially that undertaken by an organisation's management team—is important. We acknowledge that people working at the front line of human services practice often feel that recording and other forms of information generation detract from their capacity to provide much-needed assistance to their clients. Nevertheless, the chapter outlines a number of reasons why it cannot be ignored. We discuss the different types of data that organisations might generate, illustrate the steps involved in developing a management information system, outline questions workers might like to ask in any such development process, and expose the social dimensions of management information systems. Returning to context, the chapter discusses the specific difficulties posed to community-based, non-profit organisations in the contemporary mixed economy of welfare. We finish with a nod to the future, the development of knowledge management—a field of activity distinct from information management.

INTRODUCTION

Not surprisingly, people working in human service organisations are very committed to their work and to the vulnerable people with whom they work. Because of this, human service workers can become very frustrated with any organisational imperative that directs their attention away from their service users. This is particularly the case in relation to the time spent recording information for management. Often, workers challenge the utility of the information they input into management information systems, particularly when they are over-stretched and aware of the unrelenting demand for their services. Sometimes, they are concerned that the demands of such systems (in terms of what activities count as 'data') overly determine the contours of their actual practices. In such situations, it is very important to be clear about why organisations ask workers to do certain things, and in this case why developing and collecting information is a very important part of good organisational practice and governance.

Our first argument relates to a core professional skill that we hope all human service workers develop—the capacity to be critically reflective about their work overall and their engagement with service users in particular. We suggest that developing and running management information systems is the business end of critical reflectivity, but in this case at the level of the program and the organisation. What do we mean by this? All human service organisations have an ethical obligation to provide the very best service they can. To do so, they need to be able to stand back from the hurly burly of everyday practice and look critically at what is going on behind the door at the back of the reception desk. Managers and staff all have to contribute to an ongoing cycle of evaluation, looking carefully at whether the front-line practices of staff involved in delivering programs are achieving the desired outcomes. In other words, program evaluation (and other forms of assessing an organisation's performance) is a professional duty. Information about the service, not surprisingly, is the basic unit of evaluation.

The Code of Ethics developed by the Australian Association of Social Workers, for example, states that:

Social Workers should appropriately challenge and work to improve policies, procedures, practices and service provisions which:

- *are not in the best interests of the service user*
- *are inequitable*
- *are in any way oppressive, disempowering or culturally inappropriate*
- *demonstrate unfair discrimination.* (AASW, 2002: 31)

Although couched in a slightly different manner, the ethical imperative is nevertheless clear: social workers in particular must work to improve policies, procedures, practices and service provision. We suggest that a similar imperative is posed to all human service workers, not just social workers. To do this, workers (and managers, who will no doubt have similar commitments to front-line staff) must be prepared to engage in program and organisational 'critical reflexivity'—or, in technical language, evaluation. Further, as a key author on evaluation suggests, our focus on evaluation and on the information-collection systems and processes that inform evaluations should not be viewed as an imposition, but as an opportunity (Ginsberg, 2001).

A second reason for paying attention to information development and management is that all human service organisations are, as we suggested in Chapter 3, currently caught up in a broader movement affecting the entire span of interests and activities of governments—the evidence-based policy and practice movement. Occurring on a broader scale than the human services, the renaissance of evidence in the contemporary era is entirely congruent with the times. Its emergence has been spurred by a range of objectives, the most intuitively compelling of which are ethical in intent. In similar vein to our comments above, the promotion of practitioner accountability to people who use human services, as well as to other relevant bodies, is vigorously advanced as a key reason why human service workers in particular should embrace evidence-based practice (see Gambrill 2003; Rosen 2003).

An important (although not as clearly acknowledged) impetus also arises from the desire to counter the increasingly precarious image of welfare in the (unfriendly) New Public Management-inspired state. Essentially, evidence-based practice proposes that human service intervention knowledge should be developed through the application of (for the most part) sound evaluation and research methods, and that individual and organisational practice should be based on the best available evidence. Obviously, undertaking evaluation and research about the efficacy and impact of an organisation's programs and interventions requires information about an organisation's activities and those of its employees.

Finally, another very good reason to take the collection of information seriously is that it is a requirement of funding bodies—be they governments or philanthropic bodies. These days, a human service organisation would not be granted funds unless it could provide an in-depth and accurate picture of what it does. Similarly, all funding contracts require accountability because the funding itself comes from taxpayers or donors. Contemporary funding bodies assume that human service organisations have professional information-management systems, and assume that their staff engage with these proactively.

So why do human service workers react negatively to engaging in data-collection for information-management systems? Burton and van den Broek (2006) provide a number of reasons that they discovered when talking to human service workers in Queensland and New South Wales. One important reason often stated by workers is that they are fearful management information systems might compromise service user confidentiality. There are two issues here. First, workers can be worried that funding bodies might require too much potentially identifying data on the people with whom organisations work. Second, workers often do not have confidence in their own organisation's handling of the data. Burton and van den Broek cite, for example, a family therapist's concerns in relation to local data being made accessible to other sites in the organisation:

> It horrifies me because I still don't know where our computerised service users' files will be living . . . We keep all our records on computer . . .

> *That's fine at the moment because we know where our stuff goes and we know who has access to it . . . So we actually have some control over the privacy of our service users . . . With the new system it seems to me that everything we put on that system is going to be kept in head office.* (2006: 6)

Burton and van den Broek also note that human service workers are very attuned to the use of management information systems in managing risk—be it organisational risk or risk as it is perceived by the funding body. Unfortunately, as Power (1997) suggests, risk and the need to manage it are ubiquitous in the contemporary era. We use the word 'unfortunately' deliberately here because much contemporary risk management in human service organisations is not necessarily related to ensuring good service user outcomes, but rather is more related to managing the political risk of failure.

Another reason why human service workers might be wary of management information systems and evaluations is simply that the language and logic they deploy is unfamiliar. Look at the case study opposite.

DATA AND INFORMATION

In the contemporary context, virtually all human service organisations are required to develop good management information systems if they wish to receive government funds. In Victoria, for example, all organisations providing family services are required to register with the state government under the *Children, Youth and Families Act* 2005. Part of the registration standards involves the development of a management information system and over the past decade these have become increasingly more sophisticated. Our purpose in this section of the chapter is to help you begin to understand the dimensions of such systems, and what they are trying to achieve. In this way, we hope to help human service workers engage productively with them while recognising that most workers will not be involved in their design.

Case study: Program evaluation

Jan, a human service worker managing a new counselling program for victims of disasters, was asked to participate in the development of an evaluation for the program. The evaluation was commissioned by the auspicing organisation in partnership with a university. The university people would actually run the evaluation. These people were professional evaluators. The meeting Jan was asked to attend was intended to outline the design of the evaluation, and it was determined that Jan's input was important. The university people began by prompting Jan to talk about the program. Not long into the discussion, they asked her what the program's logic model was. Jan was confused. She did not understand what they were asking and she felt quite inadequate. After some time, she worked out that they were asking her to nominate the human service practice theories and knowledge the counselling program used. In this case, the practice theory was short-term crisis intervention, longer term case management where appropriate, and knowledge of people's reactions to loss, grief and trauma, as well as stages of recovery. But it took some effort for this to become clear.

Discussion questions
- How would you react if someone talked to you like this?
- Who has the problem here—Jan or the evaluators?
- Why would the evaluators need to know the logic model (practice theory and knowledge)?
- What links do you think there are between practice theories and knowledge, and management information systems?

Kettner (2002), one of the leading authors in managing human service organisations, suggests that organisations need two types of information: information about the *external environment* and information about the organisation's *internal processes*. Several types of information about the external environment are relevant. These can be reframed as questions. We suggest that readers use these questions at this beginning stage of thinking about the information needs of an organisation with which they are familiar. Accordingly, in Table 5.1 we have modified the original questions developed by Kettner for use in a simple exercise.

Table 5.1: Identifying relevant categories of external information, part 1

Question	Answers
What information do our funding bodies want?	
What information do our regulators or accreditors want?	
What information do we want about our community?	
What information do we want about our service users?	
What information do we want about our local service delivery system?	

Look at the answers you generated in these last two categories in Table 5.1. How would this information need to be translated into a management information system? With regard to service users, collecting information about the characteristics of service users at intake is the basic building block of knowing how responsive the organisation is to the needs of local people. With regard to the service delivery system, a management information system should capture the organisation's patterns of referrals—both successful and unsuccessful. If, for example, another organisation systematically refuses referrals, then the referring organisation's management needs to address this in whatever way is considered appropriate.

As previously suggested, Kettner (2002) suggests that there are significant types of internal information that organisations need for management, administrative and supervisory purposes. Most organisations, for example, will have a vision embedded in their strategic plan. That plan will also nominate cycles of review and evaluation. Internal organisational information is vital in these processes, because without it an organisation cannot tell whether or not it is progressing towards its vision. Furthermore, it cannot tell whether it is being efficient, much less effective, or whether it is targeting its undoubtedly scarce resources appropriately. Again, revising Kettner's suggestions, Table 5.2 presents some questions worth considering.

Table 5.2: Identifying relevant categories of internal information, part 2

Question	Answers
What factors need to be tracked to assess achievement of organisational purpose?	
How might these factors be measured?	
What are the performance requirements for one division, section or program in the organisation?	
What sort of data would evaluate these performance requirements?	
How can that data be collected?	

While the questions in Table 5.2 are very simple, they demonstrate that quite a lot of data is necessary to meet even the basic information needs of human service organisations. One of the hardest things to do when developing a management information system is to capture sufficient data to serve sensible purposes without going into information overload. As such, management information systems should be streamlined. The other key challenge is to develop the system in such a way that workers at the data-collection interface can easily understand the utility of the data for the organisation but also, importantly, for themselves. Such systems are often developed in layers. At the core will be what Rapp and Poertner (1992) (cited in Kettner, 2002: 162) call the 'performance guidance system'—data on all the service users serviced by the organisation; the programs within the organisation serving the service users; the volume, rate and type of service user engagement with programs in the organisation, plus any outcome variables (if these are available). As we will discuss in the next section, this last type of data is quite contentious in the human services.

As well as the core program guidance system, a typical management information system will have secondary systems focusing on the information needed for human resource management. Not surprisingly, all the parts of a management information system need to be integrated so that different parts can be interrogated in different ways, depending on the question being asked.

THE CONCEPTS BEHIND MANAGEMENT INFORMATION SYSTEMS

In the chapter's introductory comments, we suggested that human service workers often resist engagement with management information systems. In 2005, Carrilio examined the management information systems in two US human service organisations. She found that the factors which affected how staff responded to the systems were organisational culture, leadership, the extent to which the system interface was user-friendly and the overall readiness to change. In regard to the system interface, a recent Australian example is illuminating. Discussing case manager responses to a very unfriendly management information system that the Department of Education, Employment and Workplace Relations insist must be used in the Job Services Australia network of employment services, McDonald and Marston (2008b) quote one worker:

> *They need to start projecting a more accommodating and understanding image, instead of the culture of fear that they permeate through their contract managers, general staff, computer systems and general correspondence. The first thing we see each day on our computer when opening ea3000 [the system employed in the Job Services Australia network] is a message that threatens prosecution under the criminal code of conduct for providing misleading information.* (McDonald and Marston, 2008b: 112)

Clearly, confronting such an interface message every morning would not induce eagerness to engage with the system!

Keeping that in mind, it is also important that any management information system is conceptually sound. As indicated previously, this can be contentious. All management information systems are conceptually broken down into four parts—inputs, throughputs, outputs and outcomes. In Australia, up until the 1980s, most organisations collected data on inputs only, largely because they were given block grants with few specifications on how they were to spend them. Management information systems, to the extent that they existed, largely involved financial records detailing what money came in and the things on which it was spent. All that changed in the 1980s and 1990s as a new method of funding and managing human service organisations—especially non-profit community-based organisations—gradually evolved. These days, organisations work within a context in which the money they receive is given with tightly specified conditions written into a formal legally binding contract—specifications variously known as benchmarks, contract specifications, key performance criteria and key performance indicators. Organisations have to be able to nominate exactly what it is that matches the conceptual categories of input, throughput, output and outcome. See Table 5.3, in which we nominate one example.

We invite you to fill in the relevant boxes on the other examples provided.

As you can see, the final outcomes are somewhat harder to define, and as such are more difficult to measure. Because of this, it is much harder to develop reliable and valid outcome measures than it is to specify input, throughput and outputs. It is also very expensive. For this reason, the management information systems of many human service organisations only really generate information on the first three criteria. As such, they can report on what the activity actually cost but not necessarily about whether there was any significant change as a result of the activity (intervention). This does not mean it cannot be done relatively cheaply and effectively, however. Read the following case example.

Case study: Service evaluation in the field

One of us is part of a small research team that was asked by a mid-sized community-based family welfare organisation to develop an outcome measure that would help them evaluate the effectiveness of their service. They specifically asked that it be embedded in their management information data-collection processes and system. Accordingly, and after considerable discussion and research, the construct of 'wellbeing' was adopted. The rationale was that the common desirable outcome of all the organisation's interventions was that the service users felt better about their lives, as expressed by their self-reports of their wellbeing. A simple measure was constructed adopting another well-known measure of health outcomes. It is designed as a questionnaire to be applied to service users at intake and at intervals deemed appropriate by the different program area staff.

This organisation is clearly accepting the challenge of attempting to nominate desirable outcomes by developing a measure and incorporating that measure into their management information system. Hopefully others will follow suit. In developing this measure, the organisation and their university partners were very aware that the front-line service delivery staff had to engage with the process. The

Table 5.3: Service type

Service type	Input	Throughput	Output	Outcome
An anger-management program for primary school children	Resources: *Plant:* nominated room in school *Financial:* all program costs (salaries, travel, materials, advertising, on costs, program management costs) *Human* Children—their personalities, background, cognitive development. Staff—one teacher and one social worker Program design and logic	Delivery of program (i.e. a six-week program consisting of six one-hour modules developed using anger-management theory and knowledge). Delivered on site by two trained personnel with two groups of five children.	Ten children completing the program	Lower rates of inappropriate expression of anger. Sustained behavioural change. A happier school and happier children.
A domestic violence support service				
A generalist counselling service				
A disability support service				

organisation was also very aware of the social relations of management information systems. It is to this that we now turn.

THE SOCIAL RELATIONS OF MANAGEMENT INFORMATION SYSTEMS

Management information systems and organisational data-gathering do not occur in a vacuum. Human service organisations—in fact, all organisations—are patterned sets of social relations in which power is a key variable. Most human service organisations involve hierarchy to some degree, even if they are committed to democratic processes. Where there is hierarchy, there are differing degrees of power and, conversely, autonomy. In respect of management information systems, people (being people) will often attribute motives to management that management may not have intended. This is one aspect of what we mean when we invoke the notion of the social relations of management information systems. In this section, we return to the work of Burton and van den Broek (2006) and augment it by reference to a study conducted by Dearman (2005) as well as the work of McDonald and Marston (2008b), nominated earlier.

Burton and van den Broek (2006) note that many of their study participants related the management information system to control—in particular, to control mechanisms that affected the nature of their work. Talking about computerised systems, the participants in one of the studies reported by Burton and van den Broek talked about 'Big Brother', suggesting that the management information system had increased the level of management surveillance of their work. This study was situated in a call centre, a mode of operations increasingly evident in the human services. Call centres' deployment of computerised technology rapidly expands the capacity of the system to track minute details of activity. Matched, for example, with the growth of key performance indicators dictating length of calls, workers felt that their autonomy and professionalism were significantly being eroded by the management information system. Similarly, professional notions of accountability had been subsumed by bureaucratic accountability. Furthermore, the respondents in these studies claimed that they often had little input into defining what data was collected. Finally, workers suggested that there was often little realisation of the time taken to operationalise the management information system.

Similar claims were made by social workers working for Centrelink, reported in a study by Dearman (2005). In his analysis of the impact of the Centrelink Social Work Information System (SWIS) on social workers, Dearman claims that the system significantly changed the conduct of social work interviews and their follow-up, as well as restructuring the relationship between the social workers and the administrative staff. One respondent, for example, claimed that the SWIS inappropriately shaped her work in that she tended to focus more on those items of work that were recorded on the system to the neglect of others that were not. Further, the social workers to whom Dearman talked were wary of the way the data would be used, particularly in relation to workload distribution. In conclusion, Dearman suggests that the SWIS challenged social workers' sense of professional agency and independence. That said, Dearman also acknowledges that the SWIS data proved immensely useful in 'selling' the social work service in the entrepreneurial corporatised 'business' world of Centrelink, and contributed positively to increased wage claims.

In another example, McDonald and Marston (2008b) found in their work on the Job Services Australia network of employment services that a very consistent theme was significant unhappiness with the high (from their perspective, excessive) administrative load produced by the management information system imposed by the funding department. It would be almost impossible to overstate the centrality of this to the case managers' experience, and the resulting degree of frustration and job dissatisfaction. A number of case managers claimed that they spent up to and sometimes over 50 per cent of their time managing administrative requirements. Case managers claimed that the administrative overload was severely hindering their capacity to work with people to the level of intensity required to actually assist them to overcome their barriers and get into work:

We need to take the emphasis off the demanding administrative expecta-
tions so that the Job Services Australia can focus on the service user and
finding sustainable employment, rather than percentages, statistics, referrals
and so forth . . . The priority should be our service users, not whether we
are doing enough to work a difficult-to-interpret system just to keep our
jobs. (2008b: 110)

Very often, the concerns about the administrative load were couched in terms of the outcomes focus of the Job Services Australia contracts. The problem is not with delivering employment outcomes *per se*, but the quantitative output approach to reaching and measuring defined targets. That focus adds significant pressure to case managers to the point that it is 'not enjoyable to work here anymore'. In other words, the processes used to achieve successful employment outcomes are lost in the drive to meet performance targets.

These issues were widely reflected in two British studies of social work in Social Service Departments undertaken by Carey (2003) and Harris (2003). In an ethnography of care managers' practice in local authorities, Carey identifies four primary dimensions of interest. First, the majority of practice involved responding to formal paperwork and other bureaucratic processes within a rigid and highly formalised information technology-driven system. Second, the style of management provided by social work middle managers has shifted away from the developmental and supportive focus of professional supervision towards a more traditional business style emphasising authoritarianism, compliance and discipline. Third, the actual practices of care managers were 'budget led', as every intervention was defined by the (un)availability of finances. Finally, the adoption of care management in a context of constrained resources produces an increasingly de-professionalised and impoverished service to vulnerable groups.

According to Harris (2003: 66), British social workers are now 'running the business' within a 'quasi-capitalist rationality', in which social workers are 'care *managers*, putting together *packages* of care from the quasi-*market* for individual *customers*' (2003: 67, italics in original). Here, the language of 'business' used by Harris illustrates how the rationalities of such developments contrast with those usually associated with the traditional professional orientation of social work. In this case, two processes stand out: first, the intensification of work as middle managers exert pressure to extract the maximum amount of effort; and second, a narrowing and standardisation of the work processes along with increased scrutiny and control of performance, particularly through the use of standardised management information system software packages and information technology.

Despite these negative stories about the social relations of management information systems, it is possible for an organisation to develop or modify a system to be efficient, effective, responsive and inclusive. In the 'Resources' section at the end of this chapter, we have listed a number of generic management sites for community-based organisations that provide information on the development of sound management information systems.

Information management in the mixed economy of welfare

Earlier in the chapter, we alluded to the notion that the contemporary environment in which human services are delivered is not particularly friendly. This has implications for all aspects of human service management and practice, but it also has implications for how organisations are required to collect and supply information. We referred earlier to the work of McDonald and Marston (2008a) on the Job Services Australia network. This system represents an extreme example of the current relations between the funding departments and service delivery organisations—relations which are, unfortunately, putting significant pressure on service delivery organisations. In the Job Services Australia network (and largely due to the management information system imposed on Job Services Australia members), the data entry requirements are extensive and are used to oversee activity, enforce compliance and inform contract rounds by assessing member organisations' efficiency and effectiveness. This is experienced as highly controlling, intrusive and expensive, and is held to be detrimental to the Job Services Australia members' capacity to provide a meaningful service.

It is also expensive to administer. Murray (2006), for example, has calculated the costs to the Department of Education, Employment and Workplace Relations (DEEWR) of administering the Job Services Australia at $252 million, which was over 15 per cent of the total $1658 million spent on the program. Normally, administrative costs for running a program would run to around 10 per cent. He also calculated that, using the management information system, 1200 departmental staff supervise 1100 sites (that is, 1.1 staff members per site, or 11.6 per provider organisation). Overall, administrative and compliance costs to providers are also very high (Thomas, 2007). Under the last contract round, DEEWR has escalated its administrative oversight of the Job Services Australia

---

EXERCISE
- What external information does our system capture?
- What important external information is left out?
- What internal information does our system capture?
- What important internal information is left out?
- For what is the information used?
- Are the links between the system and everyday practice clear?
- Is the system interface user-friendly?
- Are inputs, throughputs, outputs and outcomes data collected?
- Is the system efficient from the perspective of the front-line staff?
- Were front-line staff involved in the development of the management information system?
- Are front-line staff involved in any review of the management information system?
- Are new staff given comprehensive training about and on the management information system?
- What impact do funder-imposed data requirements have on the organisation?
- Overall, what are the social relations of the management information system?

network, particularly in relation to what is known as the Job Seeker Accounts, monitoring how providers spend them. This has also boosted costs.

We have noted that the Job Services Australia network is an extreme example, but the reality is that, in the contemporary era, most funding departments will require extensive information from funded organisations, the generation of which imposes significant costs on service delivery organisations. While peak organisations representing the community sector continuously make representations to governments about this and related issues, it is still important that organisations and workers monitor the impact of imposed data requirements on their everyday work.

At this stage, we are ready to pose a number of questions that a worker might ask about his or her own organisation's system. We have included these in the previous exercise to assist workers' evaluations of the system and to encourage dialogue about the system at the front line.

CONCLUSION

In this chapter, we have deliberately taken a specific position in relation to information development and management in the human services, particularly in community-based human service organisations. We have assumed that most beginning workers will not be directly involved in the development of a management information system. We have also assumed that all workers will nevertheless be asked to work with one, largely because of developments in the relationships between funding bodies and service provider organisations. Our initial premise was that, because of their deep commitments to the people with whom they work, many workers are reluctant to engage in a timely and professional manner with their organisation's management information system. We have given readers a number of reasons why we think this is an inappropriate response—largely couched in terms of our ethical responsibility to promote the very best service an organisation can deliver within funding and other constraints. We then examined different types of information—focusing on external and internal information, and the conceptual blocks contributing to an effective management information system. Here we noted the difficulty many human service organisations have in accurately and efficiently determining outcomes of interventions. The chapter moved on to the social relations of management information systems, suggesting that these can be highly influential in how well a management information system works. In conclusion, we nominated a series of questions that front-line workers can ask about their own organisation's management information system. We did so to illustrate that front-line workers' experience of an organisation's system is an extremely important source of information for managers wishing to evaluate the functioning of this very important and ubiquitous part of everyday organisational practice.

Chapter review questions

5.1 Why should front-line human service workers engage with management information systems?

5.2 Give two reasons why front-line human service workers dislike management information systems.

5.3 What are three examples of external information?

5.4 What are three examples of internal information?

5.5 What is a performance guidance system?

5.6 What is the difference between a program's output and outcome?

5.7 What is meant by the social relations of a management information system?

5.8 What is the role of front-line workers in relation to the development and management of a management information system?

OTHER RESOURCES

Victorian Registration of Community Service Organisations, <www.cyf.vic.gov.au/every-child-every-chance/registration-of-community-service-organisations>.

Quality Improvement and Community Services Accreditation (Inc), <www.latrobe.edu.au/aipc/qicsa>.

IRIS (Integrated Reports and Information System), <www.cyf.vic.gov.au/family-services/iris-family-services-user-manual>.

Management Support Online, <www.managementsupportonline.com.au>.
Australian Institute of Community Practice and Governance, <www.managementsupportonline.com.au>.

KEY READINGS

Carrilio, T. 2005, 'Management Information Systems: Why are They Under-utilized in the Social Services?', *Administration in Social Work*, vol. 29, no. 2: 43–61.

Ginsberg, L.H. 2001, *Social Work Evaluation: Principles and Methods*, Allyn and Bacon, Boston.

Kettner, P.M. 2002, *Achieving Excellence in the Management of Human Service Organisations*, Allyn and Bacon, Boston.

CHAPTER SIX

Building and maintaining professional relations

SUMMARY

After establishing why a focus on inter-personal relationships is vital to producing good human service outcomes, this chapter focuses on three key dimensions of professional and collegial relationships: those between colleagues within a human service organisation; those with colleagues in other organisations; and those with significant others such as boards and volunteers. We also discuss working with cultural diversity and techniques for working with interpreters. The core assumption driving the chapter is that good professional relationships don't just happen automatically, but require you to apply continuous purposeful attention.

DEVELOPING PROFESSIONAL RELATIONSHIPS WITHIN ORGANISATIONS

Many people assume that because an organisation provides human services, and as such is dedicated to improving the wellbeing of various groups of people, the internal organisational relationships must be good. This notion is often reinforced by the fact that many of the staff in human service organisations have professional qualifications in areas such as social work, youth work and psychology, which presumably predispose them to behaving well. Unfortunately, neither condition has all that much impact on the ways in which organisations actually function. At some point, most of us have had contact with or were engaged in a group or organisation in which the relationships were 'toxic'. If so, readers will be aware of just how destructive this can be individually, as well as how these circumstances have a terrible impact on the staff and on the quality of the services the organisation provides for service users.

While it is generally understood that organisational culture is largely derived from the organisation's leadership, it is our contention that every worker has a responsibility to behave professionally and to foster good collegial relations, no matter at what level one is employed. In addition, many human service organisations are located in the non-profit sector, so often have a governing board. What sort of relationship should staff have with a board? Furthermore, most human service organisations have volunteers—generally, highly committed people who value add in all sorts of ways, and without whom the organisation would be a much poorer place. Again, how should the relationship between staff and volunteers best be managed?

Human service workers often assume that human service delivery systems (that is, the range of organisations providing human services in any particular local area) function in a coordinated manner. Unfortunately, this is often not the case. Research indicates that from a service user point of view, inter-organisational relationships can be patchy and fractured (see, for example, Spall et al., 2005; McDonald and Zetlin, 2004), and that service users can easily fall through the cracks. As a consequence of this, another imperative is that workers in human service organisations do all they can to create an effective and integrated service delivery system. Among other things, this involves developing and maintaining good relationships with colleagues in other organisations. We begin this chapter with the first of these issues: how we develop good relationships with our workmates.

Professional relationships with colleagues

Understanding yourself

Self-awareness is the fundamental building block to developing good intra-organisational relationships with your colleagues. Specifically, it is important that workers understand the impact they have on other people. This is not possible without an awareness of your personality, your style of engagement and communication, your strengths, your weaknesses, your blind spots and your fears. While it is rarely possible to 'remake' ourselves entirely, it is possible—through self-awareness—to appreciate and monitor when some aspect of yourself is having an impact (positive or negative) on a situation or a relationship. A worker can also learn to modify his or her behaviour.

There are various ways of going about developing self-awareness—for example, engaging in structured self-reflection and obtaining feedback from others. In Chapter 7, we discuss supervision in some depth, but it is important to note here that formal supervision is an important means of developing self-awareness. As well as supervision, workers need to develop a capacity to ask questions of themselves—for example, about how one typically responds to various situations, or what motivates someone to work in the human services field. Some examples might be:

- How do I respond when someone criticises me?
- How do I respond to anger?
- How do I respond to authority?
- How comfortable am I sharing ideas?
- Am I a team player or a lone ranger?

- To what extent do stereotypes shape my perception of others?
- How do I process information?
- To what extent am I 'other aware'?
- With whom do I feel comfortable?
- With whom do I feel uncomfortable?
- Am I an extrovert or an introvert?
- What in my background might impact on how I do my job?
- What in my background contributes to my values framework?
- Am I always reliable?
- How open am I to diversity?

EXERCISE

Write down your personal answers to four of the questions above. Show the questions and your answers to a friend and ask for their feedback.

An essential ingredient to building effective professional relationships is to have trust in others, as well as in the organisation. Trusting relationships depend on a number of things: integrity, competence, consistency, loyalty and openness. If you can exhibit these characteristics, then it is likely that your colleagues will be able to develop a good relationship with you. Furthermore, if your employing organisation can exhibit these characteristics in organisational operations, the overall context is set for collegiality.

Inevitably, when working in any organisation or any work context, there will be people who are quite different in background and temperament. As a consequence, one of the important foundations for good working relationships is the ability to accept and value diversity. Barriers to accepting diversity are:

- prejudices one might hold
- ethnocentrism (the tendency to regard one's own group or culture as superior—or even to only be comfortable with people of one's own culture)

- stereotypes
- discrimination.

Again, people working in human service organisations first have to admit that they do have prejudices and do hold stereotypes. The reality is that it is almost impossible to avoid them, which in turn creates the imperative to challenge and reduce them. Further, we need to actively learn how diversity plays out in terms of differences in verbal and non-verbal communication styles and in how to conduct oneself in public places. Read the case study below and answer the questions posed.

Case study: Cultural diversity

Janet is hoping to apply for a job with an organisation providing services to newly arrived refugees from a number of countries. She checks the organisation out and finds out that Sudanese and a Burmese person work there, plus a number of volunteers from various African countries. She is aware that she will probably be asked about her knowledge about cultural diversity and her skills in working with diversity. Personally, having been brought up in a very 'Anglo' part of the city and attending a private school, she has little experience. While there was plenty of cultural diversity at uni, she herself had little contact with people from other cultures and backgrounds.

Discussion question

- How should Janet answer the question when it is posed in the interview?

WORKING IN TEAMS

Inevitably, people working in human service organisations will be part of a team. There are significant benefits involved in working with a team. It can, for example, increase creativity and assist in problem-solving and innovation; it can foster higher-quality decisions; it can improve practice and service delivery processes; it can increase the quality of service delivery; it can improve communication; it can reduce turnover and absenteeism; and it can increase worker morale. Further, teams that work well are very rewarding. However, real teamwork does not come naturally to most people, but needs to be developed and learned. Reflecting on each of our pasts will illustrate that we all bring different experiences of teams with us. See the exercise.

EXERCISE

Reflect on teams with which you have engaged in the past. Try to identify the things that you liked about those teams, and things that you did not like. What role did you play in creating the team 'atmosphere'?

Successfully functioning in a team is an important factor in a worker's professional development. Perhaps the most fundamental element in promoting good teamwork is having respect for the other members and valuing team members' strengths while compensating for their weaknesses. There are several more elements to a team's success. The first of these is when a team is able to build a form of interdependence that is *productive*. Second, a team works if its members pull their weight. Third, a good team is one in which its members encourage and motivate each other. Fourth, team members who have good group skills create an effective team. Finally, good teams continuously (but not obsessively) focus on the group process, monitoring the team's functioning. Some other characteristics of good teams are:

- having a common purpose and common goals
- delineating clear roles
- having supportive leadership
- fostering trust.

Teams go through stages when they are forming. One of the most famous models of team formation—the Tuckman (1965) model—nominates four: forming, storming, norming and performing. *Forming* refers to the initial stage when people size each other up. Little tangible work is done in this phase, but a good group would focus on goals and ground rules. In the *storming* phase, the group lets its guard down and works towards constructive disagreement and contestation. Groups who cannot move beyond this may collapse into destructive conflict. Acceptance of difference and building focus on the task at hand characterise successful attainment of the *norming* stage. Finally, in the *performing* phase, the group members trust each other, enjoy the group, and engage in creative and innovative problem-solving. Another famous model of team development stages is the Cog ladder of group development—a model that nominates five steps. These are: the 'polite' stage, the 'why are we here?' stage, the 'bid for power' stage, the 'constructive' stage and the 'esprit' stage—each of which is more or less self-explanatory.

De Janasz and colleagues (2006: 192–3) nominate the following tips for effective teams:

- Be focused.
- Handle conflict directly.
- Focus on both process and content.
- Actively participate.
- Keep sensitive issues private.
- Communicate openly and positively.
- Take time to establish operating guidelines.
- Monitor what's going on with the team.
- Practise giving and receiving effective feedback.
- Work with under-performers.
- Energise the team.
- Be reliable and conscientious.
- When needed, give direction to the team's work.
- Be supportive of your team members.

EXERCISE

In respect of the list above list, nominate:

- the one or two areas that are my strengths
- the one or two areas where I need to improve
- the one thing I could do to improve in this area.

Navarra and colleagues (1990) identify a number of 'ideal' roles that people can play in teams. These are:

- *Information seeker.* Looks for facts and clarification.
- *Opinion seeker.* Exposes the values that underlie team decisions.
- *Information giver.* Gives facts based on knowledge and experience.
- *Opinion giver.* Expresses beliefs and values, and suggests them to the group.
- *Elaborator.* Expands, clarifies and anticipates the outcomes.
- *Conductor.* Combines, coordinates and suggests the relationship among ideas.
- *Orienter.* Surveys the process, raises questions and provides direction.
- *Evaluator.* Compares the group process with performance.
- *Recorder.* Documents team process to allow the group to see tangible results.

EXERCISE

Nominate which of these roles you are most likely to adopt.

DEVELOPING PROFESSIONAL RELATIONSHIPS BETWEEN ORGANISATIONS

Like 'community', partnership is a word of obvious virtue (what sensible person would choose conflict over collaboration?). (Clarke and Glendinning, 2002: 33)

Hughes and Wearing (2007: 113) nominate a range of different names given to inter-organisational relationships: collaboration, partnerships, multi-disciplinary and inter-disciplinary work. Here, we will focus on collaboration as a catch-all phrase for all of the above. Being able to collaborate with colleagues in other organisations is an essential component in the success of human service intervention. Hughes and Wearing nominate the following reasons:

- to share knowledge
- to improve the referral process
- to facilitate holistic care
- to improve continuity of care
- to enhance creativity and problem-solving.

The reality is that people who use a human service organisation's services have more complex issues and needs than the presenting problem they bring to you, and most people will need more support (probably of a different type) than you can provide. In certain fields of practice, partnerships and inter-professional networks are mandated (for example, in child protection and family support). That said, much needs be done at the ground level in order to bring the collaborative philosophy into a working reality. Indeed, trying to bridge the gap between the different types of service delivery systems in which people engage—for example, health and community welfare—can be challenging.

Collaboration can range from informal partnerships to formally planned relationships—that is, two workers in different organisations might discover that they are trying to set up a similar group project. After learning about each other, they might decide to collaborate and offer one project for both sets of potential group members. Alternatively, two organisations might have a formal memorandum of understanding (MOU) between them that stipulates that (given resource capacity) they will accept referrals from each other. (See the Other resources section at the end of the chapter for a guide to writing and using MOUs.)

Generally, the characteristics of inter-professional collaboration are that it:

- is voluntary in nature
- promotes communal trust
- has collective involvement
- has shared goals and collective responsibility
- nominates clear roles
- develops sound procedures
- agrees about problem-solving routines
- develops collaborative resources
- maintains confidentiality.

Bristow et al. (2003) identify three key reasons why collaboration occurs:

1. to increase efficiency
2. to improve inclusiveness
3. to achieve integration.

Some other advantages that inter-professional collaboration can promote include:

- shared professional competence and experience
- collective responsibility
- inter-professional communication
- increases in resource availability.

That said, some disadvantages of inter-professional collaboration can be:

- communication difficulties
- time
- commitment
- resistance
- differing professional views

- lack of collaborative skills
- poor quality of decisions
- lack of resources
- role ambiguity and duplication of effort
- low level of experience
- voluntary nature of collaborations.

We know that collaboration is not always easy, in that workers need to change the way they might be used to thinking and behaving. There is no 'right' way to implement inter-professional collaboration. It is hoped, however, that the following discussion, drawing explicitly from the work of the Early Childhood Research Institute (1995) will provide useful guidelines for workers and organisations interested in initiating similar efforts.

If one organisation wishes to develop a relatively formal partnership with another, there are a number of key tasks that need to be undertaken. The first is to identify stakeholders in any potential partnership. Key players need to be involved in identifying a shared vision and common goals for all participants, a vision that provides a foundation for collaboration. While especially important to the early stages of collaboration, this process is crucial for all phases of inter-professional collaboration. Developing a collective vision and a mission statement, then drafting operational goals, will help to clarify the roles and responsibilities of everyone involved. This process allows individuals to get to know one another on a more personal basis by providing time for communicating perspectives, beliefs and attitudes.

The success of any collaborative venture rises or falls on the basis of the nature of the personal relationships established. Moreover, the quality of collaborative relationships reflects the characteristics of the relationships of the partners. The process of identifying shared goals based on compatible or shared values allows relative strangers to join one another to work towards a common goal. Time spent developing relationships between individuals should be understood as an investment in future collaborative work. The inter-personal joining inherent in developing shared visions and goals may well provide the glue that holds individuals together when inevitable differences arise.

It should also be noted that the process of developing a sense of shared mission needs to occur at the level of management *and* at the level of service delivery. Accordingly, goals for collaboration need to be developed and consolidated by those involved in direct service delivery. This means incorporating time in busy workloads for inter-professional workers to discuss and develop mission statements as well as to identify goals for working together. Elements of collaborative practice should be included in job descriptions for all staff to validate and emphasise the importance of collaborative practice.

Collaboration cannot be imposed from above, but should nevertheless be strongly encouraged as an important theme in the organisation's culture and operational procedures. While it is important that collaboration is supported and promoted administratively, it is critical that collaborative working relationships evolve from the ground up. As front-line staff, human service workers should be empowered to create and implement their own team policies and procedures. Team-building, then, must be sanctioned as a legitimate and necessary component of service delivery by the organisational management. This means that time must be set aside for team members to cultivate and improve their working relationships with one another. Collaboration is not for everyone, and not everyone is well suited to teamwork. Performing effectively on an inter-professional team requires a unique set of professional skills and, in order for the team to function optimally, individual team members must possess the capacity to work within such a model.

All human service workers should give careful consideration to the development of their collaborative skills, as they are just as important to good outcomes as their intervention skills. A team member must possess solid professional and personal skills that will allow him or her to function effectively within the field of professional expertise as well as the capacity to work with others in such a way as to enhance overall team functioning. Traits like patience, persistence, initiative, flexibility, risk-taking, empathy, self-assurance and self-realisation are important.

In addition, workers who are non-defensive and open to other points of view, who are aware of their own personal biases, and who reflect respect for differences will contribute to a collaborative environment. There are also other qualities including the capacity to convey a sense of personal warmth and trustworthiness that contribute to effective collaborative practice. A good sense of humor will go a long way to defusing conflicts that may arise. That said, one 'toxic' team member can compromise the efficacy of the entire team, and there is a danger that team functioning will drop to the functioning level of the weakest team member. If collaboration is to work, each individual collaborator must be committed to the process.

Hughes and Wearing (2007) also note the growing trend in human service organisations for workers to be expected to work in partnership with service users and families. This wholly admirable goal poses additional challenges. Most human service organisations would argue that they do work in partnership with their service users, but the reality is often very different. Clearly, service users have limited power in service delivery relationships. Recognising this and responding to the ethical imperative to work respectfully with service users, in Chapter 9 we discuss the nature of power in worker–user relationships, and explore some techniques for working across power differentials. Here we merely note that working in partnership with service users is expected and often required in a growing number of service domains. Look at the following case study.

WORKING WITH BOARDS AND VOLUNTEERS

A significant proportion of human service work is undertaken in the non-profit sector, in community-based organisations or in religious or secular charities. The majority of these organisations will have a board of management (often known as a management committee), in many instances because the parliamentary Act that gives them legal identity stipulates that they should. Human service organisations vary enormously in the way boards operate. In some organisations—often small local organisations—the board is drawn from the local community or from interested persons committed to the activity the organisation is undertaking—either because they have needed the service themselves or because they know someone who does. In addition, it is not at all uncommon (particularly in rural and regional communities) that human service workers will sit on another board in their community. In such instances, board

Case study: Developing a partnership

Hanifa is working as a family support worker in a community-based non-profit organisation that receives referrals from the local state government Child Protection Team. Family support workers are expected to develop an intervention plan with a referred family that recognises their presenting issues, states what the family needs and wants, their goals, their concerns, and the expectations held of each partner in the plan. Workers are expected to update this plan regularly.

Hanifa receives a referral about the Watters family: mum Karen (28), dad Bill (32) and their three children (Sherrie, 10; Jamie, 6; and Carol-Ann, 2). Sherrie has been in foster care but was reunited with her family a little over two years ago, just before Carol-Ann was born. Jamie was the subject of unsubstantiated allegations when he was in kindergarten. Karen has been assessed as borderline intellectually disabled and Bill has a very intermittent attachment to the labour market, is functionally illiterate, and has limited impulse control. Both parents had contact with child welfare authorities when they were children, and are quite hostile to Child Protection.

Sherrie's school has again notified Child Protection. They visit and assess the family, but decide that rather than formally placing the family into the child protection system, the best course of action is to refer the family to Hanifa's organisation. They note, however, that the two-year-old seemed a little listless, and was not able to maintain eye contact. When Hanifa arrives with a colleague to undertake her own assessment, Karen immediately asks him whether Child Protection sent him.

Discussion questions
- How should Hanifa go about developing a partnership with the family?
- What are the factors that will hinder this process?

members can be quite intimately involved with daily activity and the relationships developed can be quite close and friendly; sadly, in some instances relationships can become quite conflictual.

In other instances, particularly in large organisations, the board may contain people drawn from quite different circles, often from business, politics, the law or academia. These boards operate very differently from the smaller community-based boards in that their interests lie primarily in formal governance, not in the daily activity of the organisation. These boards' primary relationship with the organisation is through the chief executive officer (CEO). Such boards are likely to have a formal role and a set of operational procedures mapped out, and are driven by a formal strategic plan. While the decisions of boards are usually available publicly, many boards will operate under principles of board confidentiality. Board members' liabilities and risks are actively managed through board procedures. As such, these boards are inevitably more formal in their operations.

Accordingly, the actual conduct of board meetings can be very different in each type of board. In the smaller 'working' board, the meetings might be quite informal; discussion can be wide-ranging, perhaps loosely following an agenda, often allowing side-bars and segues. The other boards are usually much more formal, with strict agendas and standardised reports and procedures. Neither board is necessarily better than the other; the small, less formal board is well suited to the early beginnings of an organisation that is responding to local issues and needs. Such boards often need to keep firmly linked to the community. As a general rule, the older and larger an organisation gets, the more likely its board will be to tend towards the latter, more formal style. Either way, all boards have a series of important responsibilities, and the smaller, less formal boards are no less accountable than the large, formal boards. Informality is no excuse for an unbusinesslike approach to the running of the organisation.

Ultimately, the board is the entity held accountable in law for the operations of the organisation. Members of the board have certain legally required duties. The ACT Council of Social Service (<www.actcoss.org.au/oik/infosheets/governance/fiduciary.html>)

Case study: Conflict of interest?

Evie is a member of the management committee of her local child-care centre. The child-care centre needs to have some fairly extensive plumbing work done but is having trouble getting a plumber to come and quote. Finally, the centre director gets a quote but it is more expensive than the committee expected. Evie says she knows a plumber (her brother-in-law, Christos) who she could ask to provide another quote. The committee says yes, so Evie rings Christos and tells him the story and asks him to come and look at the job and to advise a reasonable quote estimate. Christos does so, but he also delivers a quote considerably lower than the first one.

Discussion questions
- Has Evie created a conflict of interest in this situation?
- What should Evie have done?
- What should she do now?

notes that board members have five key duties in carrying out their responsibilities. Their first duty is to act in the best interest of the organisation—a duty of care, loyalty and obedience to the organisation's purpose, in keeping with its philosophy and objectives. Their second duty is to act honestly. Their third duty is to take care and act with diligence, abiding by the organisation's constitution and complying with legal requirements. Their fourth duty is to maintain confidentiality in respect of all organisational and board information. Their fifth duty is to declare any conflict of interest. Read the case study above and answer the questions posed.

In meeting these duties, boards have 'operations': activities undertaken by the board. These can include the development and enactment of board by-laws and other board policies; the recruitment of members; training and orientation of board members; organising board and committee meetings; and conducting board evaluations. Specifically, boards:

- direct the process of planning for the organisation
- approve long-range goals

- approve annual objectives
- monitor the achievement of goals and objectives
- oversee the evaluation of programs and services
- finalise and approve the budget
- solicit contributions in fundraising campaigns
- approve expenditures outside of the authorised budget
- insure an annual audit of the organisation's accounts
- employ the CEO
- make decisions about increases in staff profile
- interpret the organisation to the broader community
- develop a committee structure to manage the work of the board
- appoint committee members
- sign legal documents
- settle any conflict or clashes between committees.

How much contact should there be between a board and a human service organisation's staff? CEOs sometimes feel that independent board–staff contact undermines their authority. Boards usually want to respect the authority of their CEO, but they also value the independent viewpoint staff can bring. Some boards regularly ask program managers to give presentations to the board—for example, by asking a financial counselling program within the organisation about the impact of an economic downturn. Some boards assign a board member to each program manager. Restricting contact between board members and staff can result in suspicion on the part of the board and resentment from the staff. Here are some guidelines to consider:

- There is no restriction on contact, but the CEO should be informed about meetings.
- Board members can request information and reports (such as last month's intake statistics), but must stop short of directing staff work by asking for reports not already prepared.
- Personnel grievances must go through the channels specified by organisational policy.

- There should be a defined channel via which staff can express concerns to the board about the CEO, preferably through the board president or chairperson. The board president can choose to raise the concerns to the CEO, or to bring them to the board for investigation.

Finally, it is important that workers in human service organisations remember that board members in non-profit organisations are not remunerated. In other words, they are volunteers—volunteers who take on the not inconsiderable risks of being legally and financially accountable for an organisation. At those times when a worker feels frustrated by what might seem to be a risk-averse stance by a board or by board caution in the budgetary process, it is worth remembering that they adopt that stance for very good reasons. That said, well-run boards and well-managed organisations usually have potential risks well controlled, and manage to keep the organisation afloat financially.

While board members are volunteers, their relationship with the organisation is quite different from most of the other volunteers in a typical human service organisation. Sometimes the relationship between workers and volunteers can be a little unsettled. Workers may feel threatened by the presence of volunteers, and might want to confine their activities to areas that do not impinge on their 'professional' domain. If this occurs, it is actually a great pity because volunteers can add an invaluable dimension to human service intervention in particular, and service delivery overall. That said, volunteers need to be carefully managed, not only to maximise their engagement in and commitment to the organisation, but also to ensure that inappropriate behaviours do not occur.

Creyton and colleagues (n.d.) articulate twelve principles for effectively working with volunteers. These are to:

1. ensure that volunteers are considered an integral part of the mission and culture of the organisation

2. ensure that the organisation has good policies and procedures, administrative and recording systems in relation to volunteers

3. ensure that the volunteer-recruitment processes involve identification of an individual's skills, interests and potential, and that these are effectively matched to opportunities within the organisation

4. develop inclusive practices in relation to volunteers

5. provide ongoing opportunities for volunteers to be involved in organisational planning and decision-making

6. provide the same degree of learning and development opportunities to volunteers as are provided to staff

7. ensure that volunteer contributions are significantly and appropriately valued and recognised at all levels of the organisation

8. ensure that the support provided to volunteers is accessible, flexible and appropriate

9. ensure that the organisation creates an enabling environment and meaningful work for volunteers

10. ensure that the boundaries between paid workers and volunteers are clear and defined, while at the same time making an active effort to reduce unnecessary distinctions and to create teamwork between paid workers and volunteers

11. recognise and ensure that the volunteer effort contributes to overall community capacity-building

12. develop and implement appropriate evaluation and performance measures, and use information generated by these to feed back to volunteers and the organisation to inform continuous improvement of the volunteer contribution.

EXERCISE

Make an appointment with a non-profit human service organisation in your local area that has volunteers working with them. Visit the organisation and, using the above list as prompts, ask how the organisation works with its volunteers.

Whether working with colleagues, boards, volunteers or service users, another reality is that in multicultural Australia, all human service workers need to learn about how to work with people from other countries and other cultures. In addition, professionalism in human service practice means understanding the importance of personal boundaries.

Working with cultural diversity

What is culture and what do we mean by cultural diversity? Culture can be defined as a collection of ideas, values and norms specific to one particular group of people. Everyone has a culture. A specific culture can include language, race, ethnic background, country or region of origin, dress, values, religions, notions of family—the list goes on and on. Culture is what goes into defining us as belonging to a particular group. Cultural diversity, however, is understood often as a broad group of people who are 'other' than the main group in that particular society. When we think about cultural diversity in the human services industry, we are often thinking about groups of people who are not part of the mainstream group in our society. If you think about it from that perspective, cultural diversity in the human service field means that you will be working with people whose sexuality or age, class or gender, ability or race, is different to that of those belonging to the dominant culture.

If we think back to what was said about the practice of critical reflection at the beginning of this book, we ask human service workers to reflect on the role played by their social locations in their understanding and interpretation of various issues and situations. In a way, this is a reflection of your culture and the role played by the ideas and norms of the groups to which you belong. If you were to critically reflect on your culture, you would first identify what your own culture is. Think for a moment about your gender, your class, your race, your age, your sexuality, religious beliefs and abilities. Now consider those same aspects of the society in which you live. What is the dominant gender (the one that holds the power, political, legal, and financial control)? Who is rewarded in your society in terms of class, race, age, sexuality, religion, ability, and so forth? What aspects of your social location ensure that you belong to the dominant culture, and where do you differ? What groups in our society are the 'other'? What does this cultural diversity mean for the members of these 'othered' groups, and what implications does working with these groups then have for you as a human service worker?

Boundaries

Working in the human service area can be both rewarding and challenging. You will be working with services users who have complex and multiple issues, and whose lives are affected on a daily basis by the systemic discrimination that exists within the structures of our society. This is physically and emotionally demanding work, and you may find yourself in situations where service users and their families expect or need more from you than you are able to give in your role as a human service worker. You need to know what you can offer in your role and what you can't. You need to be able to set limits for both the service user and yourself—in short, you need to be able to form healthy boundaries.

Boundaries can be seen as an invisible protection between ourselves and some of the demands made on us in this work that we do. Boundaries allow us to maintain personal and professional aspects of ourselves, and allow us to protect both ourselves and our service users. Many discourses and discussions on professional and personal boundaries lack an understanding of the complexities introduced by issues such as the culture, gender, class, age, ability or sexuality of both the worker and the service user group. We will discuss much of this further when we begin to look at working within your own community. While professional ethics (discussed later in this book) are often concrete and legislated, boundaries often exist in a grey area where no 'one size fits all' rule applies. Regardless of all the complexities, the basic principle remains that healthy boundaries of some description are necessary for workers in the human services area. Without healthy boundaries, human service workers will burn out and service users may not get the professional assistance to which they are entitled.

Some basic ideas about how to keep healthy boundaries for yourself and your clients would be:

- Ensure that both you and your service user understand your role, what you can do and what you can't do at the beginning of the relationship. (You may need to review this from time to time.)

- All workers will have a different view about self-disclosure. Sometimes, discussing an incident or idea from your own life can assist a service user, shorten the distance between yourself and your service user, or assist in developing empathy. Some human service workers would insist that there is never any self-disclosure. A good rule of thumb is often to think about what you are about to share and ask yourself who it will benefit. Will this help your service user or is it for you? If it is for you, keep it to yourself.

- Ask for help when you need it. Regular supervision is essential in this area of work.

- Remember to take time away from the agency when opportunities for training and workshops present themselves.

- Maintain your beginner's mind—always learn from colleagues and clients. Try to always be learning something; it is important to have the freedom somewhere in your life to not know the answer—to take in and not give out so you can continue to be nurtured and keep your mind open.

- Remember, you are not 'it'. *You* are not the answer. Being responsive to the pain of others will make a difference to them, but you are not responsible for their lives.

WORKING WITH YOUR OWN COMMUNITY

Many workers in the human service industry come from a specific community and find themselves working for and on behalf of members of that specific community. This can pose its own issues, and many aspects of the discussion on boundaries from the previous section need to be looked at in a different light. Simple ideas (such as not giving out your home phone number or not telling service users where you live) may be irrelevant if you are from the same small or rural community. Cultural norms about participation in each other's lives, about sharing everything from food to family, need to be taken into consideration. Often workers in this situation are more motivated, more passionate and more committed to their service users than other human service workers. They have a unique role to play in advocacy for and support of members of their community. They also face unique challenges when it comes to understanding and differentiating between their role as workers and their place in their community. If, as a human service worker, you are in this position, then it is important for you to have a good understanding of why you are doing the work you are doing, what you like about it and what the challenges are for you.

As stated earlier, boundaries can be seen as an invisible protection between ourselves and the outer world that can provide a space for us that is just our own. Boundaries allow us to maintain personal aspects of ourselves and allow us to protect ourselves. Boundaries can usually say, 'This is me as a worker', as opposed to 'This is me as a member of my community'. However, other members of your community may not understand this as clearly as it is stated here, and workers from specific communities often find themselves treading a fine line between worker and community member.

The pressure to work for your community outside of your job may also come from within your organisation. Many organisations put pressure on workers from specific communities to interpret; it is easy and a money saver if the interpreting budget is tight or the monthly allowance is gone. Again, critical reflection can assist you to define healthy boundaries if you are in this situation. Ask yourself why you are doing the work you are doing, what strengths you can bring to the position as a member of the community, and what challenges this might pose. Can coming from the same community blind you at times to some aspects of the service user's dilemma? What can you do to become aware of this if it happens, and what steps can you take to address it?

Case study: Working from within a community

You are the only Indigenous support worker for a regional domestic violence program. Your role is to work with Indigenous women who are escaping violence and abuse. You offer support, advice, advocacy in court, advocacy with the police and liaison with the refuge. You often know the women, or know of the women, who come to you for assistance and this can sometimes be a bit tricky, but you have good supervision from both your agency and a respected female elder in your community. However, one day a woman comes to you for assistance who has been very badly treated by your own cousin. This is going to make things very difficult for you at home.

Discussion questions
- Identify what the issues are for you in this situation that are specific to you belonging to this community.
- Identify what your role is in this situation in terms of your work as a human service worker.
- How will you work out the differences and who will you need to talk to about this situation?

Working with interpreters

Increasingly, more and more work in the human services area will require you to work with interpreters. This work can be demanding, and there are some simple guidelines you will need to follow. Read the following case study.

This scenario is repeated daily in Australia in the human service area because human service workers lack knowledge of the proper policies and procedures needed to facilitate these sorts of situations. This practice is rude, ignorant and often racist.

Most agencies and organisations will have policies and procedures for providing interpreters in working with service users. It is your responsibility to know what these are for your particular organisation, and to advocate for better services if they fall short of effective practice. It is government policy in most human service organisations to use qualified interpreters in situations where communication is difficult, both with migrants and with deaf people.

Case study: Working with interpreters 1
Imagine for a minute that you are touring through a foreign country where you get into some kind of trouble, either with your health or legally. This is not an English-speaking country, and you are trying to make yourself understood to those who can assist you; however, they don't speak a word of English and you don't speak a word of their language. They bring out a co-worker from another department, who speaks a strain of English that has nothing to do with your understanding of the language, and your only option is to use your sixteen-year-old son who speaks a little of this language (from high school) but who doesn't know how to communicate some of the legal or health terms used. The person at the front desk is getting frustrated with you and is talking more and more loudly in the hope that an increase in volume will suddenly mean you understand what they are saying. They have no idea of the ordeal you have been through to even get to them for help, and they are now talking to co-workers and laughing. You know it is about you.

Qualified interpreters will hold a National Accreditation Authority for Translators and Interpreters (NAATI) accreditation according to their level of competence. Workers should not use co-workers who are not qualified interpreters. Often, co-workers from some smaller communities will actually know the service user, or their family or their close friends. This is a breach of confidentiality, and service users are put in an impossible situation if this is the case. Children of service users should never be used; this is not an appropriate situation. One of the authors, for example, has seen mothers struggling to find ways to describe a suspected miscarriage, trying not to say words that will startle their children (or even tell their children what is going on), resulting in medical staff dismissing them.

Qualified interpreters are highly skilled in English and other languages; they are bound by a code of ethics, which means they practise impartiality, confidentiality and accuracy. They also understand many cultural norms and practices that belong to the specific group for which they are interpreting. Most agencies and organisations will have policies and procedures for the booking and use of interpreters, so ensure that you are familiar with them.

Some 'dos' and 'don'ts' when using face-to-face or 'on-site' interpreters

When seeking an interpreter:

- **Do** only use suitably qualified interpreters and book through accredited interpreting agencies.

- **Do** try to ascertain what language dialect your client needs before booking an interpreter. The client's country of birth may mean very little.

- **Do** remember to request the specific gender of the interpreter. Matters that are particularly sensitive or clients from specific religions will often require 'same-gender' interpreters.

- **Do** remember to allow extra time for an interview such as this.

- **Don't** ever use children, relatives, friends, neighbours or the head of their particular church, even if they are available and it will save time. An accredited interpreter respects the need for impartiality and confidentiality. Sometimes a client will not be happy with the choice of interpreter (i.e. from the same small community or a distant relative). This should be respected and another interpreter arranged.

Before the interview

- **Do** brief the interpreter on the case beforehand, if this is appropriate.
- **Don't** assume that interpreting is a simple case of matching the non-English word or expression with an English meaning. Sometimes equivalents don't exist.
- **Don't** expect the interpreter to be a walking dictionary. There will be times when the interpreter will need to seek clarification or ask you to explain certain concepts.

During the interview

- **Do** introduce yourself to your client.
- **Do** use the consecutive style of interpreting. That is, pause to allow the interpreter to interpret after every few sentences.
- **Do** explain clearly who you are and what the purpose of the session is. The client should not be confused about your role, your interest in their affairs or what you can offer.
- **Do** maintain control of the interview. *You* must ask the questions and hear the replies fully. The interpreter's job is to assist in communication, not to conduct the interview alone.
- **Do** position yourself in a way that allows you to have maximum eye contact with the client. Ask questions directly to the client.
- **Don't** isolate the client by identifying with the interpreter and engaging them in a discussion. If you need to clarify or discuss something with the interpreter, request that this be explained to the client first.
- **Don't** alienate the client by having the interpreter sit too close to you.

How to work with an interpreter on the telephone

- Introduce yourself to the interpreter.
- Make sure that you tell the interpreter about the kind of telephone equipment you have (conference telephone, dual-handset, single telephone) and where you are (counter, office, hospital or ward).
- Introduce yourself and the interpreter to the client and describe the purpose of the interview.
- Limit your communication to sections of manageable length.
- Again, you want to use the consecutive style of interpreting.
- Remember, that with any telephone counselling, the person on the other end has no non-verbal cues (such as body language) to assist them.
- Clearly indicate the end of the session to the interpreter.

Case study: Working with an interpreter 2

Peter is a housing worker in a small community housing agency. The work of this organisation is to advocate for clients who are housed in Department of Housing accommodation. The previous afternoon, a 50-year-old woman had approached the reception desk, asking for some assistance. She explained in broken English that she needed a bigger house. She said that her husband and her three teenage sons were in a two-bedroom Department of Housing Unit and this was too small. The receptionist contacted Peter in his office, and explained what she thought the situation was. Peter had no time that afternoon, so he arranged for the woman to come back the following afternoon and asked the receptionist to arrange for an interpreter to be present. The following afternoon, Peter met with the interpreter prior to the woman coming to the organisation.

The interpreter was a male and was a Kurdish interpreter. When the woman came in for her appointment, she became agitated very quickly. She did not want to talk to a man (either a housing worker or an interpreter) and she was Turkish. Although the interpreter said he was fluent in Turkish, the woman refused to have anything to do with the interpreter, as the cultural conflict between the Turkish and the Kurdish communities where she had come from, would not be overcome.

Discussion questions
- If you were Peter, what would you do at this point?
- In hindsight, what should have been done to ensure that did not happen?

CONCLUSION

This chapter has demonstrated that the relationships we have with colleagues within our own organisation, between organisations, with our Board of Directors and with our volunteers are crucial ingredients in effective human service work. As we indicated in our introduction, these relationships do not necessarily come naturally, but require sustained attention. Furthermore, human service delivery is much more than the relationship between a worker and a service user. Indeed, that relationship and its outcomes depend upon the viability and quality of all the other relationships discussed here. Finally, we discussed cultural diversity and suggested techniques for working with interpreters. We suggest to you that each and every human service worker has a significant professional responsibility towards ensuring good relationships in all domains.

Chapter review questions

6.1   What is the fundamental precondition to developing good relations?

6.2   What are the benefits of working in teams?

6.3   What are some common pitfalls of working in teams?

6.4   What are the benefits of promoting inter-organisational collaboration?

6.5   What are the characteristics of inter-professional collaboration?

6.6   Identify six roles of a board of directors.

6.7   Articulate six principles for working with volunteers.

6.8   What are four key tips for working with interpreters?

OTHER RESOURCES

Writing and using memoranda of understanding, <http://ezinearticles. com/?Writing-and-Using-Memoranda-of-Understanding-(MOUs) andid=144781>.

Working in teams, <www.managementhelp.org/grp_skll/teams/teams.htm>.

Building stronger community organisations—boards, <www.ourcommunity. com.au/boards/boards_article.jsp?articleId=1309>.

Managing volunteers, <www.volunteeringaustralia.org/html/s12_content/default. asp?tnid=17anddsb%3D440>.

Rights and responsibilities in relation to volunteers <www.volunteering.com.au/ working_with_volunteers/volunteering_issues/volunteers_rights.asp>.

Victorian Department of Human Services, 2006, *Cultural Diversity Guide*, <www.dhs.vic.gov.au/multicultural/downloads/cultural_diversity_guide_ 2006.pdf>.

KEY READINGS

Creyton, M., McGarricle, A. and Olive, D. (n.d.), *Working with Volunteers: A Human Centred Approach*, Volunteering Queensland, <www.volunteering-queensland.org.au/forms/BookChapter1.pdf>.

Darlington, Y., Feeney, J.A. and Rixon, K. 2004, 'Complexity, Conflict and Uncertainty: Issues in Collaboration in Child Protection and Mental Health Services', *Children and Youth Services Review*, vol. 26: 1175–92.

Fishal, C. 2008, *The Book of the Board: Effective Governance for Nonprofits*, Federation Press, Sydney.

Hughes, M. and Wearing, M. 2007, *Organisations and Management in Social Work*, Sage, London, pp. 112–20.

Kasar, J. and Clark, E.N. 2000, *Developing Professional Behaviours*, SLACK Inc., Thorofare, NJ.

McLaughlin, H. 2004, 'Partnerships: Panacea or Pretence?', *Journal of Interprofessional Care*, vol. 18, no. 2: 103–13.

CHAPTER SEVEN | Supervision and support

SUMMARY

This chapter acknowledges that ongoing supervision and support are essential to maintaining good staff in contemporary in human service organisations. It looks at ways that, as a new human service worker, you can understand how the stress that comes with this type of work can impact on you, and more importantly, what you can do to help manage this and continue to work productively. It starts with an overview of supervision in human service organisations and the various functions this serves, including the commonly accepted core elements of administration, education and support. Next we move on to look at some of the challenges of working in the human services and the impact this may have on workers. Linked to this is a discussion of self-care and of strategies you can use to look after yourself. We then examine models of supervision that are used in the human services and discuss what they offer a new worker; we also consider where they may fail. Finally, we look at other ways of providing support and supervision. In particular, we explore peer supervision and look at how this can assist with educative and support functions and assist workers in their jobs. Throughout the chapter, we present a range of case studies to help workers understand the importance of supervision and explore how they can ensure they have access to the supervision and support they need.

OVERVIEW OF SUPERVISION AND WHY IT IS IMPORTANT

Most workers in the human service field will be engaged in difficult, sometimes distressing and always emotionally taxing work; supervision and support are among the key ways that this is managed. As discussed in Chapters 1 and 2, all organisations need to manage the work of their staff to ensure that they provide the best possible service to their clients. In social work, supervision is the way that this traditionally has been done. Supervision in human service work has been around for over 80 years, and throughout this time it has served a number of functions (Tsui, 2005). In 1976, Alfred Kadushin first published his book on social work supervision, in which he articulated the three main aspects that remain to this day: administration, education and support (Kadushin and Harkness, 2002). These have been widely accepted as defining supervision. An example of their use can be seen in the AASW supervision standards (2000), which state:

> *The primary purpose of professional supervision is to facilitate competent, independent practice and not to perpetuate dependency . . . Social work supervision encompasses administrative, educational and supportive functions, all of which are interrelated.*

Administration
This is a management function which includes: the clarification of job roles; the planning and assignment of work; the review and assessment of work; and accountability and responsibility for supervisee's work.

Education
This involves the provision of knowledge and skills, which are the worker's necessary equipment for effective practice. It includes the development of self-awareness of the social worker in relation to his/her work. Educational supervision is a core component in the professional development of the worker.

Support

The support function of supervision is concerned with helping the supervisee deal with job-related stress, and with developing attitudes and feelings conducive to maximum job performance. It helps sustain worker morale, gives the supervisee a sense of professional self worth, and a feeling of belonging in the agency.

Administration can also be seen as management; this is the component of supervision that is focused on ensuring that the work is done and tasks are allocated. In many human service agencies, this role is now performed by a manager who may or may not have formal training in human services and is less likely to be a trained social worker. This role is also specified in job descriptions and duty statements. Education is another component of supervision, which was once undertaken as a form of 'on-the-job' training for social workers and welfare staff. In the 1920s, universities and colleges took on the role of training social workers, but there was still a strong work-based focus and this continues into the current practice of student supervision. Field education is an example of the enduring master–apprentice model that was first developed as the means of social work education prior to the existence of any social work schools in universities. The final aspect of social work supervision is support. Traditionally, this formed part of the mix of supervision provided by an agency supervisor, usually a social worker, with a focus on helping the worker to adjust to job-related stress (Kadushin and Harkness, 2002).

WHAT ARE SOME OF THE CHALLENGES AND HOW MAY THEY IMPACT?

An important issue to consider is that, with recent changes in the provision of human services, the role of the professional supervisor has become more complex, as conflicting and often unrealistic demands are placed on them (Jones, 1999; Beddoe, 1997). Beddoe (1997: 10) sums it up in this way: 'Social work supervision has suffered greatly in this context and has become increasingly focused on administrative and managerial services to the neglect of educative and support functions.' She outlines the need to provide training for both new graduates and supervisors in aspects of supervision that are relevant to the field. The central purpose of supervision is to ensure best practice, with a need to focus more on service delivery and accountability. Alongside this concern for the need for improvement in the way supervision is provided, there have also been wide-ranging concerns expressed about traditional forms of supervision (Jones, 1999: 81–2). These include being too hierarchic, fostering dependence, being conducive to racist and sexist practices, and inducing conflict between the various functions.

The changes in service delivery in Western human services have placed increased pressure on the traditional social work supervision structure (Jones, 1999; Beddoe, 1997). Jones makes the point that transformation of supervision practices is required to respond to the complexities and challenges of the current environment. He concludes with the view that expectations of supervisors need to be realistic and workers should not assume the supervisors are superheroes. Clare (2001) has also written about the tensions and complexities involved in social work supervision during times of increased accountability. He suggests a model of 'developmental supervision' that, in his words, avoids the 'quick fix' of making decisions for workers. He stresses the importance of using supervision to encourage new workers to take the time to think through their own solutions and thereby address their educational and support needs. Clare sees this method as helping to overcome the tendency towards increasing powerlessness and dependency of new workers. Hughes and Wearing (2007: 122) also discuss the danger of adopting a 'problem-solving' approach in supervision, which may reduce the opportunities for longer term learning and professional development. Other significant issues to consider with supervision are power issues where performance is being assessed, differences in learning styles (Hughes and Wearing, 2007) and personality differences that will affect how someone works with other team members and their supervisor (Gardner, 2006).

The views discussed above highlight the wide range of perspectives about the role of a supervisor and what constitutes good supervision; they also show that there are many factors that will impact on your preferred learning and support needs. From this we suggest that it can be quite unrealistic to rely on your supervisor to meet all your support and educational needs, and that as a new worker you should take responsibility for understanding what these needs are and generating ideas about how you can meet them. Later in this chapter, we will focus on some forms of supervision and support that can be used.

Case study: Supervision

Leila is a new worker in a government welfare agency; she is involved in doing intake assessments. Leila has regular weekly supervision with her team leader, Jim, where she discusses cases that have been referred to her. At these sessions, Leila is asked to advise where she is up to with each case and to mention any referrals about which she is unsure. Jim is very supportive and keen to ensure that Leila does not feel overwhelmed by any cases assigned to her. He will suggest ways to complete the assessment or offer to take on work himself, or he will refer to a more experienced worker if need be.

Jim is very busy, as the team is expected to complete a set number of assessments per week; however, he is always available for the one-hour supervision session. Despite Jim's support, Leila starts to feel worried by her work. She is beginning to feel uncertain of her abilities and also wonders whether she is doing the right thing by working in this setting, as she does not fully understand or even accept some of the guidelines with which she needs to work. When she raises her concerns with Jim, he tells her that many new workers feel this way and that if she is not comfortable with any particular cases to tell him and he will reassign them.

Discussion questions
- What function of supervision is being covered here?
- Is this meeting Leila's needs? Why or why not?
- What is being left out?
- Why might Leila be losing confidence and having doubts?
- How could this be addressed?

STRESS AND SELF-CARE

Working in the human services can pose many challenges for staff (Gardner 2006: 7; Tsui, 2005: 83). Not only are workers often dealing with the most disadvantaged and marginalised people, but they will also need to work within agency (and funding) guidelines that may limit their role and place restrictions on working in the ways they feel will most benefit the service user. Also, workers are often faced with complex situations with which they may have had no specific experience or are required to work within guidelines they do not fully understand or with which they may not completely agree. All of this can result in a high degree of uncertainty and stress. Drawing on a range of authors, Tsui (2005: 83) defines stress as 'a negative feature of the environment that impinges on the individual' and burnout as 'a cluster of physical and emotional maladaptive reactions to high levels of work-related stress'. Tsui has identified major sources of work stress: the nature of the demands of the job; overwork; job insecurity; poor physical environment; a lack of clear guidelines for decision-making; and finally inter-personal difficulties between staff.

As well as stress from the nature of work undertaken and the reactions of individuals within this, the way the organisation functions and is structured can also have a positive or negative impact on the stress levels of its staff. Thompson and colleagues (1996) undertook a study looking at the effect of organisational culture on the stress levels of social workers. They concluded that the organisation itself, or staff groups within it, can develop a form of collective burnout that they describe as 'organisational stress' (Thompson et al., 1996). They conducted research with two groups of social work staff in different branches of the same organisation undertaking very similar work and found that the groups experienced quite different levels of stress, even though the client work they undertook was the same. From this they concluded that when work is poorly organised with more time pressure, and where workers have less motivation and more doubt about their effectiveness, they will experience higher levels of work-related stress. They note that workers in this situation will have a higher need of support, in particular a need for more acknowledgement from their supervisors of the stressors of their job. Their research also showed that relationships with fellow workers were of prime importance to job satisfaction.

The work of Thompson et al. (1996) highlights the importance of having an understanding of the culture in which you will work and the quality of the relationships and support that will be provided. All human service workers (but particularly those with limited experience) need to have the opportunity to be provided with ongoing education and support for undertaking their job. They need someone to keep an eye on their workload and ensure not only that they are not overloaded, but that they are not handling cases with which they do not have the experience to deal effectively. Brody (1993: 250–2) argues that many organisationally generated stresses can be addressed, and it is the responsibility of the organisation to address such stressors as role ambiguity, overload (or underload) of work, contradictory expectations, poor planning, a laid-back atmosphere, and poor matches between staff and jobs. Human service workers need to know that they are not alone with their concerns and should feel able to raise doubts and seek support as needed. Without this, they will become stressed and face what is commonly known as 'burnout' (Tsui, 2006: 83).

> *Burnout:* A state of emotional, mental, and physical exhaustion caused by excessive and prolonged stress. It occurs when a worker feels overwhelmed and unable to meet constant demands. If the stress continues, the worker begins to lose the interest or motivation that led him or her to take on a certain role in the first place.

Self-care is emphasised in social work and other courses; however, it can sometimes happen that workers get so caught up in the emotion of their work that they forget to implement self-care strategies. The stressful nature of human service work is well known and has been discussed by many authors. While the importance of looking after staff should be a high priority, the extent to which an agency can or does look after its staff will vary. The provision of supervision is the primary means by which the agency is fulfilling its requirement to support workers. This means that it is very important that you, as a new worker, can identify your own development and support needs and that you have thought about ways to achieve these. Identification of educational needs is important and self-care is a key issue.

Chenoweth and McAuliffe (2008: 256) list strategies for self-care developed by an experienced child protection worker. While these will not all be relevant to everyone, they do provide a good overview of things to keep in mind and ideas on which to draw. The strategies are:

- Manage stress through problem-solving approaches, relaxation, fun, exercise—or whatever else works for you.
- Develop and maintain hope and spirituality.
- Acknowledge the troubling and debilitating aspects of your work and also acknowledge your individual successes, achievements and the vital role that you play in our society.
- Accept that feelings of anger and sorrow are all aspects of a healthy psyche.
- Engage with your community—find a space to participate in 'health humanity'.
- Maintain clear boundaries between your work and your private life.
- Keep a life outside work—protect it and nurture it.
- Develop and use supportive workplace relationships.
- Be assertive in expressing your emotional needs at work.
- Use line-management supervision to process your emotional responses to work and to articulate your care needs.
- Become politically active on issues that are important to you in both your personal and professional life.
- Access external professional supervision.
- If needed, establish or join peer supervision or support networks.
- Write a self-care plan that outlines your strengths and vulnerabilities, maps your resources and supports and makes clear commitments about what you can do and why.

EXERCISE
- Drawing on these strategies, choose three that seem particularly important or relevant to you.
- Think of examples of how these can apply to your circumstances.
- If you wish, share this with a fellow student/worker.
- Begin to write that self-care plan!

At times, very troubling events can occur, or you may find that work or personal pressure can result in you feeling overwhelmed; you may even feel that you cannot cope. In these cases, it is important to get help. Many organisations have Employee Assistance Programs (EAPs) through which you can access confidential counselling and support. In some situations, a workplace may arrange for EAP providers to attend the agency if there has been a critical incident of some sort, such as an accident, workplace aggression, or injury to or the death of a service user or staff member. It is part of the organisation's health and safety obligations to make these types of service available to staff, and it is not a sign of weakness to avail yourself of them—particularly as by addressing these matters early on you have a greater chance of dealing effectively with them.

HOW IS SUPERVISION USED?

As a new worker in a human service organisation, you will experience some similarity and many differences from the nature of supervision and support you will have experienced as a student. Hopefully, as a student on placement, you will have had experience of supervision. Social work in particular has a very strong focus on the field education role and clear guidelines on what is expected for students in placement. Throughout your placement, while you may well have received training and support to work as a base grade worker in the organisation, the main focus will have been on your learning. There will have been a number of sources of information to guide you and your supervisor in this work, including university outlines of expectations of field placement, learning plans and texts developed specifically to assist with placement, such as *Making the Most of Field Placement* (Cleak and Wilson, 2007). As part of planning for the type of job that will suit you and the supports that you may need, it may be worth reviewing these and in particular considering your individual learning and support needs.

When you take up a formal position in an organisation, things change. You are required to meet specific guidelines regarding output of your work, often dictated by funding arrangements organisations have with governments. You are also expected to work more autonomously, although the degree of independence will vary from agency to agency. As a student, you will have had an identified supervisor who has a clearly mandated role to support you and your learning, a liaison person who can act to assist and intervene if placement issues cannot be resolved at the local level, and also access to the other university staff. Also, as a student you will have had the support of your student cohort—both through formal mechanisms such as integrative seminars and via informal catch-ups and support groups.

Once you begin employment, the amount and type of supervision you will receive will be set by the agency. The AASW has recommended standards, which state that 'Recent graduates (less than three years' fulltime experience) should receive the equivalent of weekly individual supervision of at least one uninterrupted hour per week, this can include group supervision'. However, it is up to the organisation to decide what it puts in place. The AASW notes that while attendance at staff meetings, workshops and in-house training is a valuable source of professional development, these do not replace supervision. As a new worker, however, it is essential to ensure that your professional development needs are met and that you are linked in with the rest of the organisation. Participation in these various organisational forums helps you attend to some of your own educational and support needs.

The other issue that can also occur with student supervision is a situation where, although standards are in place, they are not—for a variety of reasons—adhered to. The most common reason is the work pressures of either or both the supervisor and the supervisee. Unfortunately, it is usually during these times of high pressure and peak workloads that supervision is most needed. You can gain an understanding of the extent of support and autonomy via the job description and duty statement of your new job. There may well also be work plans developed that outline specific tasks and educational needs or opportunities. These will have some similarities to the learning plan but will have a stronger focus on job requirements.

EXERCISE

- Think about your experiences of supervision, either directly as a student, or through observation/information from other students or your experience in the workforce.
- Which styles suited you and which did you find difficult?
- You may wish to refer to Tony Morrison's book on *Staff Supervision* (2001: 76) for ideas on 'supervision histories'.
- Discuss this in pairs, focusing on what worked well and what contributed to this.
- Identify what you would like to have in the way of supervision and support.
- Think about how you can identify this in a new job or obtain it in a current position (consider job choice, organisational structure/requirements, organisational culture and commitment to supervision or reflective practice).
- If time permits, review some job descriptions and look up the agency documentation to see what is in place regarding organisational structure, lines of accountability and policy on supervision/training.

GUIDELINES FOR SUPERVISION

Given the increased focus on accountability, you can expect to have a line manager to whom you are responsible in your day-to-day practice. We will not discuss these aspects here as they have been covered elsewhere, except to note that administrative supervision will be the core form of supervision provided in your workplace. How well this relationship works and whether the administrative supervision is appropriate to your needs is another matter. At times, it can seem attractive to have minimal direction; however, you need to ensure that your basic work conditions and work allocation are covered and that you know what to expect, and that you have resources and supports in place to undertake your job. Without this, you risk the sort of workplace stress we discussed earlier in the chapter.

While the administrative aspects of supervision are fairly clear-cut, there has been a lot of debate about the point at which close supervision should end. The notion of 'interminable supervision' is discussed by Tsui (2005), who argues that once workers have a significant amount of practice they should be free to work largely unsupervised, seeking consultation as they identify the need to do so. The other factor that will influence this is the quality of your relationship with your supervisor. This can be quite an intense relationship, and it is worth considering what may prevent this. Pepper (1996) has written about factors that can impede a positive supervisory relationship or cause tension in a counselling setting. She has prepared reference tables that identify the key factors she believes are important to each of the functions of supervision. She then lists strategies for building a positive relationship and strategies for addressing tension against each of them.

Tony Morrison has written a very practical book on staff supervision in the form of a manual (2001). In this book, Morrison sets out guidelines for contracts and structures for individual supervision (2001: 99). Included in this section of the chapter are practical guidelines for setting up individual supervision and a list of rights and responsibilities. Explicitly stating what is expected of each party is one key way to ensure supervision is constructive and avoids some of the pitfalls that can occur.

EDUCATIONAL AND SUPPORT NEEDS: MODELS OF SUPERVISION

While it is commonly accepted that the administrative or management function of supervision is usually provided by the supervisor or line manager, the provision of education and support is less clearcut. There have been many approaches developed to address workers' educational and support needs, some developed by the human service organisations and others initiated by workers themselves. There is also a range of views as to whether these different methods offer improved outcomes or are a result of limited resources. Some of the other ways of meeting the support and educational needs of workers include group supervision, peer supervision, reflective groups, training courses and external supervision.

Tsui and Ho (1998: 189–92) outline a range of models of supervision that can be implemented at the agency level. These are:

- *The casework model.* This is a one-to-one relationship and the most widely used model, especially for inexperienced workers. It encompasses all three functions of supervision identified earlier in this chapter.
- *The group supervision model.* This is the second most popular model in social work supervision. It is often used as a supplement to individual supervision. The supervisor functions as the group leader and encourages staff to share difficulties and insights. As it focuses on common needs, the group should not be too diverse in terms of training or experience. The balance of power is more equal. Members are exposed to a wide variety of learning experiences, and emotional support is also provided. This is more efficient than individual supervision but relies on leadership qualities of the supervisor and motivation of staff members.
- *The peer supervision model.* There is no designated supervisor and all staff participate equally. Each staff member takes responsibility for their own work and there is no regular individual supervision; collegial consultations among staff are

common. This form of supervision creates an atmosphere of mutual help and sharing. It may not be a good choice for inexperienced staff.

- *The team service delivery model.* The supervisor takes on the role of team leader but there is no regular supervision. The team focuses on the work and collective responsibility is used for decision-making, although the team leader has the final say. Responsibility for work assignment, performance-monitoring and professional development rests with the team.

- *Autonomous practice.* For experienced, professionally trained workers there is no real need for supervision. Staff are responsible for their own professional practice and professional development. (Adapted from Tsui and Ho, 1998)

As this overview of the various models illustrates, a wide range of supervision arrangements exist. Lowe and Guy (1999: 36) argue that group supervision is the most common form of supervision for counsellors, and that many counsellors will use both group and individual supervision to address different needs. Lowe and Guy (1999) put forward a model for moving from group to peer supervision via the use of consultants who gradually move from the position of group leader to occasional guest. In many human service organisations, there can be a mixture of individual and group supervision and at times peer supervision, depending on circumstances, need and the attributes and interests of staff. Most commonly, separate administrative supervision is in place, as discussed earlier in the chapter. When you first start to work in a human service organisation, it is important to take the time to find out about the range of supervision, education and support options that are available to you.

PEER AND GROUP SUPERVISION

As indicated earlier, one form of supervision that is often used is group supervision. In this situation, there is still an administrative supervisor/senior worker who meets with a group of staff to

Case study: Debriefing sessions

Farah has recently been employed as a drop-in worker in a multi-disciplinary team that works with homeless people. She has two years' experience in the human service field and recently left her job as a child protection worker due to feeling out of her depth in her job. At the new centre, she is one of several staff who help in running activities and who are available to support homeless people who come in to participate in groups or to have a meal or shower. The agency has a policy of a debriefing meeting at the end of each day, where workers are asked to reflect on any significant issues that arose or note any concerns they may have for service users. This session is run by the agency's drug and alcohol counsellor. Farah finds the service very busy and does not yet feel comfortable with the wide range of issues with which clients may present. As there is no formal intake or appointment service, Farah is never sure who she will end up seeing and about what. She has been given a lot of reading (resources, agency guidelines and case notes) but has not been able to read them during the day. Farah decides that she does not need to come to the sessions and instead uses the time to catch up on her reading. She is annoyed when the service manager tells her that she must attend these sessions.

Discussion questions

- Why do you think these sessions are in place?
- What may be Farah's reasons for not attending?
- What is Farah risking by not attending?
- What aspects of supervision are covered by this approach?
- What would you do if you were in Farah's position?

undertake supervisory functions. While this can encompass administrative functions, it most commonly focuses on education and support, with the supervisor responsible for setting the agenda and guiding the discussion.

Kadushin and Harkness (2002: 391–402) outline a range of advantages and disadvantages of group supervision:

- It provides an opportunity for a wider range of teaching and learning experiences.

- Group members can provide an important source of emotional support.
- It provides more varied and richer sources of learning.
- It assists with morale building and the creation of a feeling of belonging.
- It can also reinforce negative views.
- It can be easier to accept criticism and advice from peers.
- It encourages interaction and group cohesion.
- It allows delegation of different roles.
- It provides a gradual step towards independence and power sharing.
- Competitiveness and rivalry can result.
- It may be daunting for inexperienced workers.
- A peer group may organise against the supervisor: the supervisor needs a high level of personal security.
- There may be strong pressure to conform: it may stifle creativity.

Group and individual supervision both offer varied and quite different opportunities, and for this reason it is important to consider where each is appropriate and use them as planned complementary processes (Kadushin and Harkness, 2002: 402). Kadushin and Harkness (2002: 406) outline the preferred arrangements for group supervision, including the set-up of the room and nominating a regular day and time to allow planning as well as to signify the importance of the sessions. They also note that while the supervisor initially may take responsibility for setting the agenda and leading discussions, by sharing this responsibility with group members, participation and autonomy can be maximised.

Following on from group supervision, peer supervision provides workers with more autonomy. In peer supervision, there is no designated supervisor; workers are all able to participate equally and take responsibility for their own work and learning. It encourages staff to be more aware of the needs of colleagues by 'creating an atmosphere of mutual help and sharing' (Tsui, 2005: 26) This form of

Case study: Group supervision

Marta works as a team leader in a large, multi-site human service organisation. The organisation provides support to people with disabilities who are living in the community. The organisation has just received additional funding to expand its services to older people. Several new workers have been employed at Marta's site and at other sites across the metropolitan area. Marta has been given the training portfolio and has spent a lot of time providing orientation and training to these new staff. Now that the orientation period is over, Marta has decided that many of these new staff will need close supervision and support to help them learn the job required of them.

Marta is also aware that several of the experienced front-line staff have been moved into new team leader positions, and believes that they are not very confident in supervising staff. Due to her involvement with the new workers, Marta has ended up cancelling many of the regular fortnightly supervision sessions she previously conducted for her team members. Marta hears from some of her team that they miss this opportunity to reflect on their practice and picks up that they are resenting the time she is spending with the new workers.

Marta decides to do two things. She sets up fortnightly group supervision for the new workers and invites some of the team leaders from other sites to also participate. She also meets with the more experienced workers in her team and suggests that they develop a monthly peer supervision group. She says that a regular time will be set aside for this and that she can come along to some sessions if the workers wish.

Discussion questions

- Why do you think Marta has set up group supervision for the new workers?
- What will be some of the advantages and disadvantages?
- What planning or other arrangements are required/desirable?
- Why do you think peer supervision is being offered to the more experienced staff?
- List some things that will be important for the success of this program.
- What may jeopardise its success?
- Draw up a checklist of how you would set up peer supervision in your workplace. If you think this is not appropriate, state why not.

supervision is 'a popular forum for the examination of practice experiences, peer review, transmitting new knowledge and preventing burnout' (Kadushin and Harkness, 2002: 434). For peer supervision to be effective, it is recommended that not all workers are inexperienced as they would then not have the required knowledge for informed discussion (Tsui, 2005). Kadushin and Harkness believe that peer supervision works best when workers have a similar level of training and experience. From this we can see that the composition of the peer group needs careful consideration to ensure that the group is constructive and provides a valuable forum for all. Groups, whether structured as in peer supervision or with the presence of a supervisor/senior staff member, can also be used for reflective practice and case presentations, and can offer valuable ways to further workers' professional development.

CONCLUSION

In this chapter, we have emphasised the importance of supervision and support for human service workers; these are essential to ensuring reflective practice and ongoing professional development. We have presented some models of supervision that can be used, and have encouraged workers to think about what is, or could be, established in their place of work. Central to this has been developing an understanding of self-care and an acknowledgement that it is sensible to play an active role in having one's own supervision and support needs met.

Chapter review questions

7.1   Why is supervision important to human service workers?

7.2   What are the three commonly agreed aspects of supervision?

7.3   What are some of the causes of workplace stress?

7.4   As a new worker in a human service organisation, what can you do to ensure you have supervision and support that meet your needs?

7.5   What is peer supervision? List three things that are important to its success.

7.6 What other ways are there of obtaining education and support in your role?

OTHER RESOURCES

Myself Care, <http://myselfcare.org/index.htm>.

Coaching and mentoring, New Zealand, <www.coachingmentoring.co.nz/resources/keywords/supervision/peer-supervision>.

KEY READINGS

Australian Association of Social Workers (AASW) 2000, *National Practice Standards of the Australian Association of Social Workers: Supervision*, AASW, Canberra.

Kadushin, A. and Harkness, D. 2002, *Supervision in Social Work*, Columbia University Press, New York.

Morrison, T. 2001, 'Group Supervision', in *Staff Supervision in Social Care: Making a Real Difference for Staff and Service Users,* Pavilion Publishing, Brighton, UK.

Tsui, M. 2005, 'Educational and Supportive Functions', in *Social Work Supervision: Contexts and Concepts,* Sage, Thousand Oaks, CA.

CHAPTER EIGHT | Managing conflict

SUMMARY

In this chapter, we explore the nature of conflict, particularly as it is experienced in community-based non-profit human service organisations. We examine models of conflict and the centrality of power. Models and stages of conflict resolution are presented, together with key communication skills—spoken and written—for managing conflict. The chapter addresses how to manage aggression and hostility, and discusses the imperative to take account of difference—for example, that arising from age, gender and culture.

INTRODUCTION

People often make unfounded assumptions about human service organisations, particularly about non-profit community-based organisations. They assume, for example, that because these organisations are, in the main, established and run within a strong values and beliefs framework and that their goal is to address disadvantage or some other form of human suffering, then the organisational culture must be one in which everyone gets along. Nothing could be further from the truth! Those who work in community-based non-profit organisations experience all the same issues around conflict that people face in other contexts. In some ways, smaller community-based organisations are more likely to be plagued by conflict because the normal inhibiting functions played by formal bureaucratic structures do not exist or are much weaker in terms of their impact on behaviour. In large bureaucracies, everyone has a clearer role in a formal structure than is usually the case in smaller organisations. Relationships are constructed by that formal structure—in particular by hierarchy. People lower down the hierarchy would rarely engage in open conflict with those higher up, not least because they would be subject to quite strict discipline if they did. In community-based or other smaller non-profit organisations, the hierarchy is much less pronounced and relationships tend to be more fluid.

Furthermore, many people who work in community-based non-profit organisations often exhibit strong commitments: to sets of beliefs, to ways of practising, to a particular service user group or to a social issue. Passion and conflict are *not* strange bedfellows. Often people will argue feverishly over quite minor differences because of these beliefs—arguments that can easily turn into conflict. Furthermore, workers can sometimes find themselves in conflict—often frightening conflict—with service users. Smaller community-based non-profit human service groups are often closer physically to their service users. Many large human service bureaucracies go to some lengths to create physical barriers between themselves and their service users, usually because of potential anger spilling over to aggression and even violence. This is not the case in smaller non-profits. In circumstances when service users are angry—reasonably or not—it is important that workers have strategies in place to manage that anger in positive ways.

UNDERSTANDING CONFLICT

Power and conflict

It is impossible to understand conflict without attending to the role of power—or, more importantly, power imbalances. Here, we take power to mean power in social relationships. (Note that we discuss power more extensively in the next chapter.) Clearly organisations are, at their very essence, constituted by structured social relationships. Although many of us might aspire to equality in most of the social settings in which we engage, the reality is that the social world is more likely characterised by inequality than equality. Organisations—even those with flat organisational structures and aspirations towards democratic functioning—are inevitably hierarchical in some form. Indeed, the legal framework that surrounds non-profit community-based organisations such as the various states' *Associations Incorporations Acts* create a degree of hierarchy. Furthermore, there is nearly always a hierarchical management structure. This has especially been the case in recent times because of the impact of increased external accountabilities on the ways in which organisations structure themselves. Most beginning human service workers are at the very bottom of the organisational hierarchy, and as such have less formal power than their bosses. As a consequence, in circumstances of conflict the imbalances of power make it difficult for the parties to engage on an equal footing.

The situation—that is, power imbalance—is even more marked for service users. For many people who use the services of human service organisations, their lives have been shaped by the impact of social structures, often resulting in injustices and oppression. Further, people rarely engage with human service organisations unless something is going badly wrong in their lives; their issues could range, for example, from chronic illness and disability to poverty and homelessness. In these circumstances, people need the organisation in quite acute ways and are, accordingly, very vulnerable. The acute power imbalances can, as suggested in the chapter introduction, induce strong reactions such as aggression and even violence—mostly as a result of despair and fear.

Case study: Managing violence

Gavin is employed by a medium-sized family support agency to provide support services to young people who have been released from state care. These young people have significant needs and few skills in negotiating the adult world (or even the city). They need a lot of support and are often a very difficult group to be with because of their substance abuse issues and hostility. Tahu is 18, homeless and has rapidly developed a drug habit. He regularly disappears into the streets and Gavin can't find him. One day he comes to the support service with several cuts and bruises and, judging from his movements, probably some broken ribs. Gavin asks him what happened and Tahu just blows up. He starts yelling and screaming and throwing furniture around. It is obvious that he is still high. Gavin is startled at the violence of the reaction and needs to do something fast. Several other kids are in the room and they look distinctly scared.

Discussion questions
- What might have happened to Tahu?
- What should Gavin do in the first instance to calm Tahu down?
- What should he do after that?
- Is it entirely Gavin's responsibility to manage Tahu's outburst?
- What sort of protocols should the organisation have in place to manage such behaviour?

Models of conflict

What exactly is conflict? In 1987, Peter Condliffe, one of Australia's leading practitioners and authors in conflict management, suggested that conflict could be defined as:

a form of relating or interacting where we find ourselves (either as individuals or groups) under some sort of perceived threat to our personal or collective goals. These goals are usually to do with our interpersonal wants. These perceived threats may be real or imagined. (Condliffe, 1987: 78)

There are three important elements in this definition: (1) that conflict usually involves a person or a group feeling threatened (irrespective of whether a threat actually exists); (2) that conflict occurs between people; and (3) that conflict is linked to our wants or desires. However, as Condliffe points out elsewhere (2002), this definition is usefully augmented by another important dimension of conflict—it is also intra-personal. We all instinctively know this; we know that when we are caught up in conflict situations we feel a range of emotions such as fear, nervousness, frustration and anger. Condliffe also makes use of the ideas of another prominent theorist, Lederach (1995), who suggests that we must think about conflict as a social phenomenon, inevitably created by human beings in the context of social relationships. Because it is a social phenomenon, all of those same processes that affect any social relationship are influential in shaping conflict—for example, class, gender, culture and age.

Given the (unfortunate) ubiquity of conflict, it should come as no surprise that social scientists have thought deeply about it and have developed different models of how conflict evolves and also what causes it. Here we will discuss one, by way of example. This model outlines phases of conflict and is drawn from Kimsey et al. (2006). We have chosen it for this discussion because it was developed in the context of a church. While clearly non-profit community-based organisations are different from churches, they nevertheless have an important characteristic in common—people participate because of their commitments to a set of values and beliefs, and to a large degree that participation has voluntaristic qualities. This model (like most of these models) suggests that conflict is cyclical and that it develops in predictable patterns of interaction. The phases are:

- *Objectification.* Parties to the conflict objectify each other and themselves and take sides.

- *Personification.* Inter-personal conversations occur that focus on the perceived personal deficits of the group or person who has been objectified. In effect, this projection of characteristics of the other party serves to reinforce objectification.
- *Magnification.* Attempts are made to transform the perceived and projected deficits of the objectified parties into 'facts', thereby bolstering the correctness of one's own position.
- *Glorification.* In this phase, the glorifiers bring into play examples of other people, usually drawn from the past, who were 'wonderful'.
- *Reification.* Creating or manufacturing situations which provide evidence for their own world-view.
- *Signification.* At this point, the parties to the conflict view events (or non-events, for that matter) as further evidence of the critical claims made.
- *Justification.* Vindication for the purpose of legitimising earlier claims made with no tangible evidence. Stages 1 to 6 provide the critical mass for their claims and criticism to achieve a 'truth' status.

How might these phases play out in a non-profit community-based human service organisation? Look at Table 8.1. The context is a feminist counselling service for victims of trauma and abuse.

Table 8.1: Phases of interaction

Objectification	One of the longer term staff members, Raquel, takes umbrage at the new director, Gail, who was recently appointed by the board. Gail is replacing a person who had been part of the service since foundation. Raquel also applied for the position. She claims Gail is making changes without fully consulting the staff.

Personification	Raquel initiates informal discussions with other staff members, questioning Gail's feminist commitments more broadly. She cites comments made by some unnamed service users about their interactions with Gail.
Magnification	Everything Gail says or does is viewed through the lens of her 'poor feminist commitments'. Attempts by Gail to get staff to make time for their annual staff reviews are seen as an unwarranted exercise of power.
Glorification	Raquel reminisces about Julia, the previous director, claiming that her commitments were almost saintly. She specifically and publicly remembers Julia's commitment to collective decision-making.
Reification	Gail's relationship with the board is questioned. It is suggested, for example, that she deliberately sought out a male accountant to be treasurer and between them they have attempted to import a business management model into the organisation.
Signification	Gail's failure to fully report her discussions with the funding department and to involve staff in the drawing-up of contract provisions is seen as further evidence of her non-collegiality. Similarly, her request that staff make appointments with her when they wish to discuss something at length is viewed as undermining the culture of the organisation.
Justification	All of the staff call a meeting and propose a motion of no confidence in Gail.

Clearly, there are lots of different reasons why conflict emerges. Condliffe (2002) cites the work of Bisno (1988), who argues that there are five sources of conflict. These are outlined in Table 8.2, which has an additional column in which you might like to think of examples from your own experience.

Table 8.2: Sources of conflict

Source	Explanation	Example
Biosocial sources	Frustration-aggression is a source of conflict. Frustration often results in aggression that leads to conflict. Frustration can also happen when people expect things to improve more rapidly than they do.	
Personality and interactional sources	These can include personality type, psychological problems, poor inter-personal skills, irritation, rivalry, jealousy, inequities in relationships.	
Structural sources	Conflict arises from organisational structure and social structures. Differences in power and status.	
Cultural and ideological sources	Conflicts can arise from differences in social, cultural, political and religious beliefs.	
Convergence	Convergence occurs when different sources of conflict emerge in one context. This is particularly the case in organisations.	

EXERCISE

Using the example of the feminist counselling service discussed above, what are the potential sources of the conflict described?

Styles of conflict

Each of us has our own particular style of engaging in conflict, a function of our unique personality and our unique history. As professionals, becoming aware of our own particular style is a foundational part of learning to engage productively with conflict. Barsky (2007: 47–8) identifies five pure styles:

Avoiders. People who are low on concern for self and low on concern for others. Avoiders may deny that conflict exists. They may also acknowledge that conflict exists but do what they can to avoid or avert the conflict.

Accommodators. People who have low concern for their own needs and high concern for the needs of others. These people value highly positive relations with others.

Competitors. People who are low on concern for others but high on concern for themselves. These are people who are out to win and who will select whatever strategy achieves that end.

Compromisers. People who pay some attention to the needs of others and some to their own needs. They favour solutions that are partial wins for both parties.

Collaborators. People who have high concerns for their own needs and the needs of others. They seek out solutions that are mutually beneficial. They encourage joint problem solving, are respectful and validating.

Of course, these are pure types and we don't necessarily all conform exactly. We can also behave differently in different circumstances.

> **EXERCISE**
> *Part 1:* Think about a conflict situation in which you have found yourself. What style or mix of styles most approximates your response?
> *Part 2:* Can you think of another example in which you displayed a different style? If so, what made it different?
> *Part 3:* Identify the advantages and disadvantages of the various styles listed above.

CONFLICT RESOLUTION AND MEDIATION

Models of conflict resolution

There are many means for addressing conflict. Perhaps the least helpful is that which reverts to a competition between parties in which the most powerful exerts their power and 'wins'. This is not a particularly helpful strategy because the 'win' is a dubious one at best, and as a tactic it breeds resentment. An example from Australia's recent history illustrates this point. In 1998, Patricks Stevedoring sacked all of its dock workers in Melbourne, locked them out using a private security firm with menacing looking dogs and attempted to use non-union labour on the docks. This action was taken with the not inconsiderable support of the Howard federal government of the time and led to a major industrial conflict—popularly dubbed a 'war'. It created great bitterness and unhappiness, and was one of the most divisive acts of what was a divisive government. The union movement never forgot and in 2007, nearly a decade later, weighed into the election campaign. Its contribution was a decisive factor in that government losing office. Nevertheless, it is an instructive example in that it shows the use of law as a mode of resolving conflict, in that case by referring the matter to the High Court of Australia.

In this way, the above example illustrates a legal response to the conflict in question. The three legal strategies that can be used to manage conflict are *arbitration* ('the hearing or determining of a dispute between parties by a person or persons chosen, agreed between them or appointed by virtue of a statutory obligation', Macquarie Dictionary, 2000: 35), *litigation* (taking a lawsuit to court) and *legislation* (a government enacting a law). Using law, or reverting to law and the courts, is not only a high-risk strategy (in that the parties can rarely be completely sure of the outcome), but it is one that is clearly out of the reach of most. Fortunately, there are other models that have the advantage of greatly increasing the power of the parties to the conflict to manage their own process, such as negotiation and mediation. Of these, the most popular these days, and the most relevant to conflict in organisations, is mediation (Martin, 2007).

Mediation is one of the most constructive ways to address conflict, as it is a tool to help people solve their own problems. Within the overall genre of activity, there are different models—for example, settlement, facilitative, evaluative and therapeutic mediation. As Martin (2007: 35) notes:

- Settlement mediation is designed to 'encourage incremental bargaining in an endeavour to reach a compromise at a midpoint of the demands of both parties'.
- Facilitative mediation is designed to 'negotiate in terms of the parties' needs and interests as opposed to legal entitlements'.
- Evaluative mediation is designed to 'reach a settlement in accordance with the legal rights and entitlements of both parties'.
- Therapeutic mediation is designed to 'improve relationships between parties by dealing with the underlying causes of conflict'.

Clearly the last of these is well suited to conflicts that arise in organisations. That said, there will be many cases where evaluative mediation would be adopted in formal disputes between employers and employees over, for example, behaviour. Other authors identify some additional models of mediation—for example, transformative mediation, which is designed to 'transform the way people deal with conflict by helping them develop mutual understanding and self-efficacy' (Barsky, 2007: 121) or solution-focused mediation, which is designed to shift the focus from the problem to the solution and in doing so is future rather than past oriented (Bannink, 2007). In all of these models, there are similarities in the way they are undertaken.

Stages in mediation

Condliffe (2002) outlines the stages of mediation in Table 8.3.

Table 8.3: Stages in mediation

Phase 1: Preparation	• Assessing the nature of the dispute • Checking the parties to a dispute • Checking the availability of resources and an appropriate location
Phase 2: Introduction	• Introduction and seating • Opening statement by mediator • Checking expectations • Confirming background case material • Discussing and clarifying terms
Phase 3: Statements	• Mediator explains process and ground rules • Parties invited to describe and explain their perspective • Mediator summarises perspectives
Phase 4: Agenda	• Request parties to suggest topics for discussion • Write a mutual list that is visible and legible • Reframe topics to mutual and positive language

Phase 5: Dialogue	
Phase 6: Negotiation	• Creating and reviewing opinions
Phase 7: Agreement	• Clarification of agreements made • Formalisation of agreements
Phase 8: Implementation review	• Review • Revision

Source: Condliffe (2002)

EXERCISE

Examine the following case illustration and plan what you, as a mediator, would do in Phase 2.

You are a social worker in a mental health service. Your service regularly takes on university students from a variety of human service backgrounds for field education. One of your colleagues is supervising two students but is not getting along with one of them. Relationships deteriorate when your colleague (Brian) claims that the student (Janeen) did not complete several reports of home visits she had undertaken. Janeen claims that she did and that Brian has lost them. Brian's history with paperwork isn't great. Janeen is very upset because she believes her placement is in jeopardy and that Brian is using this as an excuse to get her out of the agency. The other student is trying desperately not to take sides.

Communication skills for managing conflict

Most people undertaking an education to work in the human services will inevitably be exposed to the basic sets of micro communication skills necessary for managing conflict. These include active listening or the intentional use of self-talk to demonstrate to someone that you have heard and understood what they have said. Listening skills are the core building block of successful conflict management because conflict often arises when people think they have not been listened to or have been misunderstood. Good active listening serves many good functions—for example, it meets the human need to be understood and recognised by others, it creates a supportive environment for dialogue, it builds rapport and trust, and it provides a model of how communication should be undertaken.

The specific skills of active listening include attending, paraphrasing, reflecting feelings and summarising (Barsky, 2007). *Attending* refers to the behavioural or non-verbal techniques you use to demonstrate to a person that you are really listening—for example, leaning forward, maintaining eye contact, nodding. It also includes verbal utterances such as 'mmm'. *Paraphrasing*, possibly the most powerful communication skill in conflict management, is when you briefly summarise what the others have said. It is powerful because it communicates understanding, it steers the conversation into deeper reflections, it slows the conversation between parties down and it serves as a buffer. It is also useful to take the sting out of nasty or insulting statements, thereby allowing the other person to hear the message in a less emotional way.

Reflecting feelings refers to ensuring that the other person or persons knows you understand what they are feeling. Here, you are not telling someone what they *should* be feeling, but are instead acknowledging what they *are* feeling openly. *Summarising* refers to a condensed restatement of what a person has said after a significant time has elapsed. Condliffe (2002: 179) also suggests developing skills in what he terms 'transitions' techniques to encourage people to talk more directly to each other. Typical transitions are handovers and crossovers. A *handover* is when you invite one person to express their feelings directly to the other. A *crossover*, on the other hand, is when you ask each person to express their perception of the other person's point of view.

Asking questions is a key technique in conflict resolution. Used judiciously, questions are usually the best way to find out what people's thoughts and feelings are. If you are in an assessment phase of resolution or mediation, then the old litany of the five Ws ('who', 'what', 'where', 'when' and 'why') is invaluable. Questions can be either open or closed. Open questions are more conducive to encouraging dialogue because they encourage people to answer in their own words. Closed questions give a limited amount of choice and are more useful when you want to elicit specific information.

Another specific and related technique involves moving from generalities to specifics. People in the middle of a conflict often think and talk in terms of generalisations. For example, if someone is abrupt in a chance encounter, he or she may be characterised as having no respect or being rude. Conflicts can rarely be resolved when discussions are held in terms of generalities. Further, they often include unhelpful and incorrect stereotypes (for example, someone is ageist or sexist). An effective way of moving away from generalities is to ask for specific examples of the characteristic nominated.

It is also helpful is a mediator is alert to hidden offers of peace. Often, these are delivered in ways that make it appear like an accusation or an insult. For example: 'I'd be perfectly happy to renegotiate her workload if she had the sense to tell me it was too much instead of snivelling around the corridor'. The mediator could respond, 'I understand that you would adjust her workload if she communicated her issues openly and directly to you.'

Finally, obviously conflict and its management are a highly emotional process. As such, it is important that emotions—both those of the conflicting parties and those of a mediator—be acknowledged. In the first instance, it is important to acknowledge and accept emotions. It is much easier to work with something that is out in the open. Active listening and paraphrasing will reduce eruptions of feelings. It is also sensible to establish ground rules such as no name calling or personalising to prevent tensions, frustration and anger from escalating. If it does spiral, a mediator should consider either having brief individual discussions with each party or call the session to an end, to be continued on another day.

In conflict-resolution processes, written communication plays an integral role, usually in the form of formal agreements between the parties. The main aim of any form of written communication is that it be clear, concise, non-judgemental and thoughtful. The strategic purpose of any document should be kept in mind when it is being written. Furthermore, in this day and age, much writing is done in electronic form. Unfortunately—useful as email is—it can lead to many conflicts and misunderstandings—for example, confidential information being sent to someone by mistake, hurtful messages being sent in the heat of anger, and messages that are easily misunderstood because the sender was more focused on speed of response than replying accurately and clearly. As a general rule, if you are tempted to dash off an annoyed response, wait until the next day. In all instance, electronic or otherwise, the key point is care and thoughtfulness.

Case study: Conflict resolution

Carmela is the volunteer coordinator for a medium-sized organisation providing support services to newly arrived refugees. The service has been in operation for nearly 40 years and was established in the 1970s. Originally it was an unfunded organisation operated by activists who wanted to express their concern about the Vietnam War by providing services to refugees from that war. Obviously the service user population has changed considerable since then, as has the organisation. It has grown considerably, attracts significant funding and has professionalised.

There are now two distinct groups of volunteers. The first consists of the original activists, Baby Boomers who have stuck with the agency over all that time. The second distinct group comprises young people, usually university students who are really interested in gaining experience. The organisation has traditionally oriented its services to working with mothers, particularly vulnerable and isolated mothers of young children. It has been asked by the major funding department to consider pushing more of its resources to working with young people, particularly young African men. The older volunteers are outraged. The younger ones think it is a good idea. This erupted into a nasty fight at a volunteers' meeting and Carmela now has to work out what to do.

Discussion question
- Outline a fully fledged plan for Carmela.

Responding to aggression

Unfortunately, there are times when workers in all human service settings are confronted by angry people—either service users or co-workers. We need to have the ability to manage hostility when in occurs, and most of all to create environments that discourage aggressive or threatening behaviour. An important aspect of managing aggression is the ability to read early warning signs. Behaviour is a key indicator for aggression, and workers need to be sensitive to changes. Another important aspect is the ability to observe changes in a person's body language, indicating that they are getting angry.

Typical warning signs are an aggressive fixed stare, dry mouth, clenched teeth, shallow breathing, perspiration, finger drumming, darting eyes, forced or sudden silence, questioning, challenging, yelling and swearing. At this point, it is important for a worker to assess and diffuse the situation, possibly by not pursuing the issue further at that moment.

People often become aggressive because they feel wronged, misunderstood or unheard. Some other triggers, particularly for service users, are:

- fear (of the known or unknown)
- loss of personal control
- displaced anger (at the system, hospital, family)
- grief reaction
- pain (chronic or acute unrelieved pain)
- peer pressure (common in adolescents and teens).

Some simple tips for addressing anger in the moment are:

- Stay calm.
- Show respect for the person as an individual.
- Speak slowly and clearly, using short and simple sentences.
- Match the intensity of your voice (but not loudness) to that of the aggressive person.
- Make sure your non-verbal communication is not hostile or

submissive. Keep your posture open, arms uncrossed, hands visible and open. Maintain eye contact and a relaxed facial expression.

- Stand at a slight angle to the person—a metre is a safe, comfortable distance. As the individual becomes more agitated, allow more personal space.
- Don't block the person's exit.
- Ensure that you always have an exit if you need to run. (Running away is your first self-protection technique.)
- Ensure other staff know where you are if you are dealing with an individual known to be aggressive (if possible).
- Take all threats of violence seriously.
- Never try to disarm an individual.
- Never accept a weapon from an upset or agitated person. Ask for it to be placed on the ground and for the person to step away.

When the immediate situation has been resolved, it is important that you follow your employing organisation's guidelines for recording and reporting such instances. It is also very important for workers to formally and informally debrief about how it felt and how you responded. If there is no capacity for this within your organisation, it is appropriate that you ask the organisation to fund several hours of external professional supervision.

Conflict resolution across difference

Given the multicultural nature of contemporary Australian society, it is important that workers are able to explore whether a conflict is rooted in cross-cultural issues. While not automatically assuming that conflict is culturally based, there are strategies to use if it is a factor:

- Validate cultural differences (i.e. beliefs, values and ways of doing things).
- Separate interests and values.

- If you can, use cultural interpreters, someone of that culture who is not party to the conflict and who has sufficient self-efficacy to engage in the role.

In the Australian context, one of the most important manifestations of cultural difference is that provided by Indigenous Australians. When attempting conflict management with Indigenous people, it is important to acknowledge that the elders form the group that manages problems and conflict within the community. Further, anyone attempting to mediate with Indigenous people needs to be known and respected by the community as well as by the elders. Further, norms of privacy that might be appropriate to the mainstream population may not be applicable. Usually, individual problems are seen as community problems. Finally, Indigenous communities both already know about inter-personal problems and equally expect to be informed of any negotiated settlement.

It is also important to remember at all times that there are other important dimensions of difference to which we need to pay attention when managing conflict. A key factor is gender. Men and women behave very differently in conflict contexts, and the needs of both should to be taken into account. Often gender and culture can intersect. Vietnamese women, for example, consider it shameful to ask for assistance outside of the family (NADRAC, 1999). In addition, workers need to be aware of other dimensions of difference that will impact on any conflict-management process—that is, age, disability, sexuality and geography (NADRAC, 1999).

CONFLICT MANAGEMENT HEALTH CHECK

Below are some useful questions for running a conflict management health check on an organisation:

- Is adequate leadership being demonstrated within the organisation?
- What previous efforts have been made by the leader to address the conflict, and with what results?

- Is the leader comfortable with conflict resolution?
- Is the leader role-modelling effective conflict-resolution skills?
- What has the leader done to create a supportive environment within his or her group for effective conflict resolution?
- Is the leader consistent in how he or she addresses conflicts?
- Is the leader being held accountable by his or her supervisor in effectively addressing conflict-resolution issues in a particular area?
- Do team members foster a supportive or a non-supportive environment for conflict resolution?
- What previous efforts have been made by individuals or the group to address the conflict, and with what results?
- What are the defined or undefined group norms around conflict, if any?
- What isn't happening that needs to happen in this group around conflict resolution?
- How does the group, as well as the conflicting parties, see the role of the leader in all of this?
- What guidance and support does the group feel it still needs from the leader and the organisation?
- Is there an accountability factor in the organisation that supports teamwork and good communication skills?
- Are the desired conflict-resolution skills (particularly around teamwork and communication) reflected as criteria in performance review processes?
- Are there organisational core values? If so, are they reflected within performance review processes?
- Are team norms identified and established around conflict resolution? If so, are they followed in a consistent manner?
- Is the disciplinary process ever used for employees who exhibit poor communication and/or cooperation skills?
- Is the organisation (at all levels) providing skill training/ resources on an ongoing basis?

- What skill training opportunities are made available to all employees within the organisation?
- How often are opportunities made available to employees to better themselves, both personally and professionally?
- What resources are made available to employees to help in the area of inter-personal communication, teamwork and conflict resolution?
- From an organisational standpoint, what isn't happening that needs to happen in order for the conflict-resolution process to be improved?
- Are leaders/managers/supervisors provided ongoing training and development to better themselves, especially in the skills area?

(Adapted from Greg Giesen and Associates, <www.greggiesenassociates.com>)

CONCLUSION

This chapter has, of necessity, briefly touched on many issues. It is not and cannot be comprehensive. We recommend that those who wish to pursue these issues further consult the texts recommended below.

Chapter review questions

8.1   Why is it likely that conflict can erupt in small non-profit community-based organisations?

8.2   What are Bisno's five sources of conflict?

8.3   What are the five pure styles of conflict?

8.4   Why are legal solutions to conflict not always appropriate?

8.5   What are the different forms of mediation?

8.6   Name three of the core skills of active listening?

8.7   What are some of the reasons for people becoming aggressive?

8.8   What are some factors that need to be taken into account when mediating with Indigenous Australians?

OTHER RESOURCES

Australian Institute of Family Studies, Bibliography, Conflict Resolution and Mediation, <www.aifs.gov.au/afrc/bibs/mediation.html>.

Creating Common Ground, <www.commonground.net.au/index.html>.

National Alternative Dispute Resolution Advisory Council, <www.nadrac.gov.au>.

The Institute of Arbitrators and Mediators Australia, <www.iama.org.au>.

KEY READINGS

Barsky, A.E. 2007, *Conflict Resolution for the Helping Professions* (2nd ed.), Thomson, Belmont, CA.

Condliffe, P. 2002, *Conflict Management: A Practical Guide*, LexisNexis Butterworths, Sydney.

Martin, J. 2007, *Conflict Management and Mediation*, Ginninderra Press, Canberra.

National Alternative Dispute Resolution Advisory Council 1999, *A Fair Say: Managing Differences in Mediation and Conciliation*, NADRAC, Canberra.

CHAPTER NINE | Power and advocacy

SUMMARY

This chapter attends to one of the most pressing issues in human service work, the relationship between organisations, workers and service users. It acknowledges the dependency of service users and the imbalances of power between them, the various structures of society that contribute to this imbalance and the organisations responding to their issues. In this chapter, we outline processes by which workers can address these concerns.

WHY POWER AND ADVOCACY?

At all levels, social workers should be—must be—agitators. (Brake and Bailey, 1980: 225)

A deep understanding and a critical analysis of power, coupled with a sound knowledge of advocacy and ways in which to advocate, are essential tools for every human service worker. As a worker, you *need* to understand power—your own power, that of your service user, that of your organisation, and that which resides in the structures of our society. You need to know who decides, who validates and who disperses power. You also need to know who has it, who uses it, who loses out and the ways in which this happens. Further, you need some strategies regarding what to do about it. Advocacy is often the process that can guide us to challenge and negotiate inequitable power arrangements, whether it be on behalf of an individual service user, a group or an entire community.

This chapter begins with a discussion about power. We look at ways of understanding power and explore ways in which the lack of this can manifest itself in your service users or in the communities with which you work. We will examine the power you yourself hold by virtue of both your social location and your professional discourse, and look at how to productively confront and deal with these privileges. One of the ways to challenge and work through the renegotiation of power is through advocacy. We will examine and discuss what we mean by advocacy and how to ethically advocate with and on behalf of your service users.

UNDERSTANDING POWER

When we talk about power in the human service area, what is it that we are trying to understand? There are many ways of examining power. Are we talking about power between a worker and a service user, or the power held by a worker or the organisation, or the power embedded in the structures of society? The truth is that we need to have an understanding of all these facets of power when we are working in the complicated area of human services.

What is power?

The concept of power has fascinated humans for centuries. Many historical texts examining and philosophising about power are still read and discussed today. From Sun Tzu's *The Art of War*, a Chinese military treatise from the sixth century BC to *Thoughts and Meditations* of the Roman Emperor Marcus Aurelius in 161 AD, there are many explorations and ways of conceptualising power, examining who has it and how to take it. Today, many contemporary management courses and big corporations advise their managers to read and study these texts.

For human service workers, a range of authors, researchers, academics and practitioners have written and debated on this topic. These consist of the more radical writers of the 1960s and 1970s (e.g. Paulo Freire, 1970; Franz Fanon, 1967), through to those who wrote about neo-Marxist structuralism beginning in the late 1970s (e.g. Mullaly and Pease, 1997; Moreau, 1989), the many feminist theorists of the 1970s and 1980s (e.g. hooks, 2000; Fook, 1993; Tong, 1992); the postmodern theorists (e.g. Rabinow, 1984); and the critical and anti-oppressive writers of the 1990s up to today (Allan et al. 2009; Thompson, 2006). They have all have put forward explorations and arguments about power and what it means for those who are not awarded it in our society. It is not possible within this chapter to summarise the entire intellectual journey; however, we will draw on the work of many of these writers to examine and explore how power is relevant, and the ways in which it plays out in our lives, the lives of our service users and society as whole. We will also draw on them when we articulate some strategies for dealing with power in the work that you will be doing.

So what is power, who has it and how do we make sense of it for our work in the human services field?

Power is an ever present phenomenon in social life. In all human groups, some individuals have more authority or influence than others, while groups themselves vary in terms of the level of their power. Power and inequality tend to be closely linked. The powerful are able to accumulate valued resources, such as property or wealth; and possession of such resources is in turn, a means of generating power. (Giddens, 1991: 209)

There are definitely formal ways in society whereby some groups are afforded privileges and power over others. Those who hold these benefits continue to reinforce and reproduce the formal and structural methods of privilege. Think for a moment about what is rewarded in our society. People who possess many of the following attributes are rewarded: being white, middle- and upper-class, male, able-bodied, heterosexual, young (but not too young), fit, healthy, private school educated and then tertiary educated, leading to a professional, well-paid job. How many of these privileges are part of your own social location? Consider how many of these privileges may or may not exist in the lives of your service users. In so many ways, these advantages are formally protected and reproduced in our society. This should come as no surprise, as it is those who hold these privileges who are the legislators and corporate leaders.

Thompson (2006) describes power as a central feature in the struggle to promote equality. His use of the word 'struggle' is significant, as he describes the vested interests and established structures that often stand in the way of working towards equality. He goes on to argue that, as a worker in the human services field, these vested interests and established structures may assist you greatly in your life, so being able to recognise them is often the first step in being able to challenge the power you hold on both a personal and a professional level.

Allan (2009) also argues that, as a human service worker, you need to have an understanding of the ways in which power is afforded to some groups within society at the expense of others. You need to have an awareness of these patterns of domination, where they exist, how they are reproduced and within what institutions, and the ways in which they impact on and manifest themselves in the lives of our service users and ourselves.

Chenoweth and McAuliffe (2008) state that as workers in the human services field we need to understand power on two different levels. First, we need to have an understanding of how the systems and structures in society have taken power from our service users. Second, we need to understand the dynamics of power in our relationships with the service users with whom we work, their families, groups and social connections/communities.

They also argue that different human service workers have differing views of the power and control that should be afforded to their service user groups. This can be a source of tension for many workers, and for many groups advocating on behalf of specific service user groups. For example, if you are a social worker in a hospital setting, you may have different ideas about the ways in which you would keep your service users informed and involved in their treatment than a medical practitioner may have. Even the language of 'patient' compared with that of 'service user' or 'client' gives an indication of the amount of autonomy, agency and control you would afford those with whom you are working.

You need to understand, however, that working with an awareness of who holds what power in our society, is not just a 'politically correct' position or a 'nice' way to work as a human service worker. Not having a good grasp of the ways in which power plays out in society, and works towards oppressing and damaging our service users, can be very dangerous. Costello (2009) argues that a lack of information and awareness around this can lead to workers colluding with those who hold the power, and thus continuing to oppress and damage their service users. Take, for example, the ways in which society understands male violence towards women. With no gendered analysis of the ways in which our patriarchal society continues to support and reproduce family violence (and little understanding of the many myths around men not being able to control themselves and the idea that women have the responsibility to ensure that the violent outbursts don't happen when children are present in the home), many workers in the human services field continue to collude with the perpetrators. This flawed understanding has contributed to our entire child protection system leaning towards the removal of children, rather than placing the responsibility for the violence at the feet of the perpetrators, removing them from the home and working to ensure the safety of women and children.

Brake and Bailey (1980) argue that often in your work with an individual or family, a group or a community, it may become apparent that they are not aware of the public or structural dimensions of their troubling issue. If, in the course of your work with them, they still remain unaware of the ways in which their issues are defined and by whom, then the work you are doing is questionable. They state that if you do this kind of work, you are individualising—that is, you are encouraging people to view the problems they are experiencing as unique to them and as unrelated to historical and social factors. If you do so, you encourage resolution of the problem within the boundaries of the present social

Case study: Power imbalances

You are a worker in a community health centre. One of your duties is to distribute emergency relief food vouchers in line with the agency's policies and procedures during afternoon duty sessions. One afternoon, a young Indigenous single mother comes to you asking for money, and when you look in her file you find that she has been to the centre asking for food vouchers every third week for the past two months. Agency policy states that service users can only access food vouchers once in a six-month period. The last time she was at the service, she was told that she was not eligible and was turned away by another worker. She is clearly distressed and states to you that she knows she can't budget properly, that her money does not stretch through winter and she does not know what to do. On further investigation, you find that she is living in a concrete public housing house with no insulation, and that her gas bills go from $92 during summer to over $800 during winter. This is obviously not a result of her poor budgeting skills, but of her need to heat her house.

Discussion questions

- In what ways are this woman's issues connected to her social location in life?
- How could you make her aware of this in order for her to understand that this is not her personal deficit at play here?
- In what ways might you be able to advocate for this woman with your own agency, as well as with the Department of Housing and the gas utility company?

order and you reinforce values supporting the present social order.

Many workers with whom we have talked tell us that they keep politics out of the work they do and also keep their values to themselves. If you think you are doing this, then the values and political stance you are conveying to the service user is that of the status quo, which indicates that their issues are their fault. The old saying that if you are not part of the solution, you are part of the problem is never so true than when working in the human service field. As a worker, if you think you are sitting on the fence, you are actually saying that the status quo is acceptable and that there is no need to negotiate a shift in power.

In recent years, postmodern thinking and the ways in which it conceptualises power have had a big impact on workers and theorists in the human service field. When looking at power through a postmodern lens, you will develop an awareness that it is not power itself that is the problem, but rather the way in which power has traditionally been conceptualised (Allan, 2009). Allan states that Foucault (the most prominent postmodern theorist) recognised and argued that power is exercised not possessed; that power can be used over someone to control and restrict, or it can be used to inform, support or transform; and that we all have the potential to create some form of power.

In other words, Foucault and other postmodernists have maintained that power is inherent in every situation, but is open to be used in positive ways for individuals, including for you as a worker. 'Power is therefore fluid and open to constant influence and change.' (Allan, 2009: 73) Healy (2005) also states that the postmodern theorists were working towards power being exercised rather than possessed. To do this, as a worker you would view power as a product *of* a discourse (a body of knowledge) rather than it being attached to that particular discourse. This, she argues, calls for a greater capacity for shared power. This understanding can be very useful for human service workers.

If you are able to view power in this way, it can help you to work through the power that may be held by co-workers or organisations, either for yourself or on behalf of a service user. Your awareness that the power exercised by others—real as it is—is a product of the position of their profession or of their organisation can have a mobilising effect and represent a starting point to understand, negotiate and begin to challenge this power. For workers who have found themselves trapped by the feeling that they can't change a situation because the system has too much power, this postmodern take on power can be very liberating.

The reality lies somewhere between the traditional ways of viewing power and the postmodern perspective. Power is exercised, not possessed; however, the ways in which some power is exercised over the lives of service users—for example, eligibility to be included in certain categories and to receive larger amounts of income support through Centrelink—is very powerful. To take the postmodern power analysis further, using this example you would be able to gain power over the situation for yourself and your service user by having a comprehensive knowledge of social security legislation, including what categories are available and what loopholes you may be able to find. This power of knowledge can be used to your advantage, and preparing your service user with this knowledge and other information necessary to negotiate the Centrelink maze is definitely a way of recognising that power is exercised rather than possessed. However, the sharing of power can only go so far because the legislation under which social security income support has to operate is the ultimate source of power in this situation. To change and thereby renegotiate power for your service user in terms of changing legislation constitutes a much bigger battle.

How to recognise your own privilege

Being able to recognise your own power and privilege in terms of your own social location is essential if you are attempting to understand and work through power issues in the human services (Allan, 2009; Thompson, 2006). Take a moment to reflect on the ways in which society validates your position with respect to gender, class, race, ability, sexuality and your professional power. We ask you to do this not to make you feel guilty about these privileged aspects of your life, but so you can be honest about the ways in which this has worked to your advantage. If you become guilty or defensive, you will then put too much energy into surviving (or denying) this situation, rather than taking the opportunity to learn from it.

Workers can face obstacles when trying to develop an awareness of their own privileges, and through this their own role in oppression. Many workers are blind to their own privileges; most of us are more aware of how we are discriminated against than of the ways in which society generates our advantages. For many of us, our privileges are normalised and accepted by society to the extent that they are accepted as just a part of social practice—especially those privileges afforded to us through our organisation and our profession. Lack of information about living with the effects of oppression can block your ability to develop empathy. As a worker, to be able to understand the ways in which the reality of your service user's life may have worked against them or made things more difficult for them is the key to empathy.

One strategy that can help you to work through this would be to start with a clear belief that the lack of power experienced by people can lead to oppression, and that oppression hurts us all. Without concentrating only on the ways in which you are discriminated against in society, you can use your own experiences of this to recognise ways in which this may be playing out in the lives of your service users. Constantly working on your own self-awareness of this, and using your knowledge to challenge yourself and those around you, can assist you to fight the causes of oppression that your service users face on a daily basis.

As a human service worker, you already sit in a position of power relative to that of your service users by virtue of the position you hold. From a service user's point of view, some workers hold absolute power. Take, for example, the position of a worker in Centrelink or in child protection. There can be no denying that a worker from these organisations has immense power in terms of what is about to happen to service users and their families. Often families have a long history of dealing with these organisations, and it can be as a result of this history that they may afford you as a worker with more power in their minds than you actually have. It is important to be honest with yourself about this and work from this starting position.

Of course, it is the position that holds the power, due to the legislation behind the position and the organisation within which it sits. The reality, though, is that many human service workers do not critically reflect on this and can abuse the power their position affords them. As a worker, how will you view and reflect on your position of power and the ways in which your organisation treats the service users? How will you work towards ensuring that this is as evenly balanced as it can be for your service users? Take a moment to think about the power you have as a worker when you have the authority to 'label' a service user. Labelling can be useful in terms of generalising for specific issues; however, labelling also serves to keep the worker safe and the service user knowing where they sit. Much of the debate you will hear around boundaries (between workers and service users) is also about power. Professional boundaries exist for good reasons. They work to protect the service user and your-self, but it is important that you should always reflect on how you use boundaries and why. Are you using boundaries and divisions to ensure that the service user stays on the side of the 'other'? It is only through the awareness of the workers, and the workers bringing this critical analysis to the awareness of the agency or organisation where they work, that you will be able to challenge the power structures and ultimately to change them.

It is true that, in some cases, the power of the worker can be uncertain. Many workers have raised this issue with us in terms of their perceived lack of power in certain situations. Think of situations whereby your service user or a co-worker may be more privileged than you are in terms of these social locations. What if you are an Indigenous woman or you have a disability, or you work in an organisation (for example, a hospital) that privileges other pro-fessional knowledge above your own? As a human service worker, you need to be able to analyse all situations in terms of power, and recognise that a shift in power may be necessary.

Case study: Power and ethics

You are a social worker in a large public hospital. You often find yourself acting as an advocate and a mediator between medical staff, patients and families. You know that sometimes families are not given information that they can understand, or not given timely information. You have just been sitting with the mother of a 21-year-old boy who was brought into the hospital overnight. He and some friends had been taking drugs and had then decided to jump from moving trains. He did a lot of damage to himself in his fall, but he is expected to make a full recovery. His mother was extremely distressed when she came into the hospital and after talking to the medical staff at her son's bedside, she starts to cry. She tells everyone present that he cannot stay here, that the police are looking for him and that she has done her best on her own to control him, but is now at her wit's end. She says that if this gets out, she will have to leave her rental property as his good behaviour is a condition of a tenancy tribunal agreement. She sobs that it is very hard to get a good inexpensive rental property and she doesn't want to lose her house, as this won't be the first time she has had to move due to his behaviour. You walk her up to the end of the ward to sit in a sunny spot overlooking the garden, where you can attend to her anguish and distress and begin to put some practical assistance in place for her. You often take family members to this quiet spot, as it is close to patients and has a calming effect.

While you are sitting there, a couple of young interns take the window bay next to yours and start talking loudly about a patient and his mother. They refer to him as a 'no hoper drug addict', and imply that his life is his mother's fault. You and the boy's mother realise at the same time that they are talking about the woman with whom you are sitting and her son. You lean around the corner and ask them to please stop talking about a patient in this way, and tell them that this is not appropriate. They see you are with the mother. They start blaming you, as you have been talking to her in a space where they often go to talk and look out the window.

Discussion questions

- What ethical issues are evident in this situation?
- In what ways have these interns abused the power afforded to them?

- How should you, as the worker, address these issues?
- What are the broader implications for you as a social worker/ social work team in relation to the abuse of power shown by these medical practitioners?

What effects does this lack of power have on our service users?

If we take a look at the many ways in which power (or a lack of it) plays out on our service users' lives, we begin to understand the complexities involved in the ways in which our service users are oppressed on many levels. We have discussed the fact that structures within society value (and, by extension of this, also devalue) certain attributes with which we are usually born. Couple this with the power and privilege of the workers and the organisations that service users need to access for assistance, and you have multi-level oppression and discrimination playing out in many ways.

Many writers have written on oppression—what it is, and how it plays out in the lives of people (Thompson, 2006; Mullaly, 1997; Friere, 1970; Fanon 1967). Mullaly describes oppression as: 'generally understood as the domination of subordinate groups in society by a powerful (politically, economically, socially and culturally) group . . . the oppressed person experiences the full impact of multiple level oppression every day,' (Mullaly, 1997: 27). Mullaly goes on to argue that oppression impacts on identity, and on the structure of identity. A group can be defined as different and 'other' by dominant groups in society. The ways of doing things within the dominant groups become the norm, and the subordinate groups must work to fit into the dominant groups' ways of doing and knowing. If subordinate groups do not fit in with the ways of the dominant groups, their behaviour is labelled as deviant and inferior. The identity of the subordinate groups is learnt through this interaction. Subordinate groups know how society views and treats them, and this learning is reinforced throughout their lives.

Mullaly (1997) identifies five different forms of oppression: exploitation, marginalisation, powerlessness, cultural imperialism and violence. All these forms of oppression enable those in the dominant groups to maintain and accumulate status, power and assets. These forms of oppression are socially sanctioned. Our capitalist system works by having winners and losers, often with the winners being able to exploit the labour of the losers. This exploitation results in the exclusion (marginalisation) of entire groups of people from meaningful participation in our society, and can lead to severe material deprivation. On the basis of the ways in which our society supports this social and gendered division of labour, many people have a lack of access to their own income, which leads to a lack of decision-making power or choices in their lives.

Members of the dominant group universalise their experiences and culture, and this becomes the norm—or what the other groups in society should be aspiring to. Think, for example, of how some people talk about the long-term unemployed as lazy and lacking in motivation, suggesting that if they themselves can get a job, then so could the long-term unemployed if only they tried hard enough. Dominant groups blame those in the 'other' groups for not being able to gain access to the assets, status and power that they themselves enjoy, while at the same time reproducing, tolerating and accepting the structural violence that often accompanies this oppression. This is demonstrated through harassment, ridicule, intimidation and sometimes physical attacks by those in the dominant group towards those in the subordinate groups.

Thompson (2006) also discusses these processes of discrimination, and how they come about. He argues that there are eight steps in the process of discrimination:

1. *Stereotyping.* This occurs when a group is classified on the basis of cultural prejudice. If you look at the ways in which many asylum seekers have been stereotyped, it is easy to see how effective this can be in terms of keeping them different and representing them as the 'other'. This allows the process of discrimination to begin. The characteristics that are set up as stereotypical of a

specific group will almost always include deficits in relation to those of the dominant groups.

2. *Marginalisation*. Once stereotyping has occurred, it is then easy for members of this 'other' group to be pushed to the margins of society, and their needs can then be seen as less important than those of the dominant groups.

3. *'Invisibilisation'*. Stereotyping and marginalisation push a group to the edges of society and, once it is made insignificant to the running of society, work is done to 'disappear' the group further through invisibilisation. Group members will be absent in the ways in which the media represent society, and will be absent in our language and imagery. Think for a moment of the number of Indigenous young people, or people with disabilities, that you find in popular TV shows like *Neighbours*, *Home and Away* and *Packed to the Rafters*.

4. *Infantilisation*. Following on from becoming largely absent, it is then easy for the dominant group to argue for a different allocation of power, rights, citizenship and life chances to this invisible group.

5. *Welfarism*. Assistance from the government to those who are members of subordinate groups is often labelled 'welfare', whereas assistance to those in the dominant groups is often labelled a 'tax benefit'. One kind of assistance is seen as rightfully earned, while the other is touted as a handout and it comes with many rules and moral judgements. For example, welfare recipients are told when to come to appointments, when to hand forms in, who (and which gender) can sleep at their place of residence and how many nights a week this will be allowed to happen. They are given strict guidelines to get them back into the workforce; however, they are then severely penalised financially before they have a safe budget buffer that would enable them to climb out of the welfare and poverty trap in which way they find themselves.

6. *Medicalisation*. By virtue of membership of a specific subordinate group, many manifestations that arise as a result of socially

constructed circumstances will be given the status of illness and medicalised.

7. *Dehumanisation.* It now becomes much easier to dehumanise members of these groups and refer to them in impersonal ways—for example, 'queue jumpers' as opposed to 'refugees'.

8. *Trivialisation.* Not only are the needs of these subordinate groups trivialised, so are their cultures, ways of doing things and 'solutions' imposed upon them by the dominant groups to 'fix them up'. An example of this trivialisation is the policies introduced recently requiring Indigenous children in certain outback regions to have a clean face and hands before coming to school when there are no books, stationery, school buses, and very little access to libraries or computers for the majority of the children in these schools.

How many of your service user groups have systematically been discriminated against using the processes outlined above, based on the fact that they belong to a subordinate group within our society? How does this affect your service users and yourself? In what ways are these forms of oppression and discrimination manifested in the everyday lives of those with whom we will be working? Imagine, for a moment, service users who may present with avoidance behaviours, low self-esteem, depression, anxiety or fear. Service users often feel it is a result of their own failings that they cannot live on meagre income support, or cannot keep their children healthy in housing that may not reach basic health standards. These same service users often have no choice in terms of housing, location or education for their children, and very little power over what they can afford to feed their children. What might be happening in these families living with this kind of basic material deprivation brought about by entrenched structural power inequalities? How long will it be before they begin to see themselves as they are often portrayed by the dominant group—as lazy and degenerate—and what happens to them if this pathologising and stereotyping continue at the hands of a judgemental worker or organisation? Mullaly talks about this as internalised oppression, which occurs when: 'one's personal identity matches the negative portrait or social identity provided by the social world' (Mullaly, 1997: 59).

Some of the greatest thinkers of our time have thought and written extensively about internalised oppression. A famous Algerian liberationist writer, Franz Fanon (1967), argues that the acceptance of seeing yourself through the eyes of the dominant group happens unconsciously. Another equally famous liberationist writer, Paolo Friere (1970), states that critical awareness is almost impossible for a person who is immersed in such oppressive conditions. Rather than critical awareness, ignorance and lethargy, together with a lack of ability to be able to do anything about the situation, are the most likely products of this kind of structural discrimination.

What can be done about it?

As a human service worker, you are part of that social world order; therefore, it is extremely important to be able to understand the structural forms of discrimination that may be influencing the lives of the service users with whom you are working and how this is manifesting itself. We have discussed the need for you to be able to understand the ways in which power is distributed, knowing who is privileged through this distribution (including your own privilege) and who loses out, and how this may manifest itself in your service users. As well as understanding these issues, you also have to know how to work with service users to be able to educate them about these power inequalities. You need to think of ways in which to minimise the impact of yourself and your organisation on your service users' oppression. So how do you do this?

Healy (2000), states that the first thing you need to be able to do is to listen to the ways in which your service users understand their situation, and then place value on their knowledge and their ways of knowing. She says that this enables a more holistic analysis of the situation than one based on your own privileged position. In her discussion of feminist theory, Weeks (2003) argues that you need to give space to oppressed service users so they can express their pain and their negative feelings. Many service users have not had their pain, their journey and their strength validated. In a situation such as domestic violence, for example, survivors may have had difficulty identifying their feelings, their pain and their strength, as the dominant and powerful group (the perpetrators) have been validated in blaming the victim and pathologising her symptoms.

Weeks (2003) goes on to talk about the need to engage the service user in critical reflection and consciousness-raising—that is, assisting service users to link their lived experiences to their membership of an oppressed group (in this case, women), and to understand that the problem is not just an individual problem due to some deficiency within themselves, but rather a problem common to many women due to the structural implications of a patriarchal society that supports a regeneration of violence against women. She argues that this renaming of an individual woman's experience, as well as working with service users to find their own voice and to build on their strengths, will assist them in restoring a positive sense of self-esteem.

Fook (1993) argues that in your work with yourself and in your work with service users, it is necessary to first deconstruct by analysing and questioning the dominant discourses, then to resist through not accepting or participating in the aspects of these discourses that take away power. She goes on to argue that, as a worker, you need to challenge the discourse, make visible the hidden aspects that do damage, and then reconstruct by creating new models and structures. Mullaly and Briskman (2002) contend that workers can avoid blaming the victim by focusing on social and historical constructions of equality and inequality, which can also lead the worker to a better understanding of the ways in which the oppression has occurred and developed over time.

As a human service worker, it is important to continue to be self-reflective, and to strive for a greater understanding of the ways in which people cope with oppression. This can allow more empathetic dialogue and generate some alternative ways forward. Encouraging 'identity politics'—that is, doing what you can to facilitate more empowered group identities and assisting in the collectivisation of these groups—will support the sharing of stories and an increased sense of understanding of the oppression, and lead to a reclaiming of pride and a beginning development of some counter-discourses. Working like this can often lead to collective action, and the development of organisations and groups to use as vehicles for this change. Advocacy for change—whether it be within your own organisation or community, or on an even larger scale—is possible when recognition and representation are given to voices of oppressed groups through this kind of collective action.

ADVOCACY

The skill of advocacy is an essential component of human service work. As a worker, if you begin with an assumption that many structures of our society discriminate against certain categories of people, then you will spend quite a bit of time in your practice advocating for your service users—both individually and collectively. Many professional bodies take the skill and necessity of advocacy very seriously. In Australia, for example, the Australian Association of Social Workers (AASW) has a keen focus on advocacy, stating that advocacy is one of the major ways to achieve goals around the pursuit of social justice. So what is advocacy? Moreau (1989) describes advocacy as working to obtain resources through the use of pressure, and Fook (1993) explains that it involves various actions such as arbitrating and negotiating on behalf of another, in order to persuade the actions of those who make the decisions.

Advocacy occurs when the role of a human service worker extends to actively supporting or pleading the case for an individual or group. In our previous discussions on internalised oppression, we looked at ways in which some service users can come to believe the dominant discourses about their situations. However, there are many reasons why service users are often unable to advocate for themselves. They may lack confidence and/or the ability to be able to present their own case, or they may become too anxious to be able to express their views in public, as they may have tried to do so on previous occasions and been dismissed or abused. Service users may find the process of lodging paperwork too daunting, perhaps because of their limited education, low levels of literacy, language difficulties or lack of ability to be able to articulate their needs. In many situations, they may be too distressed by what is happening to present their own case.

Higham (2006) states that to be an effective advocate you need to be able to communicate confidently, articulately and factually. She says that advocates need to understand that they should not do more than necessary, and should avoid needlessly alienating others. According to Higham (2005), the main components of advocacy include being able to plant 'seeds of awareness' for future actions, avoiding unwanted conflict as you may need to work on some kind of negotiation further down the track, accepting that your plans may not always turn out the way you want them to, and being consistent about following up on any action.

In many discussions about the art of advocacy, it becomes quite clear that how you advocate is as important as the advocacy itself. Much attention needs to be paid to the ethics of advocacy. It is always important to act in the bests interests of your service user, while at the same time working in accordance with what they want. This can be sometimes be very difficult, as you may feel that what your service user wants may not be in their best interests in the long term, or may not be realistic given what you know about the rules and regulations of certain government bodies. Many service users may not understand some of the nuances of categories and rules imposed by bigger organisations (for example, eligibility criteria for 'out of turn' public housing).

It is important to always keep your service user properly informed, to do what you say you are going to do, and to recognise and talk about what you are unable to do. It is important to do what you can with the service user present and as actively involved as possible. Many times with simple acts of advocacy, a human service worker can demonstrate to a service user how it can be done, and the service user is able to make the call or write the letter the next time it is needed. Advocacy work should always try to maximise the power of the service user.

You may be called upon to do advocacy on many levels, from micro work that is for one single service user through to macro work that will benefit many.

What skills are needed in advocacy work?

Advocacy work means being effectively persuasive, even in situations when this is difficult. You may have to deal with other professionals who may have treated your service user unjustly or unfairly. You may have to deal with organisations and institutions that have rules which don't make sense (for example, having to find an address for a service user who needs to apply for a homeless allowance). Advocacy requires skilful communication in cases like this.

Chenoweth and McAuliffe (2008) discuss advocacy as taking place when workers use their professional knowledge to argue a case on behalf of a service user or group to secure a right or entitlement. They argue that many skills are needed for effective advocacy, including good and clear communication skills to enable you to be able to persuade, assert the issue and negotiate, and be able to gather relevant facts during interviews and conversations. Workers need accurate recording skills, research skills and the ability to write a report. As with any type of persuasive action, workers have to have good time-management skills. Some advocacy work will require workers to be able to present themselves to a committee or in a courtroom. Workers need to know what is expected of them and how best to argue for their service users' interests in these situations.

It can sometimes become interesting when workers have to advocate for service users within their own organisations. In these circumstances, it is important for a worker to know how to exact change within their own organisation, what works, what channels to go through and whether this change has previously been attempted. For example, if you were the worker in the Power and ethics case study on p. 193, how would you advocate for the mother of your patient in this major public hospital?

CONCLUSION

In this chapter, we have examined the issue of power from many perspectives. We have looked at who has power (generally speaking) in our society, and what happens to those who miss out. We have looked at the processes of discrimination, the oppression to which this leads and the ways in which this oppression becomes internalised. Several ways of working with service users to challenge this discrimination and oppression have been examined, including an emphasis on the importance of being able to advocate for your service user.

Chapter review questions

9.1 What are some of the ways in which power is understood in relation to working in the human services industry?

9.2 Where do you sit personally in terms of the privileges assigned by the dominant groups in our society?

9.3 Choose a marginalised group within our society and assign Thompson's eight steps in the process of discrimination. In what ways do they fail to fit any of these eight categories?

9.4 Describe the skills necessary to advocate in your role as a human service worker.

OTHER RESOURCES

Australian Government Department of Health and Ageing website, <www.health.gov.au>. This has a publications page with a practical guide to the ethics of advocacy.

The Consumer Utilities Advocacy Centre, <www.cuac.org.au>. Information on consumer rights, where to go and what to do if you need to advocate on an issue related to with a utility company.

KEY READINGS

Allan, J., Briskman, L. and Pease, B. (eds) 2009, *Critical Social Work: Theories and Practices for a Socially Unjust World* (2nd ed.), Allen & Unwin, Sydney.

Thompson, N. 2006, *Anti Discriminatory Practice*, Palgrave Macmillan, Basingstoke.

CHAPTER TEN

Administrative ethics in human service organisations

SUMMARY

After setting the context, this chapter discusses three very important concepts guiding behaviour in all formal settings, and in human service organisations in particular. These are procedural fairness (also known as natural justice), privacy and the right to information. With regard to natural justice, we also review the common forms of bias that can creep into decision-making, and look at what constitutes evidence. We discuss methods of promoting privacy, as well as preventing and managing breaches of privacy, and also explore the related issue of freedom of information. The chapter suggests that human service workers need to consider these principles, and ensure that they are applied to their own practices as well as those of their employing organisations.

NATURAL JUSTICE

Natural justice, a fundamental principle guiding organisational activity, is also known by two other terms—administrative equity and procedural fairness. It is a core idea of good governance more broadly, and is highly relevant to the human services. As we have discussed previously, generally people who use human services do so because they are experiencing some quite serious difficulty in their lives. In addition, all human services are, to a certain degree, rationed. That means organisations and the workers who work in them often have to make decisions about eligibility, and about how much help a person or a family can receive. These decisions can be very hard to make, and in the worst-case scenario a human service worker would make these decisions on the basis of bias or prejudice, or more likely on the basis of who 'fits' the organisation's image of its service users.

As we have also made clear in earlier chapters, service users of human service organisations are in unbalanced power relationships with both workers and their employing organisations. Often service users are unwell or disabled, very young or very old. For a variety of reasons (such as those discussed in Chapter 9), our service users may not be particularly good advocates for themselves and can be quite passive in their engagement with workers, accepting what they are given without complaint. In contexts where resources are scarce, and in the contemporary environment where people's needs are escalating, it is very easy to overlook a person's right to natural justice. But it is a principle that is fundamental to the operations of human service organisations. Those organisations run by the states are required by administrative law to obey the rules of natural justice. That said, there is a moral imperative for all organisations to take these rules into consideration in their daily operations. Furthermore, we are all entitled to natural justice, irrespective of who we are and what we do. Consider the three scenarios below. Each concerns an aspect of experience where natural justice is an important issue.

Case study: Natural justice

Natural justice is a universal principle that applies to all persons and in all legal systems. It applies in Australian judicial, legislative and administrative practices. Natural justice rules and principles have been developed to ensure that decision-making is fair and reasonable. It involves decision-makers informing people of the case against them or their interests, giving them the right to be heard, not having a personal interest in the outcome and acting on the basis of evidence.

Scenario 1

Tran is a 17-year-old youth who is having great difficulty living at home with his mother and step-father. He and his step-father argue a lot, and at times things have become violent. Tran has basically left home and is sleeping on a friend's couch. He has rung Centrelink but has been told different things by different customer service officers. He is confused and scared. He has been to see the social worker, who questions him closely about his eligibility for youth homeless allowance. Tran leaves Centrelink with the feeling that the social worker does not think he has a good enough reason to leave home.

Scenario 2

Carol is a front-line worker in a family support service. Her life is a bit topsy turvy at the moment because her relationship with her partner recently broke up and she has had to move at short notice. Her cat is also unwell, needing regular visits to the vet. Carol has often had to come in late to work, and sometimes also leaves a little early, mainly to get the cat to the vet. Her line manager has suggested that she needs to meet with her for a performance management meeting, and one of the issues is timekeeping.

Scenario 3

You are working in an organisation called PEOPLE FIRST, funded by the state government. Your position, along with four others, is funded by them to deliver support services to people with psychiatric disabilities living in the community. PEOPLE FIRST is in dispute with the funding body over the nature of the program, and the key performance indicators being used to monitor and evaluate the program. Basically, the department is only interested in the units of service (number of people seen and number of times they are seen). Your organisation does not believe the funding department understands the nature of the service users and their issues because if it did, it would know that it is not the number of times someone is seen that matters but the quality of the relationship developed between workers and service users. The funding department has served notice that it is going to review the funding.

EXERCISE

Re-read the scenarios above. How is the principle of natural justice relevant?

Natural justice represents an *ideal* of justice that is of unquestionable antiquity. It is a universal substantive standard that also contains procedural standards. It is also a principle with practical application. The rules of natural justice incorporate fundamental values about equality, non-discrimination, impartiality and basic fairness.

Natural justice involves three elements, the most important of which is the 'hearing rule'. The other two elements are the 'rule against bias' and the 'no evidence rule'. The hearing rule states that a person should be told the 'case to be met' and to be heard in reply. Any hearing should be set up in a way that is appropriate for the circumstances. In the case of Scenario 1 above, the social worker should explain to Tran why he doesn't think Tran is eligible for youth allowance. Further, he should put this in plain language, and he should refer Tran to a welfare rights centre so that he can access assistance to have his reply heard. If natural justice were to apply to Tran:

- The hearing should be conducted before a decision is reached or a settled view formed.

- All of the information that is being used to reach a decision should be made available prior to the hearing.

- Tran should be given a reasonable opportunity to respond, and in his case the social worker should make sure that Tran is assisted in developing and presenting his response.
- Tran would be entitled to a comprehensive consideration of his case.

Let's look at some issues that can arise with the hearing rule, in this case in the context of Scenario 3 above.

1. *A hearing held too late is not acceptable.* If the department has already decided 'in principle' that the funding will not be renewed before a hearing takes place, natural justice is constrained.

2. *A hearing held prematurely is not acceptable.* The department and PEOPLE FIRST need time to collect material and make their case. If time is not given for this, natural justice is constrained.

3. *There has been non-disclosure of information relevant to the decision.* The department and PEOPLE FIRST should have access to information used in decision-making. If this does not occur, natural justice is constrained.

4. *The department has led PEOPLE FIRST to believe that future funding will be forthcoming.* Natural justice demands that, in this instance, PEOPLE FIRST should be informed of any proposed change. Natural justice protects legitimate expectations as well as legal rights.

The other principles of natural justice identified above were the need for evidence to support a decision and the absence of bias. It is not good enough that a decision-maker is unbiased. In terms of upholding natural justice, it is particularly important that any onlooker should not suspect or perceive bias in the decision-making process. If, for example, the decision-maker has ever displayed hostility or favouritism, or clearly has a closed mind about the matter, there would be reasonable suspicion that bias exists. In the field of welfare, it is often unfortunately the case that bias can exist—particularly in contexts where untrained personnel are involved in service delivery. Furthermore, a decision cannot be made on the basis of opinion, suspicion, rumour or gossip. Rather, natural justice demands that any decision is based in evidence. It is important that the evidence used to support a decision should be disclosed to the other party in advance of a decision. In relation to Carol in Scenario 2 above, her manager would be required to demonstrate that she is not biased against Carol, and she must provide her with the information she will be using in her decision-making.

Accordingly, there should be no bias evidenced in the process. The test here is whether a fair-minded observer might reasonably apprehend that the decision-maker might not bring an impartial mind to the resolution of the question. For example, disqualifying bias will occur where a fair-minded observer might reasonably apprehend that the decision-maker has pre-judged the matter by ignoring evidence or dismissing it with insufficient reason. Furthermore, if a decision-maker has any financial or personal interest in the matter at hand, then the bias rule would be invoked. A suspicion of bias can arise from things a decision-maker says or does which might indicate that he or she is either partial or hostile, has formed pre-judgments and/or is not open to persuasion. Ignoring or downplaying evidence could be considered as the operations of bias.

It is also important that a decision-maker is aware of the tricks the mind can play in relation to bias. See the list below:

- *Confirmation bias.* Occurs when we selectively notice or focus on evidence that tends to support the things we already believe or want to be true while ignoring evidence that would serve to disconfirm those beliefs or ideas. Confirmation bias plays a stronger role when it comes to those beliefs that are based upon prejudice, faith or tradition rather than on empirical evidence.

- *Disconfirmation bias.* Refers to the tendency for people to extend critical scrutiny to information that contradicts their prior beliefs and accept uncritically information that is congruent with their prior beliefs.

- *Bias blind-spot.* Occurs when a person fails to perceive, and therefore does not compensate for, his or her own biases.

It is always worthwhile to remember that all human beings under-estimate their own biases while over-estimating those of other people. Further, we all bring unconscious attitudes and beliefs that belie our expressed attitudes. For example, in Scenario 1 above, the social worker might have a teenager himself who is giving him trouble. This conceivably could colour his attitude to Tran's claims, as well as bias him to believe Tran's parents' claims.

Some of the indicators of bias are:

- premature expression of hostility
- labelling of one of the parties
- putting one party through the hoop about proof while accepting the other without comment
- using different forms of address or different levels of familiarity
- listening differently.

EXERCISE

Looking at Scenarios 2 and 3 above, in what form might bias be expressed by the persons nominated?

- Scenario 2: Carol's line manager
- Scenario 3: The funding department's officer handling the matter.

As suggested above, the third element for natural justice to be upheld is the 'no evidence' rule. This argues that all decisions where natural justice is in play must be based on evidence rather than rumour, suspicion rather than gossip. Evidence can consist of a range of things: intake forms, emails, narratives, the decision-maker's observations or a person's demeanour. It is perfectly acceptable for a decision-maker to make further investigations— for example, to call another worker with whom the person has had contact, or in Tran's case above, to talk to his mother. If the person is in some way disadvantaged in making their case (as is often the case in the human services), a worker should consider seeking extra assistance in seeking or obtaining evidence to inform the decision about that person.

There are several types of evidence. Hearsay is one very common form of evidence in the human services, particularly from other workers, family or friends of the person about whom a decision is being made. Natural justice requires that the person has the right to rebut any evidence submitted. Furthermore, if there are conflicting accounts (which there might well be in Tran's case), it does not necessarily mean that someone is lying because it is possible (and indeed often probable) that people will perceive and remember events differently. We now turn to privacy.

PRIVACY

Maintaining citizens' privacy is an important principle in democratic societies such as Australia, and has been for quite some time. In 1948, for example, the United Nations proclaimed its Universal Declaration of Human Rights, Article 12 of which states: 'No one shall be subject to arbitrary interference in his [sic] privacy, family home and correspondence, nor to attacks upon his honour and reputation. Everyone has the right to the protection of law against such attacks.' Currently, all Australian governments have some mechanism for protecting privacy. The Commonwealth (also covering the ACT), New South Wales, Victoria, the Northern Territory, Western Australia and Tasmania have enacted specific legislation. Queensland and South Australia, on the other hand, have administrative systems. In each jurisdiction, it is primarily government agencies that are subject to privacy rules. The situation is somewhat more complex in relation to non-profit community-based organisations, particularly when they are in receipt of government funding. In Victoria, for example, organisations contracted by the state to provide statutory services are obliged to conform to the legislation. However, those merely 'funded' by the state may not be so obliged. Despite this lack of clarity, there is nevertheless a moral and professional imperative for community-based organisations to take the protection of their service users very seriously. Read the following case study.

Case study: Protecting privacy

David is a social work student on his final placement at Woodsville Neighbourhood Centre. The centre runs a number of programs for a wide range of local people. It is a busy place, with people popping in and out all of the time. One of the more troublesome programs it runs is the distribution of emergency relief—a discretionary program by which participating agencies assess claims of financial hardship and manage small temporary payments. It is difficult because it is discretionary, and there is too much opportunity for unclear or biased decisions to be made. Nevertheless, and because of funding restrictions, it is mainly volunteers who run the program. David wandered into the kitchen to get a glass of water when he spotted two of the volunteers having lunch at the table. The volunteers were discussing an applicant for emergency relief that one of them had seen that morning. She was being quite critical and dismissive of the applicant, more or less claiming that he was lying. The kitchen is open territory at the Neighbourhood Centre and anyone can (and does) wander in and out. David was concerned about the overheard conversation and asked his supervisor at their next supervision session what the centre's policy was in relation to privacy and how it was implemented. He heard that there was a policy and a set of practices with which all staff and volunteers were familiarised during induction. He was left to wonder whether this system was good enough.

This case study illustrates clearly why privacy is important in both a moral and professional sense. Unfortunately, the situation described above is not particularly uncommon. The bitter reality is that human service organisations often have to ration scarce resources, and in doing so usually base their decisions on sensitive information. Nearly every human service worker one asks will be able to talk about instances where service users' confidential case details were brought up in tearoom chatter. But, as we have said time and time again, people come to human service organisations because something is going awry in their lives. Often, people feel embarrassed or ashamed about the fact that they are not coping and they dislike having to make personal disclosures to strangers. To think that this information could be made available to other people is upsetting to say the least. Think about going to Centrelink and the experience of being asked quite personal details by a customer service officer with other officers sitting nearby and a long queue behind you. Immediately you can understand why caring about citizens' privacy in welfare settings is important. It is important morally because everyone has the right to privacy, and we are obliged as citizens to respect this right. It is important professionally because breaching privacy can seriously damage the trust a person has with a worker and an organisation, jeopardising future intervention. Here we address privacy so that if you experience something like David did in the case study, you will be able to act responsibly in relation to your organisation's policy and procedures.

Preventing privacy breaches

An organisation should have principles in relation to the collection, storage, use and disclosure of, and access to, personal information. But what information fits this category? In general, the following questions need to be posed:

- Is the information collected sensitive to the individual?
- What harm would be done to the individual if there is a breach?
- What harm is there to the organisation if there is a breach?
- How does the organisation store, process and transmit personal information?

There are a number of steps that an organisation needs to undertake to assess existing privacy protocols or develop new ones. Look at Table 10.1, read the tasks and consider what a human service or community welfare organisation would need to do in respect of each task.

Table 10.1: Service actions

Action	Human services organisational practice
Identify what personal information is necessary to be collected	
Work out how long information should be kept	
Identify the security risks to personal information and the consequences of a breach of security	
Develop a policy and a set of measures to reduce the risks	
Train staff	
Nominate a designated position to deal with personal information security breaches	
Ensure there are privacy-enhancing procedures in relation to technology	
Monitor compliance with security policy and undertake periodic assessments of new risks	
Ensure that effective complaint-handling systems are in place	
Systematically evaluate proposed or existing information systems align with good policy and practice	

People who use the services of the human services sector are entitled to know that information about them is being collected. They also need to know why, as well as what happens to the information after it is collected. The Commonwealth Office of the Privacy Commission has developed useful information sheets on a number of topics related to privacy, including this one. The first step is to ensure that reasonable steps to ensure service user awareness are in place. But how do we determine what is reasonable? What should an organisation do, for example, when it is collecting information about a service user from some other source (for example, through the process of referral or through a case conference)? A reasonable step in this instance would be to inform the person that the information had been transmitted when the person is next contacted. Where sensitive information is being collected, it is reasonable to require an individual's consent. In most human service organisations, consent would be sought formally at intake. To decide whether or not a step is reasonable usually involves making a judgement based on the facts. Generally, the more sensitive the information is, and the greater the extent of harm if information is leaked, then the greater effort an organisation should make to inform its service users that the information is being collected.

Managing privacy breaches

If a personal information breach actually happens, then an organisation will need to have a protocol for managing it. The Office of the Privacy Commissioner (2008) suggests that there are some general principles and four steps that need to be considered. The general principles are:

- Be sure to take each situation seriously and move quickly to contain the suspected breach.
- Breaches that seem immaterial may be significant when their full implications are assessed.
- The decision on how to respond should be made on a case-by-case basis.

The four steps are outlined in Table 10.2.

Table 10.2: Managing privacy breaches

Action	Human services organisational practice
Step 1: Contain the breach	Contain the breach—that is, stop the practices that led to the breach. Assess whether steps can be taken to minimise harm. Initiate a preliminary assessment: appoint someone with sufficient authority to lead the initial assessment. Assess who needs to be notified immediately.
Step 2: Evaluate the risks associated with the breach	Consider what personal information is involved. What is the context of the information (e.g. a list of service users is less sensitive than a personal file). Establish the cause and extent of the breach. Assess the risk of harm to the individual. Work out steps to mitigate harm. Identify what other harms or risks could arise. Investigate whether it is a systemic issue or an isolated issue.
Step 3: Consider notification to the individual/s concerned	In general, if personal information has been breached then the person should be notified. The preferred method is direct—in person or by phone. The notification should include a description of the incident, a description of the information, an account of what the organisation is doing, an offer of assistance to the individual, organisational contact details, how the individual can lodge a complaint.

Step 4: Prevent future breaches	Develop a breach-response plan: set out contact details of staff who should be notified, clarify roles and responsibilities, document organisational procedures, review the response plan regularly.

EXERCISE

Read the case below and work through Steps 1 to 4 outlined in Table 10.2.

Case study: Privacy breaches

Rosa works in a domestic violence service for women from culturally and linguistically diverse backgrounds. Her job is to place women and their children referred to them from the domestic violence hotline into women's refuges and then to support them for as long as they need it. Like all such services, the organisation takes the security of its service users very seriously. Rosa has been working on her case notes, which are getting behind. She keeps getting interrupted by various things so she asks her coordinator whether she can work on them at home the next day. She is given permission to do this. She loads the files needing to be updated on her pen drive, which she puts in her backpack. The next day, she goes to retrieve the files and cannot find the pen drive. She makes a call to work and asks her colleague to search around her desk. The pen drive is not found.

Finally, we turn to the third principle drawn from administrative ethics, one which is clearly related to privacy—the right to information.

FREEDOM OF INFORMATION

A cornerstone of contemporary democracy, freedom of information is one of the most important means we have to hold governments accountable. In fact, the importance of information in a representative democracy has been acknowledged by the Australian High Court (e.g. the 1992 cases of *Nationwide News v Wills* and *Australian Capital Television v The Commonwealth*).

As well as a desire to maximise accountability, underpinning formal freedom of information mechanisms are other philosophical principles. It is generally held that:

- If citizens are adequately informed and have access to information, there is likely to be more public participation in policy-making processes and in government itself.
- Groups and individuals affected by government decisions should know the criteria applied in making those decisions.
- Every individual has a right to know what information government is holding about him or her personally, to inspect files held about or relating to him or her, and to have inaccurate information corrected.

Nevertheless, freedom of information provisions and the ways in which governments enact them can be highly political and often controversial. Many commentators have raised concerns about how, over the last decade, access to information via freedom of information legislation has become increasingly difficult, as well as increasingly out of reach for people on limited incomes. Furthermore, the formal systems associated with freedom of information legislation in different jurisdictions require a significant degree of knowledge about government and bureaucracy, as well as a willingness to have a go. Many of the people who use human services are unwilling or unable to take bureaucracy 'on'. Fortunately (and with hindsight), in 2006 the Australian High Court made a particular decision in relation to a case brought by Michael McKinnon, the freedom of information editor for *The Australian* newspaper. He made a seemingly innocuous request to access federal Treasury documents related to taxation and bracket creep, and also on the first home-owners' scheme. The request was blocked by the then Treasurer, Peter Costello, who was concerned about the capacity of the public service to give frank advice if their advice was going to be open to public scrutiny, a position that was upheld by the Administrative Appeals Tribunal. The High Court made a decision on the Appeals Tribunal ruling which many interested observers regarded as pivotal to the whole future of freedom of information. See, for example, the Greens' leader Bob Brown's response:

High Court blow against democracy
Media Release | Spokesperson Bob Brown
Wednesday 6th September 2006, 12:00am

The High Court 3–2 decision against Michael McKinnon's Freedom of Information appeal is a blow against democracy, Greens Leader Bob Brown *said today.*

Senator Brown, who introduced Freedom of Information to Tasmania in 1991, said the Court's finding should lead to reform of the law.

'I call on Attorney-General Ruddock to amend the Freedom of Information Act *so that any reasonable public interest would ensure the information is released,' Senator Brown said.*

'Information is the currency of democracy. Beyond clear defense of national security, it is difficult to argue that ministers should be able to keep the public in the dark. I will look at bringing in an amendment to fix the problem which allowed the High Court majority to keep people in the dark,' Senator Brown said. Senator Brown added that former Liberal Senator Allan Missen, the father of Australia's Freedom of Information laws, always intended that the public's right to know should override ministers protecting their political patch.

Source: <http://bob-brown.greensmps.org.au/taxonomy/term/122/all>, accessed 26 May 2009

It is controversies such as this that prompted a move by the Rudd Labor government to reform the federal *Freedom of Information Act*, a development we discuss later. All Australian governments have legislative mechanisms to facilitate freedom of information for their citizens. In Australia, the *Freedom of Information Act* was passed at the federal level in 1982, applying to all ministers, departments and public authorities of the Commonwealth. There is similar legislation in all states and territories:

- Australian Capital Territory: *Freedom of Information Act* 1989
- New South Wales: *Freedom of Information Act* 1989
- Northern Territory: *Information Act* 2003
- Queensland: *Freedom of Information Act* 1992
- South Australia: *Freedom of Information* Act 1991
- Tasmania: *Freedom of Information Act* 1991
- Victoria: *Freedom of Information Act* 1982
- Western Australia: *Freedom of Information Act* 1992

In 2009, the Rudd Labor government announced an overview of the 1982 *Freedom of Information Act* to overcome what many believed to be significant problems in its operationalisation, particularly in terms of the organisational culture in many government departments that undermined the Act's democratic intent. Specifically, it was suggested that government departments became increasingly less willing to engage with the legislation in the manner intended, and were in fact often obstructing people's access to information. The new proposals suggested by the government include the following:

- ensuring the right of access to documents is as comprehensive as it can be, limited only where a stronger public interest lies in withholding access
- giving greater weight to the role of the *Freedom of Information Act* in the proactive publication of government information
- introducing structural reforms designed to make the system more cohesive, accessible and transparent
- establishing an Office of the Information Commissioner.

While it is good to know that governments are trying to strengthen our right to access information, issues remain about the implications of freedom of information for human service work, particularly that undertaken in community-based non-profit organisations. As with the other two issues discussed in this chapter, there are clear ethical issues around why workers should think about the right to information, particularly the rights of human service organisations' service users to information held about them. It is easy, for example, for us to understand that organisations such as Centrelink and the Australian Tax Office have sensitive information about individuals in their records. So too do state government authorities such as child protection services, corrections and mental health services.

While it is clear that state organisations must comply with freedom of information legislation, what is the case for the community-based non-profit sector? Under the previous Act, the sector was exempt. The reforms mooted in the new Act suggest that the sector—as government contractors—might have to comply. Not surprisingly, this makes some people quite unhappy, as there are concerns that compliance will be too intrusive and the administrative systems to manage freedom of information will be expensive. The Public Interest Advocacy Centre, for example, has suggested to the federal government that contracted charitable and non-profit organisations should be exempt from the Act because they carry out other services in addition to those contracted by government.

In reality, most human service organisations, public and non-profit, record and store sensitive information. Furthermore, most of us would consider it ethically appropriate for people to have access to information that we record about them. In addition to information, human service workers often write case notes about people, which include observations about a person's presenting appearance and behaviour. This latter information is essentially a worker's opinion. It might well be informed opinion, but it is still opinion. As discussed in the chapter on writing and recording, the general rule when recording information about people is to avoid intemperate language. Consider the following two case studies and exercises.

Case study: Freedom of information 1

Kristy is a social worker with a church-based non-profit organisation that provides outreach services to young homeless people. The service users often behave in quite scary and wild ways, for a whole range of reasons including substance abuse, cognitive impairment and anger. After an incident in which an alcohol-affected young man threatened to bash up a colleague, Kristy was obliged to write an incident report.

EXERCISE

Write the incident up. After you have finished, hand it to another class member and ask them to assess how much opinion and how much fact is in the report. Ask the question of how would the young man react if he read the report.

Case study: Freedom of information 2

Mohamed works as family support worker for in a program in a community sector agency that is trying to get young fathers engaged with their babies and the children's mothers. Eddie is a young Indigenous man who has a 1-year-old son living with his girlfriend. Eddie has many personal issues, including the very real possibility that he has foetal alcohol syndrome with all the attendant cognitive difficulties. Mohamed knows this because he took Eddie for a full assessment with a cognitive psychologist. Mohamed is very unsure about what he should record in the file, and how any information should be recorded.

EXERCISE

How should Mohamed record this information? Will his record be based on opinion or fact? Is the report of the cognitive psychologist opinion or fact?

Chapter review questions

10.1 What are the three elements of natural justice?

10.2 What are the three types of bias that can work against natural justice?

10.3 Why is privacy important, morally and professionally?

10.4 What are the four steps recommended by the Office of the Privacy Commissioner for managing a breach?

10.5 Why is freedom of information important in a democracy?

10.6 Why is freedom of information important in human service organisations?

OTHER RESOURCES

Victorian Government Solicitor's Office, *Procedural Fairness: The Hearing Rule*, <www.vgso.vic.gov.au/resources/publications/adv/proceduralfairness-thehearingrule.aspx>.

Australian Government Solicitor, *Natural Justice and the 'Hearing Rule': Fundamental Principles and Recent Developments*, <www.ags.gov.au/publications/agspubs/legalpubs/legalbriefings/br78.htm>.

Australian Government, Office of the Privacy Commissioner, *Guide to Handling Personal Information Security Breaches*, <www.privacy.gov.au/publications/breach_guide.pdf>.

National Welfare Rights Network, *Freedom of Information: How to Request a Copy of Your File from Centrelink*, <www.welfarerights.org.au/pages/factsheets.aspx>.

KEY READINGS

Administrative Review Council 2007, *Decision Making: Natural Justice*, Best Practice Guide 2, Administrative Review Council Best Practice Guides, Commonwealth Government of Australia, Canberra.

—— *Decision Making: Evidence, Facts and Findings*, Best Practice Guide 3, Administrative Review Council Best Practice Guides, Commonwealth Government of Australia, Canberra.

Wallace, J. and Pagone, T. 1990, in *Rights and Freedoms in Australia*, Federation Press, Sydney.

CHAPTER ELEVEN | Preparing for and dealing with complaints

SUMMARY

This chapter discusses why it is important that human service workers pay serious attention to service users' complaints. We provide advice about developing and implementing a complaints mechanism. This advice can also be used to evaluate an existing complaints mechanism in a human service organisation. Following this, we discuss how workers themselves should respond to complaints, particularly complaints about their colleagues, the organisation or another organisation. Finally, the chapter discusses whistleblowing as one major tactic human service workers might use if they are seriously disturbed by practices they witness.

WHY COMPLAINTS MECHANISMS ARE NECESSARY

Many human service organisations, particularly those in the non-profit community sector, are afflicted by what an influential scholar of the non-profit sector, Lester Salamon (1995), has called the 'myth of pure virtue'. In coining this term, he was trying to persuade the non-profit sector in particular to face up to the fact that, in many ways, it does not necessarily function in the manner its organisations tend to assume. In other words, non-profit community-based organisations are not automatically more participatory, more responsive or more flexible than state bureaucracies. This is especially the case in relation to their relationships with service users. Australian author Michael Wearing (1998), for example, undertook a major study of the functioning of non-profit human service organisations, illustrating the presence of many processes with service users that were less than desirable. Generally, workers in human service organisations tend to assume that the value base of professions such as social work influences and shapes how service users and service providers interact. These assumptions lead workers and organisations to also suppose that service users are happy with the service, that the organisation is respectful and responsive and that service users are not harmed through their engagement.

Unfortunately, such assumptions are ill-advised. This in turn can mean that formal accountability to service users is not particularly well developed in many human service organisations, particularly non-profit or non-profit community-based organisations. In 1995, McDonald and Crane undertook a qualitative study of consumer rights in a sample of Australian non-profit community-based human service organisations. They found that, contrary to human service workers' beliefs, the implementation of consumer rights procedures such as complaints mechanisms were rudimentary at best. These results are supported by two other more recent Australian non-profit researchers. Jo Baulderstone (2007) presents good evidence that non-profit accountability to service users is more rhetoric than reality. Comparing non-profit human service organisations with government and businesses, Richard Mulgan (2001) shows that community sector agencies are less accountable than organisations in the other sectors across a number of dimensions. For our purposes here, he found them less accountable than the others in their treatment of service users. Nevertheless, all three acknowledge that funding organisations—particularly government departments—are requiring funded organisations to develop and implement user complaints mechanisms.

Even though most of us would consider it a standard of good and ethical organisational practice to have a sound and effective complaints mechanism in place, Hasenfeld (2000) provides us with a solid *intellectual* reason as well. Human service organisations, he argues, are moral settings; everything about them—their structure, their policies and their daily practices—are moral practices. By this he means that organisational structures and practices articulate and reaffirm the moral status of service users, positioning them within a particular hierarchical stratification that determines their rights. If an organisation has a poorly functioning (or no) complaints mechanism, then service users are clearly positioned as people with no rights. This situation is, according to the service users' movement, more widespread than we would like to believe (Barnes and Wistow, 1994). Read, for example, the Service users' rights case study.

Social workers in particular are uneasy with formal calls for increased accountability to service users, and this unease arises because of the shift in the power balance between users and professionals involved in proper accountability. Nevertheless, improving organisational accountability to service users is not only the ethically correct thing to do; it is increasingly an instrumental requirement of funding. So, for both ethical and instrumental reasons, we now turn to a discussion about how to develop a good complaints system.

DEVELOPING AND IMPLEMENTING COMPLAINTS SYSTEMS

Australia has formal systems for managing complaints at the federal and state government levels. The state systems consist of such bodies as the various Ombudsmen, the anti-discrimination agencies, the courts and tribunals, as well as institutional processes such as freedom

Case study: Service users' rights

Marika is a 30-something refugee from Eastern Europe. Since arriving in the country, she has successfully studied for a Master's degree. She is nevertheless having extreme difficulty in getting a job and has to attend an employment services organisation to receive her social security payment. After attending one for some time she got fed up with the fact that the organisation did not seem to want to really help her to get a job matching her capacities and her education. Instead, her case manager kept sending her to interviews for menial jobs. She tried to switch to another organisation in the same field, but was not allowed. She then decided she needed another case manager who was more likely to be less 'rule bound' and more likely to help her. She tried to complain to the organisation but was told she had to complain to the funding department. When she investigated this option, it seemed an overwhelming task. She subsequently accepted a job as a cleaner.

Discussion questions

- What is Marika's moral status or identity constructed in this organisation's practices?
- Do you know of any other human service organisations or organisational practices that negatively constitute service users?
- Do you think Salamon's notion of the myth of pure virtue operates in Australian non-profit community-based agencies?

of information. These are usually augmented with department-specific complaints procedures and internal reviews. It is fortunate that government has developed these systems, because they provide the community sector with very useful ideas about how to go about developing a good system themselves. Increasingly, governments and businesses are adopting international best-practice standards for developing complaints mechanisms. These standards are developed by the International Standardisation Organisation (ISO). Within what is known as the ISO 9000 series, there is ISO 10002.2004. The Australian Standards Association, the body charged with developing all of Australia's formal standards and benchmarks, officially adopted it in 2006.

The ISO 10002.2004 provides guidance on the process of complaints handling related to products within an organisation, including planning, design, operation, maintenance and improvement. The complaints-handling process described is suitable for use as one of the processes of an overall quality management system.

It is also intended for use by organisations of all sizes and in all sectors. ISO 10002:2004 addresses the following aspects of complaints handling:

- *enhancing customer satisfaction by creating a customer-focused environment that is open to feedback (including complaints), resolving any complaints received, and enhancing the organisation's ability to improve its product and customer service;*
- *top management involvement and commitment through adequate acquisition and deployment of resources, including personnel training;*
- *recognizing and addressing the needs and expectations of complainants;*
- *providing complainants with an open, effective and easy-to-use complaints process;*
- *analysing and evaluating complaints in order to improve the product and customer service quality;*
- *auditing of the complaints-handling process;*
- *reviewing the effectiveness and efficiency of the complaints-handling process.*

Source: <www.iso.org/iso/catalogue_detail?csnumber=35539>

Drawing on these standards, Ombudsman Victoria (2007) has, among other things, outlined the features of a good complaint mechanism. These are:

- *Commitment.* It should be very clear that the organisation takes seriously any complaints it receives. This can only come about if (a) the organisation develops a culture that actively welcomes complaints, and (b) sufficient resources are devoted to managing complaints.
- *Fairness.* The rules of natural justice should be applied to all parties to a complaint—the complainant, and the person from the agency about whom a complaint is made.

- *Transparency and access.* Every employee and volunteer in the organisation and every service user should be familiar with the process. It must be easily understood and written in plain language—and, where appropriate, in other community languages.
- *Responsiveness.* Complaints should be quickly, courteously and fairly dealt with within publicised established guidelines.
- *Privacy and confidentiality.* All complaints should be conducted in such a manner that identities are secure, all legal requirements to privacy are maintained and confidentiality is protected.
- *Accountability.* A complaints management system and its operations should be made accountable to the relevant people—for example, service users and boards of management.
- *Service improvement.* A complaints-management system should provide useful data for improving the functioning of the organisation. There should be mechanisms built into the organisation's management to ensure that this information is taken up in appropriate ways.
- *Internal review.* A complaints-handling system should allow a complainant to express grievances about how his or her complaint was managed.

That same document from Ombudsman Victoria (2007) outlines the steps to building good complaints systems. First, the document suggests that organisations review and evaluate the existing policy, resources, procedures and practices. Many organisations will already have a system in place but may, after review, decide that it is inadequate. It is also a very good idea to have this done externally—to ask a *critical friend* (someone who has your organisation's best interests at heart but who is not afraid to point out weaknesses) to do this. In many instances, non-profit boards of management may include a regular evaluation of the organisation's complaints-management system as part of their overall risk-management strategy. After reviewing the existing system, an organisation is then advised to identify areas for improvement and develop an action plan for doing this.

The first step is to develop a policy that sets out the orientation of the desirable complaints system. Such a policy should:

- be clearly labelled
- contain a policy commitment statement
- outline the definition of terms used in the policy
- provide a model for complaints
- outline roles and functions
- detail complaint categories
- outline how complaints trends will be reported
- outline the communication mode
- outline safeguards against retribution
- list remedies
- link to the organisation's strategic goals and risk-management strategy
- nominate resources available
- indicate the implementation date
- outline the evaluation or audit process and the policy review date.

EXERCISE

Write a brief outline of a complaints management policy for:

- a women's refuge
- a community legal centre
- a needle exchange service.

What, if any, are the differences between them?

After the policy is written, the organisation needs to start thinking about who is going to run the complaints system. Clearly, whoever does it needs to be well trained with a good knowledge of the services offered, have good inter-personal skills, be non-judgemental, be sensitive to cultural and linguistic differences, be adequately resourced to do the job and have appropriate delegated authority to make required decisions.

Any robust complaints system needs to be resourced with appropriate information and communication technology skills, and the complaints staff need permission to access all levels of the organisation. All complaints systems need a simple yet thorough recording system that should record the complainants' details, the nature of the complaint, the desired remedy, the mode of complaint (telephone, email or letter), the responsible staff member, procedures identified, action taken, response time and outcome, and recommendations for improvements to the organisation's processes. The very last step is to make sure any complaint is lodged with complaints of a similar nature so that any patterns over time can be discerned.

Case study: Complaints policy

A child and family welfare organisation in an Australian state was required by its funding body to develop a series of policies, one of which was a complaints policy. The board of this organisation established a sub-committee (a Policy and Standards Committee), which oversaw the establishment of a small staff committee that developed, planned and implemented a range of policies, including the complaints policies. The board sub-committee was charged with the responsibility of reviewing the policies and associated procedures on a regular basis. In this way, the introduction and review of the policy provided a means for continuously evaluating the organisation's practices.

RESPONDING TO COMPLAINTS ABOUT THE ORGANISATION AND STAFF

Many people working in human service organisations do so because they have commitments to the wellbeing of the people who come to the organisation for help. Often these people are on low incomes and are experiencing other quite serious and disabling issues that impair the functioning of their families and their own lives. Because of their commitment, human service workers often assume that their motives are sufficient to ensure that their practices (and those of the organisation) are unilaterally in the best interests of service users.

When human service workers hear of complaints about their own practice, they often are quite hurt and react defensively. While this is understandable, it is not particularly helpful because complaints are one sure way to point to issues workers and organisations might like to review. Social workers, for example, are enjoined to engage in critical reflection about their practice. As such, they should actively seek out perspectives on their engagement with themselves and with the organisation. They should also model this orientation for other staff.

The first thing front-line staff need to understand is why people make complaints. Usually, it is because they are not happy with a decision made about them, or they do not believe they have been given sufficient or appropriate service. Sometimes they are not happy with the way staff have interacted with them. In non-profit community-based organisations, the quantity of service given to people may be limited because of resource constraints. Most non-profit community-based organisations are funded through contracts with governments, which often specify what the organisation should do and for how long the service should be provided. Furthermore, not many organisations have sufficient independent revenue to offer services over and above what they are contracted to do. This dilemma can easily lead to complaints by service users.

Often service users won't complain at all, even though they may be unhappy. As suggested above, most people who engage with human service organisations face significant difficulties in their lives. In such contexts, people have little alternative—or, in the language of management, feel constrained in their exercise of voice (complaining) and exit (moving to another organisation). Using human services is not like going to a restaurant. If a person is unhappy with the food or the service at a restaurant, they will probably leave no tip, may well complain, and will certainly not return to that restaurant. Human service organisations are not like that, and the act of service use and the identity of the service user is quite different from that of what is known as the 'sovereign consumer'. That identity is one that applies to all of us when we engage in consumption for most goods and services—for example, in the retail sector.

To understand the difference, think about organisations that provide emergency relief (cash payments made by funded human service organisations to people suffering from extreme financial stress). In these instances, the desperation of service users is so great that they will be unlikely to complain about how a worker treats them. Indeed, in many instances in the past, emergency relief recipients had to agree that the money would not be spent on certain items (such as cigarettes or cakes) or were given emergency relief vouchers to present at the supermarket checkout. These vouchers clearly marked them out in public contexts as poor and as human service users, an experience many found unnecessarily humiliating. Victorian researchers Frederick and Goddard (2008) recently described the experiences of people receiving emergency relief. While acknowledging that people often have good experiences, this is clearly not always the case. Read, for example, the experience of 'Jim':

> *Some of the women who work there, I know they are only just helping out, but they stick their noses in. It's really none of their business. They shouldn't stick their noses in, because it's embarrassing to go. One of them said to me once, 'This isn't a supermarket you know'. You're feeling bad enough as it is, you don't need that.* (2008: 276)

For many users of human service organisations, it is hard enough to merely make an inquiry, much less make a complaint. How the organisation treats people in the first instance is very important. Most of the time, people are happy if they are treated courteously, respectfully and professionally, and are listened to and not judged. Because of this, the front line is very important in managing service users' response to staff and organisational practices. Being responsive at this level can effectively respond to 8 per cent of complaints service users might make. So a very important problem faces front-line workers (and as the example above indicates, volunteers): what should a person do when they become aware of inappropriate or less than professional behaviour from colleagues?

Case study: Unprofessional behaviour

Susan is a social work student on placement in an inner city Centrelink office. When near the front counter, Susan overheard a customer service officer being rude and dismissive to an elderly woman whose English is rather unclear. It was also unclear what the woman wanted from the organisation. The customer service officer raised her voice and spoke very loudly to the woman. The woman looked quite frightened, plainly did not know how to put her case more clearly and evidently did not understand what the officer was saying.

Discussion questions

- What is likely to be Susan's immediate response to this?
- What should Susan do in this circumstance?
- What should Susan's social work supervisor do?

To date, our comments have largely been confined to instances where an organisation's or a worker's practices have induced (or had the potential to induce) a complaint. There are other more serious instances that can confront workers either in their own organisation or in another. Here we are referring to ethical breaches where someone behaves in such a way as to contravene an endorsed code of ethics. The complex issues surrounding ethical practices are discussed in considerable depth in Chapter 12. Here, our discussion is limited to the situations where a complaint is made as well as some steps individual workers can take to minimise the possibility of exploitative *dual relationships*.

The Australian Association of Social Workers has a code of ethics (AASW, 2002). While that code of ethics covers a range of issues, the excerpt below contains the entry for professional integrity.

Professional integrity

a) *Social workers will carry out professional duties with integrity, refraining from any behavior which contravenes professional principles and standards or which damages the profession's integrity.*

b) *Social workers will represent their professional qualifications, competence, experience, achievements and affiliations with honesty and accuracy.*

c) *Social workers' private conduct will not compromise the fulfillment of professional responsibilities.*

d) *When making public statements or performing public actions social workers will clarify whether they are acting as private individuals, or as representatives of the social work profession, an organisation or group. When representing the profession or an organisation, social workers will correctly reflect policies, procedures and services and distinguish between personal and official views or positions.*

e) *Social workers will ensure that professional relationships are not exploited to gain personal, material or financial advantage.*

f) *Social workers will avoid any form of physical contact which may violate professional boundaries, result in unintentional psychological harm, or damage the professional relationship. Social workers will remain sensitive to the variety of ways in which service users and others may interpret physical contact, with particular reference to cultural and gender differences.*

g) *Recognising that conflicts of interest can arise from engaging in dual or multiple relationships with service users, former service users, research participants, students, supervisees or colleagues, social workers will set and enforce explicit, appropriate professional boundaries to minimise the risk of conflict, exploitation or harm. (Practitioners are called upon to defend their behaviour in the event of complaint or investigation regarding professional misconduct.)*

h) *Social workers will not engage in any form of sexual conduct with service users, students, supervisees, research participants or others directly involved in a professional relationship which invites trust and confidence in the practitioner's role and/or involves an unequal distribution of power or authority in the social worker's favour.*

i) *Where the potential for exploitation or harm exists, social workers will not enter into an intimate or sexual relationship with a former service user. In circumstances where any such relationship is considered, professional consultation is essential.*

Of these factors that erode professional integrity and about which a complaint could be made, one of the most common is what is known as dual or multiple relationships. Dual relationships occur when a worker engages with service users (or in some instances, colleagues) in more than one relationship. These are considered unethical if they have the capacity to be exploitative. Reamer (2003: 124) outlines in Table 11.1 what he calls the central themes in dual relationships.

Table 11.1: Central themes in dual relationships

Type	Example
Intimate relationships	Sexual relationships Physical contact Services to former lover Intimate gestures
Personal benefits	Monetary gain Goods and services Useful information
Emotional and dependency needs	Extending relationships with service users Promoting service user dependency Confusing personal and professional lives Reversing roles with service users
Altruistic gestures	Performing favours Providing non-professional services Giving gifts Being extraordinarily available
Unanticipated circumstances	Social and community events Joint affiliations and memberships Mutual acquaintances and friends

Reamer (2003: 130) again suggests that workers should develop personal 'risk-management' protocols in regard to their own activity. These are:

- Be alert to potential or actual conflicts of interest.
- Inform service users, colleagues and supervisors about potential or actual conflicts of interest and explore reasonable remedies.

- Consult colleagues and supervisors, and any relevant professional literature, regulations, policies and ethical standards to identify pertinent boundary issues and constructive options.
- Design a plan of action that addresses the boundary issues and protects the parties involved to the greatest extent possible.
- Document all discussions, consultation, supervision and other steps taken to address boundary issues.
- Develop a strategy to monitor implementation of any action plan.

Naturally, adopting protocols such as these is as much a function of an organisational culture as it is a professional imperative. For that reason, organisations themselves need to take the issue of promoting ethical organisational conduct very seriously. Chapter 12 outlines strategies for promoting an ethical organisational environment overall, including the development and operation of clearly defined organisational standards regarding dual relationships and written, operationally defined procedures. While being aware of one's own conduct, unfortunately—as indicated above—there will be occasions when workers observe dual relationships (or other questionable issues) operating between a fellow worker and a service user. What should an individual worker do when confronted with evidence of a dual relationship?

This is a difficult issue because the temptation is to do nothing because of concerns about the possible unpleasantness and conflict that might ensue. This is no small matter. Nobody likes to have a complaint lodged about them, and inevitably, no matter how effective an organisation's complaints-management system is, emotions will run high and feelings will be very fragile. Assuming that the organisation has a formal process for handling ethical breaches, it is clearly the responsibility of a worker to indicate his or her concerns to the nominated person. While it is not strictly necessary in any legal or ethical sense, it is morally appropriate to talk to the person concerned and tell them (a) of your concerns, and (b) of the steps you intend to take. This takes moral courage. In some instances,

Case study: Dual relationships

Janet is the recreation officer in a daycare centre for elderly people and people with disabilities. This is a non-profit agency run by a local community-based management committee whose members mainly consist of local business people and two ministers of religion. The centre receives funds from the government, but like all such agencies is forced due to funding limitations to hire some staff with no professional qualifications in some roles. These staff are supervised by three professionally educated staff—a social worker (and manager), Janet the recreation officer, and a nurse. It is the practice of the centre to take small groups of service users away on weekend trips to the beach. Usually, these trips are staffed by a driver, several of the untrained staff and one professional staff member. On the last trip, the professional rostered on—the nurse—became ill at literally the last moment and there was no one else available to accompany the party. The manager decided to let the trip go ahead as everyone was packed and ready, actually sitting in the bus and the accommodation had already been paid for. Several weeks after the trip, Janet became aware of a serious issue when she accidently viewed a visual recording left on the centre's video camera. The recording showed scenes of a female worker and the driver in swimming costumes mucking about in a spa bath with several of the centre's disabled service users. The film also revealed several cans of beer on a table next to the spa. The scene appeared to be one of a party. The workers were touching the service users in what could be interpreted as sexually suggestive ways.

Discussion questions
- What should be the first thing Janet does?
- What should the organisation do to investigate the issue?
- What is the likely outcome for the staff members involved?
- What is the likely outcome for the organisation's manager?
- What should the organisation do with regard to the service users?
- What should the organisation do to ensure that such an occurrence does not happen again?

it might be appropriate to talk the whole process through with an ethical adviser or human resource management-appointed employee assistance adviser. If the worker is from another organisation, then the appropriate protocol would be an organisation-to-organisation discussion between the respective chief executive officers. In both instances, the worker making the complaint should make every effort to document in full the incident or incidents that worry them, as well as their concerns about the wellbeing of any service users. If an organisation does not have any protocols for organisation-to-organisation complaints (or, for that matter, for managing ethical breaches and promoting an ethical culture), then workers should ask that these be developed in a consultative and comprehensive manner.

WHISTLEBLOWING

There is a final category of complaint which is in a class all on its own—whistleblowing. What is whistleblowing? Social work authors Greene and Latting (2004) argue that there are three criteria which consistently appear in the many definitions that exist:

1. The act involves notifying powerful others of wrongful practices in an organisation.
2. The act is motivated by the desire to prevent unnecessary harm to others.
3. The act is an action of an employee or former employee.

For an action to be regarded as full blown whistleblowing, the whistleblower would make the complaint to an external agent.

For unknown reasons, very few papers on whistleblowing and social work have been published in social work or other human service peer-reviewed journals. Because of that, we turn to other work to understand whistleblowing. Fortunately, in 2008 the Australian National University published one of the largest studies of whistleblowing in the Australian public sector (Brown, 2008), a study which is illuminating. From the more than seven thousand public servants surveyed, the following activities were considered to constitute wrongdoing and thereby were potentially the subject of whistleblowing:

- misconduct for material gain (e.g. stealing, bribes, kickbacks, rorting overtime or leave provisions)
- conflict of interest (e.g. failing to declare a financial interest, intervening in a matter pertaining to a friend or relative)
- improper or unprofessional behaviour (e.g. downloading pornography, being intoxicated or drugged, sexual assault, stalking, sexual harassment, racial discrimination, misuse of confidential information)
- defective administration (e.g. incompetent or negligent decision-making, endangering public health or safety)
- waste or mismanagement of resources (e.g. negligent purchases or leases)
- perverting justice or accountability (e.g. covering up poor performance, hindering an official investigation)
- personnel and workplace grievances (e.g. bullying, favouritism, unfair dismissal).

Greene and Latting (2004) argue convincingly that whistleblowing should be seen as part of the advocacy role of all human service professionals, particularly social workers. The AASW Code of Ethics, for example, states that:

> Social workers will address suspected or confirmed professional misconduct, incompetence, unethical behaviour or negligence by a colleague through the appropriate organisational, professional or legal channels. Social workers should familiarise themselves with the complaints processes of their workplace and with the AASW procedures for complaints against members. (AASW, 2002: 18)

Often, people believe that whistleblowers come to a sticky end in that they are subject to reprisals by the targeted organisation. Certainly there have been some very public examples, of which the mysterious death of Karen Silkwood features prominently. Unfortunately, in a review of studies of whistleblowing, Dawson (2000) found that few whistleblowers seem to have deeply considered or were even aware of the likely personal consequences of external disclosure. In a study by De Maria and Jan (1997) reported in Dawson's paper, 71 per cent of the sample stated that they had suffered official reprisals, and a telling 94 per cent had suffered unofficial reprisals. Unofficial reprisals are 'hard to investigate because the offending action is ambiguous, subtle or deniable' (De Maria and Jan, 1997: 46). Dawson suggests that the most common is workplace ostracism. Other forms of unofficial reprisal noted by Dawson include the questioning of and attacks on motives, accusations of disloyalty and dysfunctionality, public humiliation, and the denial of work necessary for promotion.

Fear of unofficial reprisals can stop people from speaking up when perhaps they should. To avoid negative reprisals, it is important that if a worker has encountered wrongdoing and is considering blowing the whistle, it be done properly. Fortunately Greene and Latting (2004) have developed guidelines for responsible whistleblowing. They suggest that it is important to assess the situation and one's own preparedness to go forward. They suggest that practitioners should ask themselves:

- Is the wrongdoing severe enough to warrant intervention?
- Is the potential benefit to the service users worth the threats to the organisation's public image?
- Is the evidence credible and sufficient?
- Am I motivated by unresolved anger from my past or present?
- Can I live with myself if I remain silent?
- Can I live with myself if I speak up?
- Am I prepared to face adverse consequences?

The following strategies may be a good way to proceed:

- *Begin first with offending colleagues.* The AASW Code of Ethics suggests that social workers thinking of whistleblowing should first talk to that colleague (or colleagues). If that does not work, more action is required.

- *Establish a track record of credibility.* This implies that it is difficult for new workers to be taken seriously. Effective whistle-blowers are respected people. This reality was well illustrated by the success of senior nurse and intensive care manager Toni Hoffman when she alerted the Queensland public to the activities of surgeon Dr Jayant Patel at Bundaberg Base Hospital in Queensland.

- *Assume others in the organisation are concerned.* Workers should make an effort to see whether their immediate supervisors and colleagues share the concerns. If so, they should attempt to solicit their collaboration.

- *Obtain corroborating evidence and supporters.* It is important to investigate thoroughly. If possible, support should be gained from anyone who has witnessed the activity in question.

- *Keep careful records.* Workers should remember that whistle-blowing often ends up in legal contexts for resolution. Careful documentation and a clear chronological record help maintain credibility.

- *Use the chain of command.* Unless the situation is an immediate emergency, workers should respect organisation's (usual) practice of preferring an internal investigation initially. Only if frustrated at all levels of the chain of command should a worker take a complaint outside of the organisation.

- *Obtain the advice of dispassionate, expert outsiders.* Advice can be sought from a range of bodies. For example, most state Ombudsmen have advisers who will consult with people. In addition, most professional bodies such as the AASW and the Australian Psychological Association (APA) have ethics committees that can also be consulted (Greene and Latting, 2004).

CONCLUSION

This chapter has provided a preliminary overview of the reasons why human service organisations should develop effective complaints mechanisms. Culminating in a discussion about whistleblowing, we considered some guidelines for developing a workable complaints mechanism as well as guidelines for responding to problems or concerns that workers may witness. In this concluding section, it is important to note that human service organisations should themselves take the development of formal complaints mechanisms very seriously. In fact, a professional organisation would monitor complaints over the years and use them to pinpoint areas or activities that need scrutiny, evaluation and perhaps reform. After all, a person complaining or a whistle-blower can often be the canary in the mineshaft, warning of potential catastrophe. While this is clearly important, the real reason for developing an effective complaints-management process is to build the professionalism of both human service organisations and human service workers in the interests of promoting service user wellbeing.

Chapter review questions

11.1 What is the intellectual reason developed by Hasenfeld (2000) for developing effective complaints mechanisms?

11.2 Why are social workers a little uneasy when it comes to discussing accountability with service users?

11.3 What are four features of a good complaints mechanism?

11.4 Why are service users often unwilling to complain?

11.5 What are dual relationships?

11.6 What are the steps a worker should take before blowing the whistle?

OTHER RESOURCES

The Victorian Ombudsman *Whistle Blowers Protection Act* 2001, <www.ombudsman.vic.gov.au/www/html/37-whistleblowers.asp>.

The New South Wales Ombudsman's handbook, *Investigating Complaints*, <www.ombo.nsw.gov.au/show.asp?id=132>. This is one of the more extensive and thorough publications available about handling complaints.

The Joint Parliamentary Ombudsman *Unreasonable Complainant Conduct: Interim Practice Manual*, <www.ombo.nsw.gov.au/show.asp?id=456>. This publication provides many 'scripts' that can be used to facilitate the handling of complaints.

Electronic copy of *Whistleblowing in the Australian Public Sector*, <http://epress.anu.edu.au/whistleblowing_citation.html>.

KEY READINGS

Greene, A.D. and Latting, J.K. 2004, 'Whistle-blowing as a Form of Advocacy: Guidelines for the Practitioner and Organisation', *Social Work,* vol. 49: 219–30.

Reamer, F.G. 2003, 'Boundary Issues in Social Work: Managing Dual Relationships', *Social Work*, vol. 48: 121–33.

Reamer, F.G. and Siegel, H.D. 1992, 'Should Social Workers Blow Their Whistles on Incompetent Colleagues?', in E. Gambrill and R. Pruger (eds), *Controversial Issues in Social Work*, Allen and Bacon, Boston, pp. 66–73.

CHAPTER TWELVE

Professional ethics and ethical reasoning

SUMMARY

In this chapter, we begin with the concept of multiple truths, an idea that is particularly useful for studying the professional ethics of human service workers. It features in case studies that illustrate dilemmas facing practitioners in diverse settings. Reference is made to how professions justify their codes of ethics. We then present an introduction to the ethical theories that impact most upon human services, followed by different models for ethical reasoning and the skills required to respond to ethical dilemmas. Key components of the professional code of ethics of three human service occupations illustrate significant commonality, which in turn supports our argument for situating professional ethics within a social justice framework and a broader global human rights paradigm.

INTRODUCTION

The notion that there are multiple truths is especially applicable to work in the human services. Lishman (1998: 90) refers to the way ethical issues arising out of tensions between individual rights, public welfare, inequality and structural oppression challenge our interpretation of rights, duties and responsibilities. Indeed, there may be no 'right answer' (Banks, 1995). The complexity of working with many different 'others' (in terms of race, class, gender and culture) in human service work highlights the significance of the notion of multiple truths. The different ways, for example, in which workers respond to certain tasks that, at face value, may present as straightforward procedural matters can lead to outcomes that may have a long-term critical impact on service users.

Working in a non-profit community-based organisation providing services and programs to refugees, can present workers with significant challenges. Service users of such organisations often seek help with their applications to the government to sponsor relatives to join them in Australia. When assisting refugees to fill out the appropriate forms, a worker will hear a 'truth' in the applicants' spontaneous responses to each question. Should a worker tell the applicants that, on the basis of the information provided, their relative will not be granted a visa if that is their opinion? Or should the worker provide all the information he or she has to people wanting to sponsor relatives to come to Australia prior to assisting with the application process? We would suggest that the latter approach is more appropriate, with the worker carefully explaining current refugee intake policy and alerting potential applicants to the criteria used to determine eligibility for a family reunion visa. Such an approach empowers potential applicants in that they can shape their applications to 'fit' policy, and in doing so maximise their chances of success.

As you read this chapter, we encourage you to refer back to this scenario, relating it to the different types of ethical reasoning and decision-making models, and reflecting upon where you would 'fit' in terms of your personal, professional and political identity.

Should the worker be completely impartial when providing refugee applicants with information? Alternatively, should the worker unashamedly promote the applicants' and their family members' human rights? Should the worker expect the service user to tell the 'truth' in answering the questions on the application form, or should the worker encourage the applicant to respond with information articulated in such a way that a more strategic alternative 'truth' is articulated? What is the correct ethical response in such situations?

WHAT IS THE MEANING OF ETHICS?

Ethics is the branch of philosophy that deals with morality, distinguishing between the good and evil, the rights and wrongs in human actions. Ethics also involves questions of duties, obligations and values. Generally, ethics presents as both a set of principles guiding human conduct and a theory or system of moral values. Professional ethics—such as legal and medical ethics—refers to the principles of conduct governing an individual, a professional or a group. Rather than thinking about ethics as a system of neatly developed and unambiguous rules, we suggest you view ethics as a form of discourse—a particular type of conversation, for example, that shapes conduct as it is undertaken (Dabby et al., 2008: 199). This approach acknowledges the significance of context and is compatible with the concept of ethics involving 'multiple truths'.

Over the past decade, several theorists have promoted the view that ethics and ethical conduct are dynamic and actively devolving through collaborative discourse. Values—for example, those embedded in human service organisational policies and practices—are openly reviewed, engaging service users and other relevant sections of the community as stakeholders in developing responses to common critical issues. Goldstein, cited in Dabby et al. (2008: 243), takes us even further away from the traditional professional approach to ethics as a fixed set of rules as reference points for action, suggesting that 'ethical and moral understanding is best learned through the experience of human relationships and its many variations'. Like artists, human service workers engage with 'clients, colleagues, environments and experiences' (2008: 243) to create our approaches to ethics.

THE ROLE OF PROFESSIONAL ETHICS

According to Skene (1996), professions generally have a code of ethics to justify self-regulation (as opposed to government regulation), to maintain standards, to secure compliance, to promote internal cohesion and to regulate entry into their profession. Professional codes of ethics generally 'attempt to outline a fair balance of interests by reducing the power difference among clients, workers, and agencies' (Weaver, 2001: 7). Ethical principles provide overall guidelines about how professionals should act.

Banks (2006) presents five main reasons why professions have their own codes of ethics:

1. to contribute to the 'professional status' of an occupation
2. to establish and maintain professional identity
3. to guide practitioners about how to act
4. to protect service users from malpractice and abuse
5. to discipline and regulate the profession.

While codes of ethics are closely associated with professionalism and professional identity, some American writers have drawn attention to difficulties in applying these to the complexity of human service practice (Chenoweth and McAuliffe, 2008: 78). It has been suggested that codes are designed more to protect professionals than to protect clients, and to deal with conflicts between professional ethics and institutional policies and practices. The following case study highlights the ethical complexities that can arise when a critical issue involves multiple parties.

In contrast to the 'macro' community issue of homelessness, the following case study portrays the ethical dilemma facing family and medical staff regarding an individual patient.

Case study: Ethical complexity

A public park with gardens near the beach in an inner urban munici-pality has been used by homeless people since the 1990s. The same three men have been taking shelter there at night for the past few months. Some local residents complain to the local council, requesting that 'the park be returned to the ratepayers'. The park residents maintain that 'we have been advised by police that it is perfectly legal for us to sleep in the area as the police told us this is a "free country"'. They have expressed concern, however, about the loss of their personal belongings, with allegations that the council workers have been stealing their sleeping bags, blankets and tent.

Councillor A to the Council CEO: 'You might remember I raised this issue a couple of weeks ago about social inclusion on the streets. I mentioned this issue as there are some very dirty mattresses, pillows and blankets left there for people to sleep overnight, with the place being used during the day for the people having a bar-beque or using the playground. It's a tough one, not sure what is the best way to handle it.'

Councillor B to the CEO: 'I hear there have been three homeless men taking shelter in the gardens overnight. I have been told that one of them may be Aboriginal. I have been told that they were last week given an "eviction" notice. I further hear that their blan-kets are being removed from behind the shelter during the day. If this is true, it may be potentially very bad publicity, and illegal. Who in the parks area and the council community services unit might know about this?'

Discussion question
- As the Council Community Services Housing Worker, what will you say at the public meeting called to address this?

ETHICAL THEORIES

Ethical theory gives us ways of articulating decisions that have a moral or value basis to them. (Chenoweth and McAuliffe, 2008: 53)

The following overview of theories influencing human ser-vice policies and people draws considerably upon Banks (1995, 2006) and Chenoweth and McAuliffe (2008). Chenoweth and

Case study: Ethics of care

An elderly female patient with Alzheimer's disease and a certain type of aggressive cancer is attending hospital to receive blood transfusions to keep her alive. Transfusions were initially every three months, then bi-monthly, then fortnightly. The patient, who is in a wheelchair, is able to walk about semi-independently for only one day after each transfusions and then becomes bedridden. The doctors are wondering about continuing the transfusions because of the inability of her body to manage the burden of disease, and with the likelihood of transfusions becoming weekly, and possibly even daily. The doctors are now saying that they can't do much more; that they can't see how increased transfusions will save her life, or improve her everyday experience of her life. The family are aware of all these facts but still want the transfusions to continue. If transfusions are stopped, their mother will die; she will also die with the transfusions but the question is when.

Discussion question

As the hospital social welfare worker, what would you say to the family, knowing that either way the outcome is that the patient will die?

McAuliffe point out that ethical theories are either consequentialist or non-consequentialist. Consequentialist theories take the possible consequences of actions into account, while non-consequentialist theorists see the consequences as irrelevant. The most commonly referred to ethical theory that is not concerned with possible consequences is *deontology*. Deontology theory considers that what is right is: determined by duty, rights or obligations; assumes that all human beings are rational; and assumes that moral rules are universal and apply across all culture and times. A deontological thinker is grounded in the belief that actions can be determined as right or wrong, good or bad, regardless of their consequences. Adherence to rules is the central imperative. Once formulated, the ethical rules should hold under all circumstances. In contrast, a teleological (or consequentialist) thinker believes in the importance of consequences (Mattison, 2000). A non-consequentialist deontology takes no account of culture or circumstances. a consequentialist teleology places importance on both.

In explaining ethical theories influencing human services practice, Banks (2006) groups them into two approaches: those that focus on principles of action and those that are character and relationship based. Included in principle-based theories are the Kantian and utilitarian approaches and the radical and anti-oppressive approaches which have emerged in human services since the 1970s.

The Kantian core principle stipulates that 'we should treat others as beings who have ends . . . not just as objects or a means to our own ends' (Banks, 2006: 29). This principle of respect for persons is integral to work in the human services. Rationality and a sense of duty (as opposed to inclination) are key factors in Kantian ethics. Utilitarianism is defined as 'the right action is that which produces the greatest balance of good over evil (the principle of utility)' (Banks, 2006: 36). Utilitarianism has played a key role in the public life of Western society, shaping the framework of the parliamentary and justice systems, political liberalism, and the 'welfare state' (Bessant, 2009).

> *Both Kantian and utilitarian theories of ethics are premised on the assumption of the human being as a freely acting individual . . . [and] . . . reflect the twin values of freedom and individualism that lie at the heart of western capitalist societies.* (Banks, 2006: 38)

From the 1970s up to the present, radical movements followed by anti-oppressive and critical approaches have emerged as a recurrent theme in the human services practice literature, promoting collective action for social change and calling for alliances across industry, church and community sectors. Jordan (with Jordan, 2000) refers to 'anti-oppressive approaches', which include anti-racist and anti-discriminatory, anti-ageist, anti-ableist, feminist and anti-heteronormative modes of practice. The 'persona is political' concept associated with the rise of these movements has had a significant impact upon the education and identity of human service workers during the decades since the 1970s. Its significance lies in the way it allowed many issues previously relegated to the private domain to be brought out into the open for redress.

Banks (2006) includes the principle of social justice in what she nominates as the principle-based approaches, which she suggests links with both utilitarian and radical approaches to ethics. Social justice is founded upon the concepts of equality, justice and 'distributive justice'. The notion of distributive justice, a principle of significant importance in modern Western ethical thinking, is especially relevant to those who are responsible for distributing public resources such as counselling, care or money. It is a complex set of ideas that attempts to provide a means for making important decisions about who gets what in societies such as Australia. Its complexity, however, is beyond the scope of this chapter to address. For those who wish to explore it further, see the link at the end of the chapter for more information.

Banks groups virtue ethics, 'the ethics of care' and 'post-modern ethics' under the character- and relationship-based approaches. Virtue ethics emphasises the role of character, with the term 'virtue' referring to traits such as courage, prudence, rationality and temperance. Virtue ethics originates from classical Greek philosophers like Socrates, Plato and Aristotle, who regarded virtue as the basis of collective justice and of a life lived well: 'A key element of virtue ethics involves understanding how we identify ourselves as a particular kind of person.' (Bessant, 2009: 429–30) It also values the particular relationships people have with each other (Banks, 2006). For this reason, virtue ethics is particularly relevant to professions in the human services, as ethical issues so often arise from 'the nature of the relationships and our responsibilities in those relations—to the client, other colleagues, our supervisors, the agency itself' (Rhodes, cited in Banks, 2006: 56)

The 'ethics of care' approach takes into account the particularity of each situation and people's relationships with each other. Chenoweth and McAuliffe (2008) point out that this approach moves beyond the focus on the individual to consider the individual in their relationships with significant others as well as their socio-political context. They suggest that ethical decisions relate to what a caring response would involve, rather than nominate what would be the universal right or correct response.

Although generally associated with principle-based ethics or the 'ethics of justice', rights-based approaches to ethics have also been developed independently of ethical theories based on foundational principles (Banks, 2006). Other theories referred to by Chenoweth and McAuliffe (2008) include the:

> *protection of civil, human, legal and politics status of individuals through a social contract (contractarianism); and the viewing of individuality as part of a community (communitarianism). Contractarianism . . . focuses on social order and the agreements that people have with each other about how they should be governed in relation to principles of justice and fairness. Communitarianism . . . requires us to look more closely at social context.* (2008: 55)

ETHICAL REASONING

To date, we have used the term 'ethical issues' fairly generally. Banks (2006), however, refers to the need to distinguish between ethical issues, ethical problems and ethical dilemmas.

Ethical issues

These frequently arise in the context of state welfare systems where the professional has decision-making power (on behalf of the state) in their relationship with the service user. Banks (2006) identifies four main types of ethical issue that frequently face workers in human services, and that may become ethical problems and dilemmas. These are:

- *Individual rights and welfare.* The service user's right to choice in decision-making; the worker's responsibility to promote the welfare of the service user
- *Public welfare.* The rights and interests of parties other than the service user

- *Equality, difference and structural oppression.* Balancing equal access and opportunities with the responsibility to work for changes in policy and society for those especially disadvantaged—due, for example, to culture, age or residence (i.e. those living in rural, remote or isolated places)
- *Professional roles, boundaries and relationships.* Adapting according to the nature of the position and context (e.g. a case manager in a bureaucracy or a community worker with a neighbourhood centre residing in an urban or rural area).

Ethical problems

This refers to different moral decisions for which the right course of action is clear. Such is the situation when a worker becomes aware of unethical practice in his or her workplace and feels obliged to expose this—an act sometimes referred to as 'whistleblowing' (see Chapter 11). How this is approached will depend upon whether the situation arises from the unethical behaviour of another individual (for example, a counsellor overstepping the professional relationship boundaries with a service user) or an issue that may impact (directly or indirectly) upon service users generally (for example, disclosure of long waiting list statistics for families 'at risk' who require speedy services).

Reamer (2001) recommends caution in addressing such scenarios. By this he is suggesting that you: assess the severity of the situation; examine the quality of evidence available to verify the ethical abuse; weigh up the likely effect of exposure on all parties and organisation/s involved; and reflect upon your motivation for taking up the matter. What is the viability of achieving the long-term outcome by alternative means?

In contrast we are sometimes faced with situations that are unethical but for which there is no professional or legal mantle to draw upon. An ABC *Four Corners* television program (5 April 2010) exposed the damage experienced by several individuals and families participating over a number of years in week-long 'therapy' programs provided in a rural retreat in Australia by an unqualified counsellor. The professional counsellors interviewed on *Four Corners* expressed concern about the abuse of ethics that was occurring, but were unable to take action owing to lack of relevant professional registration or government legislation.

Ethical dilemmas

Ethical dilemmas are those where the worker is faced with 'a choice between two equally unwelcome alternatives, which may involve a conflict of moral values, and it is not clear which choice would be the right one' (Banks, 2006: 12). Our view, expressed in the introduction to this chapter, is that often there is no 'right' decision. Banks refers to the complexities associated with ethical decision-making in human services when each person involved in the situation sees it differently according to their knowledge, experience and values. This is illustrated in the Multiple truths case study about Martha, a service user with a regional care network.

Ethical dilemmas may often arise from competing values and loyalties. As indicated in the Martha scenario, the principle of self-determination can conflict with how the case manager interprets a duty of care. Competing interests may emerge from different members of a group with which you are working, or there may be conflict between welfare for the individual and the service needs of the majority.

Chenoweth and McAuliffe (2008) present models for ethical reasoning in three different ways: a process model, reflective models and the inclusive model. A useful ***process model*** is the ETHIC model of decision-making (developed by Congress, 1999), whereby the following steps/checklist will facilitate a 'reasoned decision'.

1. **Examine** relevant personal, societal, agency, client and professional values.
2. **Think** about what ethical standard of the relevant mode of ethics applies to the situation, as well as about relevant laws and case decisions.
3. **Hypothesise** about possible consequences of different decisions.

4. **Identify** who will benefit and who will be harmed in view of social work's commitment to the most vulnerable.

5. **Consult** with supervisor and colleagues about the most ethical choice.

Case study: Multiple truths

Martha, a woman in her eighties, has been assessed as being in the 'high-care' need category. Although she is separated from her partner, he plays an important caring role. She is still very mentally alert and self-determined, maintaining as much control as possible over her situation—in other words, as expressed by her case manager at the carer coordination agency, 'she directs everything'. This involves determining how her 'package money' ($500 per week) is to be spent. Certain types of naturopathy are included in services negotiated to date, as well as her request for kinesiology—'so the agency has to pay for this'. Although Martha's need for care is increasing, she rejects admission to a nursing home. An important part of her day is meditation between noon and 2.00 p.m. She does not approve carers visiting her during these hours.

Tension has arisen between the carers employed to attend to Martha at home (twice daily, seven days a week), their employing agency, the case manager and Martha about each of their views in relation to:

- how Martha is allocating her 'package money'
- flexibility of access hours for carers visiting Martha in relation to visits required to other service users
- her attitude towards future care/accommodation.

Discussion question

- What would be your plan of action as the case manager working with Martha?

REFLECTIVE MODELS

These are based on feminist perspectives, with emphasis on service user empowerment through a meaningful relationship with the worker, active engagement in addressing the issue and inclusion in the decision-making process. Within the reflective models are emerging alternative models that promote collectivist cultures and group solidarity in contrast to those of our Western individualist culture. Approaches such as these raise tension for human service workers, who are often constrained by the organisational culture to which they are accountable, themselves often informed by an individualised model of Christianity. Banks points out, for example, that the International Statement of Social Work Principles tend to be based on 'Judeo-Christian and humanistic traditions', which reflect the individual as the fundamental unit in society (Chenoweth and McAuliffe, 2008: 28).

The *inclusive model* integrates key components of the above with accountability, critical reflection, cultural sensitivity and consultation—the four dimensions Chenoweth and McAuliffe (2008) consider critical to sound ethical reasoning. Using a spiral approach, each step involves 'asking questions, finding out information, assessing alternative actions, implementing action and evaluating outcomes' (2008: 100).

Reamer's (1999) ethical decision-making framework (below) is based upon a set of guidelines consistent with the overall values of human service occupations, to help workers identify the nature of ethical dilemmas and critically reflect upon how to resolve them.

- Rules against basic harm to an individual's survival take precedence over rules against harms such as lying or revealing confidential information or threats to additive goods.
- An individual's right to self-determination takes precedence over his or her right to basic wellbeing.
- The obligation to obey laws, rules and regulations to which one has voluntarily and freely consented ordinarily overrides one's right to engage voluntarily and freely in a manner that conflicts with these.
- Individual's rights to wellbeing may override laws, rules, regulations and arrangements of voluntary association in cases of conflict.
- The obligation to prevent basic harms and to promote public goods such as housing, education and public assistance overrides the right to complete control over one's property.

Steps recommended by Reamer (1999) to make decisions about ethical dilemmas are:

1. Identify the ethical issues, including the professional values and duties that conflict.
2. Identify the individuals, groups and organisations likely to be affected by the ethical decision.
3. Tentatively identify all viable courses of action and the participants involved in each, along with the potential benefits and risks for each.
4. Thoroughly examine the reasons in favour of and opposed to each course of action, considering relevant
    *   ethical theories, principles and guidelines
    *   codes of ethics and legal principles
    *   professional practice theory and principles
    *   personal values (including religious, cultural, and ethnic values and political ideology), particularly those that conflict with one's own.
5. Consult with colleagues and appropriate experts (such as agency staff, supervisors, agency administrators, attorneys, ethics scholars).
6. Make the decision and document the decision-making process.
7. Monitor, evaluate and document the decision. (1999: 76–7)

Previous case studies have highlighted dilemmas that we have left open for resolution. The following Ethical dilemma case study about a hospital social worker includes the outcome of the situation after following Reamer's first four steps.

In the case study, Laura followed steps one to four suggested by Reamer. However, the nature of this dilemma necessitated discrete consultation (step 5) prior to decision-making. Documentation referred to in steps 6 and 7 regarding the entitlement to payments following the motor accident was not appropriate in these circumstances.

Case study: Ethical dilemma

Laura is a social worker in the Intensive Care Unit (ICU) of a large public hospital where ethical dilemmas frequently arise when compassion for service users conflicts with institutional regulations. She engages with the family of a man admitted with brain injuries who is deemed non-survivable after involvement in a single-car motor vehicle accident. The man, self-employed, was supporting his wife Melissa (32) and two sons aged 7 and 9. Overcome by grief, Melissa is further stressed about potential loss of their house and way of life. As this was a car accident and he was not over the limit in terms of drugs or alcohol, Laura assisted Melissa in dealing with the formal motor accident insurance system to help out with some of the immediate anxieties. In the course of the conversation, Melissa tells Laura that she thinks it was suicide. She has not spoken of this fear to anyone, as she feels it would devastate his parents (whom Laura has also met and who are understandably shattered), and would have a terrible impact on his sons and his friends.

Melissa tells Laura that for the past two months he has been talking about killing himself, telling her that she and the boys would be better off without him, telling her that he 'had to go' as a way of keeping her safe. Melissa says that she would try to joke these conversations off, but on the night before his accident, he was talking very much like this. On the day of the accident, she said he woke happy and told her he had everything figured out and she need not worry anymore. He took the lunch she had packed for him and headed out the door as usual. He did not drive towards work, but instead headed out to the country— where after two hours of driving, he ran into a tree.

Laura knows that if this is suicide, Melissa and her sons will not be eligible for any insurance claim. Laura also has considerable empathy for Melissa and her sons, and knows that the accident claim payment will assist in helping them financially through this difficult time. Laura also knows that suicide makes for a very complicated grief, and Melissa feels her sons and family don't need to know this.

Discussion questions

- What would you do if you were the social worker?
- What did Laura do?

Laura talked this through with Melissa. She had not recorded Melissa's interpretation of her husband's death. Together they agreed that there had been no discussion about this factor. Laura focused on helping Melissa cope with her grief and reducing the financial impact of her husband's death upon loved ones, aware that no other individuals would be harmed by this approach.

INDIVIDUALIST AND COLLECTIVIST MORAL REASONING

Jordan (with Jordan, 2000) maintains that current political morality in Western society is attempting to combine two different modes of ethical reasoning—the liberal individualist and the egalitarian collectivist traditions. In social policy, the collectivist approach suggests that services are provided as a basic right to all citizens. The individualist approach involves provision according to membership or entitlement, determined on what the person merits or deserves. Individualism favours institutions that promote individual responsibility, with individuals being accountable for the outcomes of their decision and choices. Collectivism, on the other hand, favours institutions that promote care, mutuality, solidarity and interdependency, facilitating support and cooperation (Jordan with Jordan, 2000: 43).

SERVICE USER/COMMUNITY INVOLVEMENT

Briskman and Noble (1999) refer to the fact that users increasingly are demanding that their services be delivered in terms of their own values, not those of the professionals (as portrayed by the case study of Martha developed above). Agencies are becoming obliged to frame codes of ethics specific to their clientele. Examples of this in Australia can be found in the codes of ethics developed by sexual assault centres (CASAs), Indigenous organisations and some of the consumer-led agencies for people with disabilities. Briskman and Noble suggest the use of a community development model whereby service users are able to meet together and define the nature of the service required, as well as appropriate ways of providing this. At the individual level, Dabby et al. (2008) argue that if a moral dilemma involves the worker's interface with the service user, the service user should be engaged in the perception, construction and resolution of the dilemma facing the worker.

RURAL CULTURES

Ginsberg's (2005) study of workers in rural communities, cited in Dabby et al. (2008) found that 'dual relationships' may be inevitable in a rural context. Dual relationships occur when a worker has more than one relationship with a service user. For example, a dual relationship would exist when a worker in a small town was also a member of the local council. In this situation, the worker might be called on to make decisions in one arena that could countermand decisions made in the other. In the special circumstances found in small communities, individualistic 'clinical' approaches to professional ethics and professional boundaries are not necessarily appropriate to community practices. In a small community, where communal relationships matter, rigidly defined professional role boundaries will constantly be challenged.

MULTICULTURAL COMMUNITIES

Similar to the types of rural contexts discussed above, when working with small culturally and linguistically diverse community organisations, the professional term we assign to the 'other' (for example, patient, client, customer, service user, consumer, community member, local citizen) will impact on our relationship with them, and our response to certain cultural acts that may present as ethical issues.

> *Receiving gifts ranging from a dozen spring rolls to four new car tyres in acknowledgement of assistance provided, being requested to name the new-born child of a young couple with whom I had had close and significant contact for several months. What should the professional's response be, given*

the interplay of two different value systems; that is, white Anglo-Social Work values embodying a commitment to independence, separation of the private from the public, and demarcation; and the Cambodian system embodying hospitality and reciprocity? [this] . . . reminded me constantly of the importance of acknowledging the values of the other. I had to learn to receive as well as give. I had to be prepared to challenge the values which informed my practice. (Fook et al., 2000: 149)

ORGANISATIONAL CULTURES

In contrast to professional ethics, Sinclair (1996) draws attention to the fact that mechanisms to enforce the enactment of organisational ethics are swift and powerful, whereas the procedures required in addressing breaches of professional codes are prolonged and cumbersome. Moreover, conflicts may arise amongst different professional codes and organisational codes when organisations comprise several different groups of professionals:

For example, a consulting organisation may contain groups of engineers, architects and social workers or planners. On any one project the various professional codes and the organisational code might suggest different norms of disclosure of information to the client. A matter regarded by social workers as an essential subject for client consultation might be regarded by partners as a managerial decision within the overall terms of the contract and by the engineers as a professional practice requiring reference to a professional body. (Sinclair, 1996: 91)

SKILLS REQUIRED FOR ETHICAL DECISION-MAKING

Critical factors in the ability to engage meaningfully in ethical discussions and decision-making are: first, knowledge about your professional code of ethics; second, familiarity with your organisations code of ethics or guidelines; third, frameworks to help clarify conflicting values and ethical dilemmas; and finally, awareness of your own personal values through critical reflection.

Cleak and Wilson (2007) provide a useful framework for

analysing ethical dilemmas. Below is an adapted version of the text that aims at helping students in *Making the Most of Field Placements*.

1. Define the ethical issue/problem/dilemma.
2. Gather all relevant information, then analyse the situation through discussing it with peers, team members and people with previous experience in this matter who may be aware of precedents. Consider the perspectives of all parties involved.
3. Identify broad ethical principles that could guide action.
4. Refer to your profession's code of ethics, the agency's code of conduct for guidance and any relevant rights-related bodies (for example, Guardianship Advocacy Board, Legal Aid).
5. Explore the situation of the service user/s involved; where appropriate, engage them in dialogue to reflect on different perspectives.
6. Define your options. After discussion with your supervisor/manager, arrive at a resolution. In reflecting on the ethical basis of your practice, it is important to remain open to other options and possible outcomes.

HUMAN RIGHTS: TOWARDS RIGHTS-BASED PRACTICE

In his contribution to a volume devoted to global ethics in the new century, Jones (2001) refers to human rights and the principle of national self-determination as the two global norms that are most widely recognised in our world. So where does our obligation to professional ethics fit in relation to human rights? In referring to alternatives to the conventional framing of professional ethics that many workers are seeking, Ife (2001) believes that the human rights paradigm is a viable alternative. Ife views rights and ethics as complementary to each other, but with important differences. He sees less worker-imposed control function attached to the discourse of rights. The assumption is that we follow a rights perspective 'as a result of moral suasion rather than fear of sanctions' (Ife, 2001: 104).

Ife also argues that professional ethics are essentially individualist in their orientation—as an individual professional engages in individual decisions. This is reflected in the International Federation of Social Workers' statement of ethical principles, which:

> *aims to encourage social workers across the world to reflect on the challenges and dilemmas that face them and make ethically informed decisions about how to act in each particular case* (IFSW, 2004: i).

It acknowledges that 'social workers are often in the middle of conflicting interests and may function 'as both helpers and controllers' (IFSW, 2004: 1).

McDonald (2006) promotes a human-rights based practice as the way forward for human services in the twenty-first century. Reasons for this relate to it providing:

- 'an unambiguous and inspiring morality and politics' for workers operating in a withering welfare state
- a framework for conceptual links across the private–public sectors, facilitating constructive public engagement with the expanding private sector
- internationally acknowledged documents for reference in the form of the Universal Declaration of Human Rights, the International Covenant on Civil and Political Rights and the International Covenant on Economic, Social and Cultural Rights (2006: 177).

CODES OF ETHICS FOR HUMAN SERVICES

In Australia, the social and community services industry auspices a diversity of occupations and positions in human services. Major professions in this sector for which there are accredited higher education/tertiary programs and specific industry awards are social work, welfare work, youth work and community work. Here we list the overall aims of each group as stated in the codes of ethics developed by their professional associations, looking particularly at commonalities across the different professional codes. As formal government registration has not been obtained by any of these occupations, membership of the professional associations is voluntary, as is adherence to their codes of ethics.

Social work: International federation

The Australian Association of Social Workers (AASW), a national body, is a member of the International Federation of Social Workers (IFSW). The IFSW outlines twelve general areas of professional conduct for inclusion in the codes of ethics of member countries. Listed below (in a more succinct manner than in the original) these stipulate that social workers:

- are expected to develop and maintain the required skills and competence
- should not use their skills for inhumane purposes such as torture or terrorism
- should act with integrity
- should act with compassion, empathy and care to service users
- should not subordinate the needs or interests of service users to their own needs or interests
- have a duty of self-care, personally and professionally, to ensure provision of appropriate services
- should maintain confidentiality, an exception relating to a greater ethical requirement (e.g. preservation of life)
- are accountable for their actions to service users, colleagues, employers, professional associations and the law, and that these accountabilities may conflict
- should collaborate with schools of social work to support high-quality student field education
- should foster and engage in ethical debate with colleagues and employers, taking responsibility for ethically informed decisions
- should be prepared to justify their decisions and be accountable for the outcomes
- should work to create conditions with employers and nationally

whereby the IFSW principles and national code of ethics are maintained, evaluated and upheld. (adapted from IFSW, 2004c)

Australian Association of Social Workers

The purpose of the AASW Code of Ethics is to:

- identify the values and principles that underpin ethical practice
- provide guidance and standards for ethical conduct and accountable service
- provide a foundation for ethical reflection and decision-making
- guide social workers in determining the demands they may legitimately make on their employers, colleagues and the AASW
- clarify social workers' actions in industrial or legal disputes
- act as basis for investigation and adjudication of formal complaints about unethical conduct.

Key components of the AASW Code of Ethics are:

- *human dignity and worth*—demonstrate respect for clients, and seek to promote their dignity, individuality, rights, cultural affiliations, and their participation in the decision-making process
- *social justice*—promoting policies, practices and social conditions that uphold access, equity, participation; acting without prejudice; aiming to empower individuals, families, groups and communities; promoting public participation
- *service to humanity*—including 'duty of care' and facilitating access to resources, services and rights, including undertaking advocacy
- *integrity*—taking care of the profession, truthfully representing your qualifications, ensuring that professional policies and procedures are upheld (not personal views or policies) and recognising conflicts of interest if they arise

- *competence*—as a worker, expanding levels of knowledge, theory and skill, utilising an appropriate supervisor or appropriate forms of supervision.

From the above general code of ethics are drawn guidelines linking ethics and values to responsibilities to significant others in different contexts. These are one's responsibilities to clients, responsibilities to colleagues, responsibilities in the workplace, responsibilities in particular settings and responsibilities to the profession.

The Australian Institute of Welfare and Community Workers

The Australian Institute of Welfare and Community Workers (AIWCW) is a national body comprising a range of human service workers employed in the social and community services sector. This includes welfare workers, community workers, youth workers, group workers, project officers, counsellors, case managers, residential care workers, home and community care workers, neighbourhood centre coordinators, disabilities workers and advocacy workers (Chenoweth and McAuliffe, 2008). The AIWCW's aims are to:

- promote public awareness of AIWCW aims and objectives
- promote relevant education and training of employees or potential workers in welfare and community work
- identify and document competency standards for welfare and community work
- register qualified persons and promote practice standards consistent with the AIWCW Code of Ethics
- uphold the rights and improve, protect and foster the interests of AIWCW members through liaison with appropriate industry bodies
- maintain the employment standards of the welfare and community work field
- influence social change where inconsistencies, deficiencies and injustice appear in the field

- consult with associated organisations within the industry. (AIWCW, in Chenoweth and McAuliffe, 2008: 96–7)

Chenoweth and McAuliffe point out the similarities in aims, principles and language of the AIWCW Code of Ethics and that of the AASW.

Youth work: Youth Affairs Council of Victoria

The Code of Ethical Practice for youth workers, written by the Youth Affairs Council of Victoria, is based on a human rights framework. It draws upon the UN Convention on the Rights of the Child, the Declaration of Human Rights and the Declaration on the Rights of Indigenous Peoples. The Code of Ethical Practice is based on the following principles of youth work. The code will guide youth workers to enable and ensure:

- the empowerment of young people
- young people's participation
- social justice for young people
- the safety of young people
- respect for young people's human dignity and worth
- young people's connectedness to important people in their lives, such as family and community
- positive health and wellbeing outcomes for young people
- the positive transitions and health development of young people. (Youth Affairs Council of Victoria, 2008: 9)

Below are the areas of practice responsibilities required to work ethically with young people:

- recognition of Indigenous peoples
- duty of care
- young people as the primary consideration
- boundaries

- privacy and confidentiality
- transparency, honesty and integrity
- social context
- anti-oppressive practice: non-discrimination, equity and self-awareness
- cooperation and collaboration
- knowledge, skills and self-care.

Assessing these summarised codes of ethics of social work, welfare and community work, and youth work, it is clear that the commonalities across these human service professions outweigh the differences.

CRITICAL SELF-REFLECTION: PERSONAL, PROFESSIONAL AND POLITICAL 'ME'

What are my ethical values and where do I 'fit'? These are core questions facing every human service worker. Workers have responsibilities to service users, their profession and/or their union, their employing organisation and to society more broadly (adapted from Banks, 2006: 129). Underlying these formally acknowledged duties is a worker's personal, professional and political identity. Banks identifies three 'typical models' of human service practitioner: the committed/radical; the professional; and the technical-bureaucrat. While she presents them as distinct, it is clear that workers can exhibit a mix of all three in varying balances, which in all likelihood will shift given different contexts and circumstances.

The position and context in which you choose to work differs according to whether you are committed to bringing about change beyond empowering individual service users (committed/radical model), whether you place priority on the professional image with autonomy enabling you to concentrate on the rights and interests of individual service users (professional model) or whether you feel comfortable confining your roles and duties to those prescribed by the agency (technical-bureaucratic model).

Field experience often provides a valuable opportunity to explore your identity and the workforce to discover where you fit comfortably in relation to your personal, professional and political persona. In the current 'risk'-dominated climate in Western society (most visible in the child protection arena), positions in the technical-bureaucratic context are increasing. However, other growing areas of response to social needs provide openings for alternative models. Banks (2006: 139) refers to the 'new professionalism', an approach that has elements of the technical-bureaucratic approach 'while still retaining the notion of professional expertise'. An example of this can be found in the social care case-management positions working with elderly people and with people who have disabilities. Moreover, there is a diversity of innovative outreach programs to specific isolated highly vulnerable and disadvantaged people (for example, streetwork with drug- and alcohol-dependent people or with sex workers) in our cities, as well as increasing opportunities as volunteers or project workers to learn about alternate ways of living and working in international aid/development work in other countries. All of these provide contexts where different ways of working can be explored.

CONCLUSION

This chapter has provided an introduction to the meaning of professional ethics and ethical theories that are particularly relevant to the human services. We have outlined how our ability to effectively respond to ethical issues, problems and dilemmas is dependent upon our understanding of different approaches to ethical reasoning, our knowledge of our own profession's code of ethics and our critical decision-making skills. Reflection upon your own persona will help you identify where you situate your professional ethics in the broader human rights philosophy.

We end this book with an acknowledgement that working professionally in the human services and in human service organisations is very challenging—intellectually, emotionally, morally and politically. While we have given you some pointers, we suggest that you should continue to seek knowledge about your organisational context, your service users, your practice, your beliefs, your values and your personal politics. All human service workers are engaged in a continuous process of becoming a *better* worker, committed to progressing on the journey of lifelong learning.

Chapter review questions

12.1 Why does each profession have a code of ethics?

12.2 What are the differences between ethical issues, ethical problems and ethical dilemmas?

12.3 What are the three different models for ethical reasoning referred to by Chenoweth and McAuliffe (2008)?

12.4 What steps would you follow in handling an ethical dilemma when it arises in your work with a service user?

12.5 What reasons promote human rights-based practice?

12.6 Reflecting upon your personal experience, field education and work experience, with which of the three 'typical models' of human service practice—committed radical, professional or technical bureaucratic—do you identify?

OTHER RESOURCES

AASW Code of Ethics 1999, <www.aasw.asn.au/document/item/92>.

Google Cultural Dictionary, Legal Dictionary, Medical Dictionary, Distributive Justice, <www.distributive-justice.com/mainpage_frame-e.htm>.

KEY READINGS

Banks, S. 2006, *Ethics and Values in Social Work* (3rd ed.), Palgrave Macmillan, Basingstoke.

Chenoweth, L. and McAuliffe, D. 2008, *The Road to Social Work and Human Service Practice* (2nd ed.), Cengage Learning, Melbourne.

Ife, J. 2001, *Human Rights and Social Work: Towards Rights Based Practice,* Cambridge University Press, Melbourne.

REFERENCES

Allan, J. 2009, 'Doing Critical Practice', in J. Allan, L. Briskman and B. Pease (eds), *Critical Social Work: Theories and Practices for a Socially Unjust World* (2nd ed.), Allen & Unwin, Sydney, pp. 70–87.

Allan, J., Briskman, L. and Pease, B. (eds) 2009, *Critical Social Work: Theories and Practices for a Socially Unjust World* (2nd ed.), Allen & Unwin, Sydney.

Aurelius, Marcus 2008, *The Thoughts of the Emperor [161 AD]*, available at <www.MobileReference.com>, accessed 20 March 2010.

Australian Association of Social Workers 2000, *National Practice Standards of the Australian Association of Social Workers: Supervision*, AASW, Canberra.

—— 2002, *Code of Ethics*, AASW, Canberra, available at <www.aasw.asn.au/adobe/about/AASW_Code_of_Ethics-2004.pdf>, accessed 18 November 2008.

—— 2003, *Practice Standards for Social Workers: Achieving Outcomes*. AASW, Canberra.

—— 2006, *Continuing Professional Education: Policy*, AASW, Canberra.

—— 2008, *AASW Practice Standards for Mental Health Social Workers*, AASW, Canberra.

Banks, S. 1995, *Ethics and Values in Social Work*, Macmillan, Basingstoke.

—— 2006, *Ethics and Values in Social Work* (3rd ed.), Palgrave Macmillan, Basingstoke.

Bannick, F.P. 2007, 'Solution-Focused Mediation: The Future with a Difference', *Conflict Resolution Quarterly*, vol. 25: 163–83.

Barnes, M. and Wistow, G. 1994, 'Learning to Hear Voices: Listening to Users of Mental Health Services', *Journal of Mental Health*, vol. 3: 524–41.

Barsky, A.E. 2007, *Conflict Resolution for the Helping Professions* (2nd ed.), Thomson, Belmont, CA.

Baulderstone, J. 2007, 'Accountability to Service Users: Rhetoric or Reality', *Third Sector Review*, vol. 13: 9–19.

Beddoe, L. 1997, 'A New Era for Supervision', *Social Work Now*, no. 7, August.

Beddoe, L. and Maidment, J. 2009, *Mapping Knowledge for Social Work Practice: Critical Intersections*, Cengage Learning, Melbourne.

Benjamin, M. 2008 'Creating E-mail Policies at Work', *Auto Dealer Monthly*, vol. 4, no. 12, available at <Mhtml:file://J:\email%20lit\Creating%20Email%20Policies%20At%20Work%20%20.3/04/210>.

Benner, P. 1984, *From Novice to Expert: Excellence and Power in Clinical Nursing Practice*, Addison-Wesley, Menlo Park, CA.

Berg-Weger, M. and Birkenmaier, J. 2000, *The Practicum Companion for Social Work: Integrating Class and Field Work*, Allyn and Bacon, Boston.

Bessant, J. 2009, 'Aristotle Meets Youth Work: A Case for Virtue Ethics', *Journal of Youth Studies*, vol. 12: 423–38.

Bisno, H. 1988, *Managing Conflict*, Sage, Beverly Hills, CA.

Bloom, M. and Fischer, J. 1983, *Evaluating Practice: Guidelines for the Accountable Professional*, Prentice-Hall, Englewood Cliffs, NJ.

Boyle, S., Hull, G. Jr, Mather, T., Smith, L. and Farley, O. 2006, *Direct Practice in Social Work*, Pearson Education, London.

Brake, M. and Bailey, R. 1980, *Radical Social Work and Practice*, Edward Arnold, London.

Briskman, L. and Noble, C. 1999, 'Social Work Ethics: Embracing Diversity?' in B. Pease and J. Fook, (eds), *Transforming Social Work Practice: Postmodern Critical Perspectives*, Allen & Unwin, Sydney: 57–69.

Bristow, G., Entwhistle, T., Hines, F., Martin, S., Morgan, K. and Pithouse, A. 2003, *Partnerships Between the Public, Private and Voluntary Sectors in Wales*, Cardiff University Press, Cardiff.

Brody, R. 1993, *Effectively Managing Human Service Organisations* Sage, Thousand Oaks, CA.

Bromfield, L. and Higgins, D. 2005, 'National Comparison of Child Protection Systems', *Child Abuse Prevention Issues*, no. 22, Australian Institute of Family Studies, Melbourne.

Brown, A.J. (ed.) 2008, *Whistle-blowing in the Australian Public Sector*, Australian National University Press, Canberra.

Buchanan, D. and Huczynski, A. 2004, *Organisational Behaviour: An Introductory Text* (5th ed.), Pearson Education, London.

Burton, J. and van den Broek, D. 2006, 'Information Management Systems and Human service work', in *Proceedings, Social Change in the 21st Century Conference 2006*, Queensland University of Technology, Brisbane, available at <http://eprints.qut.edu.au>, accessed 20 May 2010.

Carey, M. 2003, 'Anatomy of a Care Manager', *Work, Employment and Society*, vol. 17: 121–35.

Carrilio, T. 2005, 'Management Information Systems: Why are They Underutilized in the Social Services?' *Administration in Social Work*, vol. 29, no. 2: 43–61.

Chenoweth, L. and McAuliffe, D. 2008, *The Road to Social Work and Human Service Practice* (2nd ed.), Cengage Learning, Melbourne.

Clare, M. 2001, 'Operationalising Professional Supervision in this Age of Accountabilities', *Australian Social Work*, vol. 54: 269–79.

Clarke, J. and Glendinning, C. 2002, 'Partnership and the Remaking of Welfare Governance', in C. Glendinning, M. Powell and L. Rummery (eds), *Partnership, New Labour and the Governance of Welfare*, Policy Press, Bristol: 15–40.

Cleak, H. 2009, *Assessment and Report Writing in Human Services*, Cengage Learning, Melbourne.

Cleak, H. and Wilson, J. 2007, *Making the Most of Field Placement*, Thomson, Melbourne.

Cog's Ladder of Group Development, available at <www.loris.net/ndindex/Cogs.html>, accessed 10 May 2010.

Condliffe, P. 1987, 'Conflict Management', in K.G. Vallence and T. McWilliam (eds), *Communication That Works*, Nelson Wadsworth, Melbourne: 120–39.

—— 2002, *Conflict Management: A Practical Guide*, LexisNexis Butterworths, Sydney.

Congress, E. 1999, *Social Work Values and Ethics: Identifying and Resolving Professional Dilemmas*, Wordsworth, Belmont, CA.

Costello, S. 2007, Notes on Case Recording, unpublished teaching materials, RMIT University, Melbourne.

—— 2009, 'Reconstructing Social Work Practices with Families', in J. Allan, L. Briskman and B. Pease (eds), *Critical Social Work: Theories and Practices for a Socially Unjust World* (2nd ed.), Allen & Unwin, Sydney: 180–208.

Coulshed, V. and Mullender, A. 2001, *Management in Social Work*, Palgrave, Houndsmills.

Creyton, M. McGarricle, S. and Olive, D. (n.d.), *Working with Volunteers: A Human Centred Approach*, Volunteering Queensland, available from <www.volunteeringqueensland.org.au/forms/BookChapter1.pdf>, accessed 10 May 2010.

Cumming, S., Fitzpatrick, E., McAuliffe, D., McKain, S., Martin, C. and Tonge, A. 2007, 'Raising the *Titanic*: Rescuing Social Work Documentation from the Sea of Ethical Risk', *Australian Social Work*, vol. 60: 239–57.

Dabby, M., Holliman, D., Karliner, S., Pearl, D. and Silverman, B. 2008. 'Ethics as Activity: Building Collaborative, Expansive and Just Social Work', *Journal of Social Work Values and Ethics*, vol. 5: 22–35.

Darlington, Y., Feeney, J.A. and Rixon, K. 2004, 'Complexity, Conflict and Uncertainty: Issues in Collaboration in Child Protection and Mental Health Services', *Children and Youth Services Review*, vol. 26: 1175–92.

Davis, I. and Reid, W. 1983, 'Event Analysis in Clinical Practice and Process Research', *Social Casework*, no. 69: 298–306.

Dawson, S. 2000, *Whistle Blowing: A Definition and Some Broad Issues for Australia*, Working Paper No. 3/2000, Victoria University of Technology, available from <www.uow.edu.au/~bmartin/dissent/documents/Dawson. html>

D'Cruz, H., Gillingham, P. and Melendez, S. 2007, 'Reflexivity: A Concept and Its Meanings for Practitioners Working with Children and Families', *Critical Social Work*, vol. 8, available from <http://uwindsor.ca/criticalsocialwork/reflexivity-a-concept-and-its-meanings-for-practitioners-working-with-children-and-families>, accessed 10 May 2010.

Dearman, P. 2005, 'Computerised Social Casework Recording: Autonomy and Control in Australia's Income Support Agency', *Labor Studies Journal*, vol. 30: 47–65.

Department of Education, Employment and Workplace Relations 2009, *Australian Labour Market Update*, available from <www.workplace.gov.au/NR/rdonlyres/D6914740-DE0B-44FB-AFE7-364037CC0820/0/ALMUOcto-ber2009.pdf>, accessed 10 May 2010.

Department of Health and Ageing 2006, *The Kit: A Guide to the Advocacy We Do: Submission Writing*, available from <www.health.gov.au/

internet/main/publishing.nsf/Content/mental-pubs-k-kit-toc-mental-pubsk-kit-ski-mental-pubs-k-kit-ski-3-mental-pubs-k-kit-ski-3-6-mental-pubs-k-kit-ski-3-6-wri>, accessed 10 May 2010.

De Janasz, S.C., Dowd, K.O. and Schneider, B.Z. 2006, *Interpersonal Skills in Organisations*, McGraw Hill, New York.

De Maria, W. and Jan, C. 1997. 'Eating Its Own: The Whistleblower's Organization in Vendetta Mode', *Australian Journal of Social Issues*, vol. 32: 37–59.

Dickey, B. 1987, *No Charity There: A Short History of Social Welfare in Australia*, Allen & Unwin, Sydney.

Donovan, F. and Jackson, A. 1991 *Managing Human Service Organisations*, Prentice Hall, Englewood Cliffs, NJ.

Early Childhood Research Institute 1995, *Building Bridges: Lessons Learned in Inter-professional Collaboration*, available from <http://clas.uiuc.edu/fulltext/cl00910/cl00910.html>.

Elpers, K. and Westhuis, D.J. 2008, 'Organisational Leadership and Its Impact on Social Workers' Job Satisfaction: A National Study', *Administration in Social Work*, vol. 32: 26–43.

Fanon, F. 1967, *The Wretched of the Earth,* Penguin, Harmondsworth.

Faulkner, J. 2009, *Freedom of Information: Companion Guide*, available from <www.dpmc.gov.au/consultation/FreedomofInformation_reform/docs/Companion_Guide.pdf>, accessed 10 May 2010.

Fishal, C. 2008, *The Book of the Board: Effective Governance for Nonprofits*, Federation Press, Sydney.

Flanagan, J. 1954, The Critical Incident Technique', *Psychology Bulletin*, vol. 51: 327–58.

Fook, J. 1993, *Radical Casework: A Theory of Practice*, Allen & Unwin, Sydney.

—— 1996, *The Reflective Researcher: Social Workers' Theories of Practice Research*, Allen & Unwin, Sydney.

Fook, J., Ryan, M. and Hawkins, L. 2000, *Professional Expertise: Practice, Theory and Education for Working in Uncertainty*, Whiting and Birch, London.

Ford, K. and Jones, A. 1987, *Student Supervision*, Macmillan, London.

Fox, R. and Gutheil, I. 2000, 'Process Recording: A Means for Conceptualising and Evaluating Practice', *Journal of Teaching in Social Work*, vol. 20: 39–55.

Frederick, J. and Goddard, C. 2008, 'Sweet and Sour Charity: Experiences of Receiving Emergency Relief in Australia', *Australian Social Work*, vol. 61: 269–84.

Freire, P. 1996 [1970], *Pedagogy of the Oppressed*, Penguin, London.

Gambrill, E. 2003, 'Evidence-Based Practice: Sea Change or the Emperor's New Clothes?' *Journal of Social Work Education*, vol. 39: 3–23.

Gambrill, E. and Pruger, R. (eds), *Controversial Issues in Social Work*, Allen and Bacon, Boston, pp. 66–73.

Gardner, F. 2006, *Working with Human Service Organisations*, Oxford University Press, Melbourne.

Giddens, A. 1991, *Modernity and Self Identity: Self and Society in the Late Modern Age,* Stanford University Press, Stanford, CA.

Giesen, G. n.d., *Organisational Conflict: What You Need to Know*, available from <www.greggiesenassociates.com/pdf/ORGANISATIONAL_CONFLICT.pdf>, accessed 5 January 2009.

Ginsberg, L.H. 2001, *Social Work Evaluation: Principles and Methods*, Allyn and Bacon, Boston.

Gonzi, A., Hager, P. and Anasthasou, J. 1993, *The Development of Competency-based Assessment Strategies for the Professions*, Australian Government Publishing Service, Canberra.

Greene, A.D. and Latting, J.K. 2004, 'Whistle-blowing as a Form of Advocacy: Guidelines for the Practitioner and Organisation', *Social Work*, vol. 49: 219–30.

Halfpenny, N. 2009, 'Enacting Critical Social Work in Publicly Funded Contexts', in J. Allan, L. Briskman and B. Pease (eds), *Critical Social Work*, Allen & Unwin, Sydney, pp. 255–67.

Hamilton, M. 2009, 'Thoughts on Writing Reports and Assessments: A Reader's Perspective', in H. Cleak, *Assessment and Report Writing in Human Services*, Cengage Learning, Melbourne, pp. 40–51.

Hansman, H. 1980, 'The Role of Nonprofit Enterprise', *The Yale Law Journal*, vol. 89: 835–902.

Hardina, D. 2005, 'Ten Characteristics of Empowerment-Oriented Social Service Organisations', *Administration in Social Work*, vol. 29: 23–42.

Harris, J. 2003, *The Social Work Business*, Routledge, London.

Hartman, A. 1991, 'Words Create Worlds', *Social Work*, vol. 36: 275–6.

Hasenfeld, Y. 1983, *Human Service Organisations*, Prentice Hall, Englewood Cliffs, NJ.

—— 2000, 'Organisational Forms as Moral Practices: The Case of Welfare Departments', *Social Services Review*, vol. 7: 329–51.

Healy, K. 2000, *Social Work Practices: Contemporary Perspectives on Change*, Sage, London.

—— 2005, *Social Work Theories in Context: Creating Frameworks for Practice*, Palgrave Macmillan, Houndsmills.

Healy, K. and Lonne, B. 2009, *The Social Work and Human Service Workforce: Report from a National Study of Education, Training and Workforce Needs*, Australian Learning and Teaching Council, Sydney.

Hettlage, R. and Steinlin, M. 2006, *The Critical Incident Technique in Knowledge Management-Related Contexts*, Swiss Association for International Cooperation, Zurich.

Higham, P. 2006, *Social Work: Introducing Professional Practice*, Sage, London.

Hogan, F. 2001, 'Letter Writing and Collaborative Note Making in Social Work Practice: The Ethics of Participation and Transparency in an Information Age', *Irish Social Worker*, vol. 19: 11–15.

hooks, b. 2000, *Feminism for Everybody: Passionate Politics*, Pluto Press, London.

Hughes, M. and Wearing, M. 2007, *Organisations and Management in Social Work*, Sage, London.

Ife, J. 2001, *Human Rights and Social Work: Towards Rights Based Practice*, Cambridge University Press, Melbourne.

International Federation of Social Workers (IFSW) 2004, *Ethics in Social Work: A Statement of Principles*, available at <http://www.ifsw.org/cm_data/Ethics_in_Social_Work_Statement_of_Principles_-_to_be_publ_205.pdf>, accessed 10 May 2010.

Jackson, A. and Donovan, F. 1999, *Managing to Survive*, Allen & Unwin, Sydney.

Jenkins, P. and Potter, S. 2007, 'No More "Personal Notes"? Data Protection Policy and Practice in Higher Education Counselling Services in the UK', *British Journal of Guidance and Counselling*, vol. 35: 33–7.

Johnson, P. 2009, 'Writing Emails and Business Letters', RMIT University Open Program Notes, 6 May.

Jones, A. and May, J. 1992, *Working in Human Service Organisations: A Critical Introduction*, Longman Cheshire, Melbourne.

Jones, M. 1999, 'Supervisor or Super Hero: New Role Strains for Frontline Supervisors in Human Services', *Asia Pacific Journal of Social Work*, vol. 9: 79–97.

Jones, P. 2001. 'Individuals, Communities and Human Rights', in K. Booth, T. Dunne and M. Cox (eds), *How Might We Live? Global Ethics in the New Century*, Cambridge University Press, Cambridge: 172–90.

Jordan, B. (with Jordan, C.) 2000, *Social Work and the Third Way: Tough Love as Social Policy*, Sage, London.

Kadushin, A. and Harkness, D. 2002, *Supervision in Social Work*, Columbia University Press, New York.

Kasar, J. and Clark, E.N. 2000, *Developing Professional Behaviours*, SLACK Inc., Thorofare, NJ.

Kettner, P.M. 2002, *Achieving Excellence in the Management of Human Service Organisations*, Allyn and Bacon, Boston.

Kimsey, L., Trobaugh, S.S., McKinney, B.C., Hoole, E.R., Thwelk, A.D. and Davis, S.L. 2006, 'Seven-Phase Model of Conflict: Practical Applications for Conflict Mediators and Leaders', *Conflict Resolution Quarterly*, vol. 23: 487–99.

Lawler, J. 2007, 'Leadership in Social Work: A Case of Caveat Emptor', *British Journal of Social Work*, vol. 37: 123–41.

Lederach, J. 1995, *Preaching for Peace: Conflict Transformation Across Cultures*, Syracuse University Press, New York.

Lipsky, M. 1980, *Street-Level Bureaucracy*, Russell Sage, New York.

Lishman, J. (1998) 'Personal and Professional Development', in R. Adams, L. Dominelli and M. Payne (eds) 1998, *Social Work Themes, Issues and Critical Debates,* Macmillan, London: 189–215.

Little, P. 1995, 'Records and Record Keeping', in P. Carter, T. Jeffs and M.K. Smith (eds), *Social Working*, Macmillan, London, pp. 32–48.

Lowe, R. and Guy, G. 1999, 'From Group to Peer Supervision: A Reflective Team Process', *Psychotherapy in Australia*, vol. 6: 79–90.

Macquarie Dictionary 2000, Macquarie Dictionary Publishers, Sydney.

Martin, J. 2007, *Conflict Management and Mediation*, Ginninderra Press, Canberra.

Mary, N.L. 2005, 'Transformational Leadership in Human service organisations', *Administration in Social Work*, vol. 29: 105–18.

Mattison, M. 2000, 'Ethical Decision Making: The Person in the Process', *Social Work*, vol. 45: 201–12.

McDonald, C. 1999, 'Human Service Professionals in the Community Services Industry', *Australian Social Work*, vol. 52: 17–25.

—— 2006, *Challenging Social Work: The Institutional Context of Practice*, Palgrave Macmillan, London.

McDonald, C. and Crane, P. 1995, 'Mask or Mirrors? The Emergence of Consumer Rights in Nonprofit Human Service Organisations', *Third Sector Review*, vol. 1: 19–38.

McDonald, C. and Marston, G. 2008a, 'Re-visiting the Quasi-Market in Employment Services: Australia's Job Network', *The Asia Pacific Journal of Public Administration*, vol. 30: 101–17.

—— 2008b, 'Motivating the Unemployed? Attitudes at the Front Line', *Australian Social Work*, vol. 61: 315–26.

McDonald, C. and Warburton, J. 2003, 'Stability and Change in Nonprofit Organisations: The Volunteer Contribution', *Voluntas: International Journal of Voluntary and Nonprofit Organisations*, vol. 14: 381–99.

McDonald, C. and Zetlin, D. 2004, 'The Promotion and Disruption of Community Services Delivery Systems', *Australian Journal of Social Issues*, vol. 39: 267–81.

McGhee, S. 2009 *Independent Schools Queensland Admin Link*, no. 4, November, available at <www.aisq.qld.edu.au/files/files/Communications/AdminLink/AdminLink4_09.pdf>, accessed 10 May 2010.

McLaughlin, H. 2004, 'Partnerships: Panacea or Pretence?', *Journal of Interprofessional Care*, vol. 18, no. 2: 103–13.

Meagher, G. and Healy, H. 2006, *Who Cares? Volume 2: Employment Structure and Incomes in the Australian Care Workforce*, Australian Council of Social Service Paper 141, ACOSS, Sydney.

Mendelsohn, R. 1979, *The Condition of the People: Social Welfare in Australia 1900–1975*, Allen & Unwin, Sydney.

Miley, K., O'Melia, M. and DuBois, B. 1998, *Generalist Social Work Practice: An Empowering Approach*, Allyn and Bacon, Boston.

Mintzberg, H. 1989, *The Structuring of Organisations*, Prentice Hall, Englewood Cliffs, NJ.

Moreau, M. 1989, *Empowerment Through a Structural Approach to Social Work: A Report from Practice*, Maurice J. Moreau in collaboration with Lynne Leonard, École de service social, Montréal.

Morrison, T. 2001, *Staff Supervision in Social Care*, Pavilion, Brighton.

Mulgan, R. 2001, 'The Accountability of Community Sector Agencies: A Comparative Framework', *Third Sector Review*, vol. 7: 89–105.

Mullaly, B. 1997. *Structural Social Work: Ideology, Theory and Practice* (2nd ed.), Oxford University Press, Toronto.

Mullaly, B. and Briskman, L. 2002, *Challenging Oppression: A Critical Social Work Approach*, Oxford University Press, Toronto.

Mullaly B. and Pease B. 1997, *Structural Social Work: Ideology, Theory, and Practice*, Oxford University Press, New York.

Munn, P. and Munn, P. 2003. 'Rural Social Work: Moving Forward', *Rural Society*, vol. 13: 22–34.

Murray, P. 2006, *A Job Network for Job Seekers: A Report on the Appropriateness of Current Services, Provider Incentives and Government Administration of Job Network*, Catholic Social Services, available from <www.catholicsocialservices.org.au/system/files/CSSA_Job_Network_Discussions_Paper_0.pdf>, accessed 6 May 2008.

National Alternative Dispute Resolution Advisory Council 1999, *A Fair Say: Managing Differences in Mediation and Conciliation*, NADRAC, Canberra.

Navarra, T., Lipkowitz, M. and Navarra, J. 1990, *Therapeutic Communication: A Guide to Effective Interpersonal Skills for Health Care Professionals*, SLACK Inc., Thorofare, NJ.

New South Wales Ombudsman 2004, *The Complaint Handler's Toolkit*, available at <www.ombo.nsw.gov.au/show.asp?id=107>, accessed 12 November 2008.

O'Connor, I., Wilson, J., Setterlund, D. and Hughes, M. 2008, *Social Work and Human Service Practice* (5th ed.), Pearson Education, Sydney.

Office of the Privacy Commissioner, *Guide to Handling Personal Information Security Breaches*, <www.privacy.gov.au/publications/breach_guide.pdf>.

O'Hara, A. and Weber, Z. 2006, *Skills for Human Service Practice: Working with Individuals, Groups and Communities*, Oxford University Press, Melbourne.

Ombudsman Victoria 2007, *Ombudsman Victoria's Guide to Complaint Handling for Victorian Public Sector Agencies*, available at <www.ombudsman.vic.gov.au/www/html/93-foreword.asp>, accessed 12 November 2008.

Osborne, D. and Gaebler, T. 1992, *Reinventing Government*, Addison Wesley, Reading.

Packard, T. 2009, 'Leadership and Performance in Human Service Organizations', in R. Patti (ed.), *The Handbook of Human Services Management* (2nd ed.), Sage, London: 310–30.

Patti, R. (ed.) 2009, *The Handbook of Human Services Management* (2nd ed.), Sage, London.

Pepper, N. 1996, 'Supervision: A Positive Learning Experience or an Anxiety Provoking Exercise?', *Australian Social Work*, vol. 49: 55–64.

Power, M. 1997, *Audit Society: Rituals of Verification*, Oxford University Press, Oxford.

Rabinow, P. (ed.) 1984, 'An Interview with Paul Rabinow and Hubert Dreyfus', in *The Foucault Reader*, Penguin, Harmondsworth: iii–x.

Rapp, C. and Poertner, J. 1992, *Social Administration: A Client-centred Approach*, Longman, New York.

Reamer, F.G. 1999, *Social Work Values and Ethics*, Columbia University Press, New York.

—— 2001, *Tangled Relationships: Managing Boundary Issues in the Human Services*, Columbia University Press, New York.

——2003, 'Boundary Issues in Social Work: Managing Dual Relationships', *Social Work*, vol. 48: 121–33.

—— 2005, 'Documentation in Social Work: Evolving Ethical and Risk-management Standards', *Social Work*, vol. 50: 325–34.

Reissman, C. and Quinney, L. 2005, 'Narrative in Social Work: A Critical Perspective', *Qualitative Social Work*, vol. 4: 391–412.

Rosen, A. 2003, 'Evidence-based Social Work Practice: Challenges and Promise', *Social Work Research*, vol. 24: 197–208.

Ross, K. 2004, *How to Write a Press Release in One Easy Lesson*, Research Hub, Australian Council for the Arts.

Salamon, L. 1995, *Partners in Public Service: Government Nonprofit Relations in the Modern Welfare State*, Johns Hopkins University Press, Baltimore, MD.

Shaefor, B., Horejsi, C. and Horejsi, G. 2003, *Techniques and Guidelines for Social Work Practice*, Pearson Education, London.

Schneider, B. 2001, 'Constructing Knowledge in an Organisation: The Role of Interview Notes', *Management Communication Quarterly*, vol. 15: 227–55.

Skene, L. 1996. 'Codes of Ethics and the Professions: A Legal Perspective', in M. Coady and S. Bloch (eds), *Codes of Ethics and the Professions*, Melbourne University Press, Melbourne: 162–80.

Sinclair, A. 1996, 'Codes in the Workplace: Organisational versus Professional Codes', in M. Coady and S. Bloch (eds), *Codes of Ethics and the Professions*, Melbourne University Press, Melbourne: 182–204.

Sinnott, M. 2007, *E Referral in South West*, available from <http://health.vic.gov.au/pcps/coordination/e_referral/session2a.htm>, accessed 10 May 2010.

Smith, S.R. and Lipsky, M. 1993, *Nonprofits for Hire: The Welfare State in the Age of Contracting*, Harvard University Press, Cambridge, MA.

Spall, P., McDonald, C. and Zetlin, D. 2005, 'Fixing the System? The Experiences of Service Users of the Quasi-market in Disability Services in Australia', *Health and Social Care in the Community*, vol. 13: 56–63.

Sun Tzu 1993, *The Art of War*, trans. Roger Ames, Random House, New York.

Taylor, C. 2008, 'Trafficking in Facts: Writing Practices in Social Work', *Qualitative Social Work*, vol. 7: 25–42.

Thomas, M. 2000, *A Review of Developments in the Job Network*, Research Paper No. 15, Parliamentary Library, Department of Parliamentary Services, Canberra.

Thomson, D. 1998, *A World Without Welfare: New Zealand's Colonial Experiment*, Auckland University Press, Auckland.

Thompson N. 2006, *Anti Discriminatory Practice*, Palgrave Macmillan, Basingstoke.

Thompson, N., Stradling, S., Murphy, M. and O'Neil, P. 1996, 'Stress and Organizational Culture', *British Journal of Social Work*, vol. 26: 647–65.

Tilbury, C., Osmond, J., Wilson, S. and Clark, J. 2007, *Good Practice in Child Protection*, Pearson Education, Sydney.

Tong, R. 1992, *Feminist Thought: A Comprehensive Introduction*, Routledge, London.

Tsui, M. 2005, *Social Work Supervision: Contexts and Concepts*, Sage, Thousand Oaks, CA.

Tsui, M. and Ho, W. 1998, 'In Search of a Comprehensive Model of Social Work Supervision', *The Clinical Supervisor*, vol. l: 181–205.

Tuckman, B. 1965, 'Development Sequence in Small Groups', *Psychological Bulletin*, no. 63: 384–9.

United Nations 1948, *Universal Declaration of Human Rights*, available at <www.un.org/en/documents/udhr>, accessed 10 May 2010.

Wearing, M. 1998, *Working in Community Services: Management and Practice*, Allen & Unwin, Sydney.

Weaver, D. 2001, 'Being a Voice in a Foreign Language', in S. Abels (ed.), *Ethics in Social Work Practice: Narratives for Professional Helping*, Love Publishing, Denver, CO: 170–82.

Weeks, W. 2003, 'Developing Feminist Practice in Women's Services', in J. Allan, L. Briskman and B. Pease (eds), *Critical Social Work: An Introduction to Theories and Practices*, Allen & Unwin, Sydney: 93–110.

Westbrook, T., Ellis, J. and Ellet, A.J. 2006, 'What Can We Learn from the Insights and Experiences of Committed Survivors?', *Administration in Social Work*, vol. 30: 37–62.

Wint, E. and Healy, L. 1998, *Social Work Reality: Illustrative Case Studies*, Woodside, Kingston, Jamaica.

Woodside, M. and McClam, T. 2006, *Generalist Case Management: A Method of Human Service Delivery*, Thomson Brooks/Cole, Pacific Grove, CA.

Youth Affairs Council of Victoria Inc. 2008, *Code of Ethical Practice: A First Step for the Victorian Youth Sector*, available at <www.cardinia.vic.gov.au/files/Code_of_ethics_for_youth_workers.pdf>, accessed 10 May 2010.

INDEX